The Spectatorship of Suffering

Lilie Chouliaraki

D1453813

⑤ SAGE Publications

London ● Thousand Oaks ● New Delhi

To Daphne

 SAGE Publications Ltd
1 Oliver's Yard
55 City Road
London EC1Y 1SP

SAGE Publications Inc.
2455 Teller Road
Thousand Oaks, California 91320

SAGE Publications India Pvt Ltd
B-42, Panchsheel Enclave
Post Box 4109
New Delhi 110 017

British Library Cataloguing in Publication data

A catalogue record for this book is available from the
British Library

ISBN-10 0 7619 7039 8   ISBN-13 978 0 7619 7039 2
ISBN-10 0 7619 7040 1 (pbk)   ISBN-13 978 0 7619 7040 8

Library of Congress Control Number available

Typeset by C&M Digitals (P) Ltd., Chennai, India

CONTENTS

ACKNOWLEDGEMENTS

I would like to thank BBC World Television, Danish National Television (DR) the Greek television channels MEGA and NET and the Getty Image Bank for kindly providing permission for the use of news material analysed in this book. I would also like to thank MODINET, the Research Project on 'Media and Democracy in the Network Society' funded by the Danish Research Councils, for financial support.

I am grateful to my colleagues Ib Bondebjerg, Bessie Dendrinos, Jan Ekecranz, Hans Krause Hansen, Rasmus Helles, Dorte Salskov Iversen, Henrik Søndergaard and Delia Tzortzaki for their continuing support and encouragement.

My editor, Julia Hall, has shown much understanding and patience during the most difficult stages of this project. I am grateful to her for this. My deepest appreciation goes to Professors Dimitris Vassilopoulos and Georgia Kostopanayiotou and my family, Thomais, Mikhail, Yiorgos and Elias, for being next to me.

INTRODUCTION: DISTANT SUFFERING ON TELEVISION

This is a book about the relationship between us as spectators in the countries of the West, and the distant sufferers on our television screen – sufferers in Somalia, Nigeria, Bangladesh, India, Indonesia, but also New York and Washington DC. How do we relate to television images of distant sufferers? Do we switch off, shed a tear or get angry and protest? Do we forget about them or seek to do something about their suffering? Such questions touch on the ethical role of the media in public life today. They address the issue of whether or not the media can cultivate a disposition of care for and engagement with the far away other; whether or not television can create a global public with a sense of social responsibility towards the distant sufferer.

These issues have always been on the agenda of public debate and the social sciences. Nevertheless, we know little about the role of the media in shaping an ethical sensibility that extends beyond our own 'neighbourhood'. On the one hand, as television news constantly bombards us with humanitarian emergencies, arguments about the compassion fatigue of the general public abound. On the other hand, the Asian tsunami emergency turned out to be 'a unique display of the unity of the world', as the Secretary General of the UN, Kofi Annan, put it.[1] Never before had the international community responded to distant suffering as it did in the event of the catastrophic tidal wave along the Indian ocean coastline, which swept away more than a quarter of a million people in December 2004.

The Secretary General explained the unique international response to tsunami-hit nations as being due to two factors:

- global footage – the whole world saw this human tragedy
- global suffering – over 40 countries lost their own citizens in the disaster.

This response tells us something important about the spectacle of suffering in the media. It tells us that witnessing the event and its disastrous aftermath on screen is important in evoking emotion and, thereby, a sense of care and responsibility for the distant sufferer. It also tells us how important is the fact that 40 nations, many of them Western, not only witnessed but also experienced the feeling of loss.

Even though the UN Secretary General was quick to celebrate the response to tsunami survivors as a display of global unity, a number of questions still beg a response. Is it enough to witness the scene of distant suffering, in all its intensity and drama, in order to engage with suffering? What forms can our engagement with distant suffering take? Is charity enough to make a difference in the life of the sufferer and what about traditional forms of public action? Do political protest and social solidarity have a place in television's mediations of distant suffering? Finally, it is crucial to turn the UN Secretary General's assertion into a question: under which conditions is it at all possible for the media to induce displays of global care for people we know nothing about and will never meet?

This is what this book is about: the conditions under which it is possible for the media to cultivate an ideal identity for the spectator as a citizen of the world – literally a cosmo-politan.[2] Central to this issue is the problem of public action as action at a distance. Public action has always been action at a distance – at least in modern times – but the mass media have intensified the tensions involved in the enactment of public action because they constantly confront us with realities that occur too far away from everyday life for us to feel that we can make a difference to them. No other spectacle can raise the ethical question of what to do so compellingly as suffering. The most profound moral demand that television makes on spectators, Ellis claims, is to make us witnesses of human pain without giving us the option to act on it (2000: 1).

We might, however, wish to reverse the claim. We might wish to assume, instead, that the spectacle of suffering puts under pressure not the spectator per se, but the norms that dominate the ethics of public life today. The ethics of public life insist that suffering invites compassion, it must be acted on and on the spot if it is to be an effective response to the urgency of human pain. Its ideal moral citizen is the figure of the good Samaritan. This dominant discourse is, evidently, out of pace with our contemporary experience of suffering, which is thoroughly mediated and impossible to act on in a compassionate manner. One of the key problems that surrounds the debate on cosmopolitan citizenship, I argue in this book, is that public action is still understood as compassion – that is, on-the-spot action on suffering – but now needs to be acted as pity that is action that incorporates the dimension of distance.

Mediation and discourse

The mediation of suffering is an important focus of study precisely because it problematizes the nature of public action under conditions of mediation. The question of how distant misfortune becomes a story to be told throws into relief the strategies of discourse that accommodate the demand for action on suffering given that, for the majority of us, physical closeness to the sufferer is impossible. These strategies of discourse – what Boltanski (1999: 7) calls a 'politics of pity' – refer to the ways in which television uses image and language so as to render the spectacle of suffering not only comprehensible but also ethically acceptable for the spectator. This book, it follows, is neither about news production (the chain reactions between the site of suffering, news room and broadcast studio), nor news interpretation (audience responses to the news). This book is about the news text that reaches our living rooms.

What I seek to study is the choices made when creating the news text concerning how the sufferer is portrayed on screen and how the scene of suffering is narrated. Even though such choices are part of everyday journalistic routines rather than ideologically motivated calculations, they always carry norms as to how the spectator should relate to the sufferer and what we should do about the suffering. It is these ethical values, embedded in news discourse, that come to orientate the spectator's attitude towards the distant sufferer and, in the long run, shape the disposition of television publics vis-à-vis the misfortune of far away others.

This is not a new insight. Social and political theories of the public sphere emphasize the crucial relationship between media discourse and the norms of public life.[3] We have yet to comprehend, however, just how news texts shape public ethics, by shaping the spectator's encounter with distant suffering. What we need to do, as Corner (1995: 143) proposes with respect to the documentary, is to 'develop closer and better microanalysis, of the language and image of the media' and locate media texts within broader contexts of social practice and public conduct.[4]

The concept that connects the media as discourse and text with the media as institution and technology is the concept of *mediation*. As Silverstone argues, the study of mediation requires giving attention to both the institutions and technologies via which the circulation of news discourse takes place (2004a). The institutional perspective deals with the practices of news production in the journalistic field and seeks to understand how media organizations link up to transorganizational networks (notably in the political field) or other transnational media. In insisting on news making as the activity of organisations and networks, what the institutional perspective often fails to appreciate is the nature of news discourse itself. However, in so far as both perspectives address the social production of news, the news as discourse perspective is itself an indispensable component of institutional analysis. It couples the study of media institutions with that of mediated discourse and the technologies that disseminate it across the globe.

Chapters 1 and 2 – 'Mediation and public life' and 'The paradoxes of mediation' – take as their point of departure on social theory seeking to understand the impact of media and their discourse on public life today. These chapters show that, in order to talk about how public norms change as a result of mediation, we should focus on mediation as not only institutionally driven but also technologically driven discourse. In fact, Chapter 1 argues, the ethical question of how television shapes the disposition of the spectator vis-à-vis the distant sufferer always stumbles over this troubled relationship between discourse and technology. Either celebrated for expanding discourse beyond the here and now or criticized for undermining the authenticity of discourse, the spectre of technology deeply haunts the visions and hopes, but also misconceptions, of social theory about the moral citizen and the cosmopolitan public.

Mediation and power

If it is news discourse that concerns me here, this is because our relationship with distant suffering is made possible, or thinkable at all, by means of this discourse. To be sure, questions of discourse depend crucially on money and technology – on the transnational networks that enable news flows across the globe.[5] The development of satellite technologies, for example, lies behind every picture of Banda-Aceh, Baghdad or Darfur that reaches our home. Despite the instantaneous and global reach of visibility that such technologies have achieved, the optimistic celebration of our planet as a global village or the satellite viewer as a new cosmopolitan should be held in check.[6]

Current regimes of television viewing are not simply unified by technology. Rather, they embed new transnational technologies of communication in existing and relatively stable transnational relationships of power and these map out an asymmetrical and unjust landscape of news flows. The consequence is new divisions rather than simply new unifications. The parallel to the digital divide in new media is the satellite divide in global news flows.[7]

The division between safety and suffering captures a fundamental aspect of this asymmetry in the viewing relationships of television. This is the asymmetry of power between the comfort of spectators in their living rooms and the vulnerability of sufferers on the spectators' television screens. The viewing asymmetry of television does not explicitly thematize the economic and political divisions of our world but reflects and consolidates them. Who watches and who suffers reflects the manner in which differences in economic resources, political stability, governmental regimes and everyday life enter the global landscape of information. Similarly, who acts on whose suffering reflects patterns of economic and political agency across global zones of influence – North and South or East and West. Safety and suffering, then, are apt categories for understanding television's power to represent the world to the world, its power to map information flows in terms of geographical neighbourhoods, cultural affinities and political alliances and, by this token, to 'other' those who live in poverty or with war.[8]

In this politics of discourse over who belongs where and who cares for whom, the contemporary relationships of viewing are neither identical nor radically different from previous critical accounts of world divisions and global relationships of subordination. Echoing Hall's work on the exercise of white power over colonized people, contemporary relationships of viewing reflect a similar symbolic struggle for power, territory and identity. In the same spirit, Said would call this viewing asymmetry a contemporary mutation of the old divide between the West and the 'orient'.[9] It is to both the unique quality of contemporary relationships of power and their continuity with historical relationships of power that I repeatedly return in this book.

At the same time, the representation of suffering in terms of hierarchical zones of viewing construes the space of safety as a homogeneous space – the space of routine everyday life, predictability, relative prosperity.[10] Media theory is responsible for the legitimacy of this construction. Theories on the mass media as devices for the re-enchantment of the world or agents for the enhanced reflexivity of our societies acknowledge the suffering 'others' only in their role of forging the togetherness and sociality of Western audiences.[11] However, this aggregate function of television – often celebrated as evidence of a new 'communitarian' ethic – is only possible on the condition that it separates itself from the zone of suffering and deprives the suffering 'others' of their own sovereignty as human beings.[12] Instead of making the disturbing spectacle of distant sufferers the object of critical reflection, much theory on the media places the content – ethical and political – of mediation outside the agenda of research and debate.

Chapter 3 – 'Mediation, meaning and power' – takes issue with this attitude found in theory. It deals with theories on the media that understand media discourse in a simplified manner, as image only. Despite their critical spirit towards the society of the spectacle or the culture of the simulacra (disappearance of the real into a mirror image of reality, which is the only reality for today's spectators), these aesthetic narratives of mediation have more to say about the life of spectators than the ethical dilemmas that the life of the distant sufferers may press on our societies.

Chapters 1 to 3, together, point to a crucial weakness in contemporary theory on the media. This is the tendency of theory to hover unproductively between the 'paradoxes' or 'impossibilities' of mediation. Does technology facilitate an ethical public life or undermine this possibility? Does media discourse deliver the promise of a reflexive and active public or seduce and disempower spectators? This dilemmatic approach to mediation does not help us, I believe, to understand the question of ethics and public life in its full complexity. Importantly, it does not help us find ways to redress the bias and inequality in current practices of mediation.

Phronesis in social research

Questions about the ethical role of the media and the power of public action are, indeed, 'grand' questions. They are usually dealt with in 'grand' theory. They become the topic of philosophical arguments on the existence of universal moral standards or political debates about the rise or decline of communitarian and cosmopolitan values. The perspective I adopt in this book is different. I approach these 'grand' questions by means of particular examples.

Drawing on Aristotle's advice that our enquiries into social life should be driven by the practical consideration of what 'is good or bad for man', I focus on the ways in which particular news texts present the sufferer as a moral cause to western spectators.[13] This concrete engagement with values – what Aristotle calls *phronesis* (prudence) – grasps the question of ethics from the pragmatic perspective of praxis.[14] This is the perspective that takes each particular case to be a unique enactment of ethical discourse that, even though it transcends the case, cannot exist outside the enactment of cases. Does the news text construe the misfortune of distant sufferers as a case of action – whose action or with what effects – or does it construe the scene of suffering as being of no concern to the spectators?

The nine news texts that I look into in Chapters 5, 6 and 7 tell us different stories about their sufferers and about what we can do for them. Some of them tell stories that we are bound to forget as soon as we turn away from the television set. An accident in the remote Indian state of Orissa, ambush killings in West Papua and floods in Bangladesh do not present suffering as a cause for the spectators' concern or action. Some other pieces of news tell stories that beg for, and get, our attention, even if it is momentarily. Reports on how illegal African immigrants fought the stormy Mediterranean, how starving children pay the price for Argentina's economic crisis, or the imminent death by stoning of a Nigerian mother present us with suffering as a cause for concern, if not practical action. There are those rare pieces of news also, such as the tsunami catastrophe or September 11th attacks, that linger on our television screens, with their urgent demand for engagement, and will haunt our lives with their lasting impact. In a phronetic spirit, I take each of these nine news texts to be, at once, a discursive event 'reporting the news' and a practical logic that reflects a specific ethical value about how important this particular sufferer is and what there is to do to about his or her suffering.

The practical perspective on ethical value is important because much social science today formulates the question of ethical value in either/or terms. In foundationalist epistemologies, ethical value is either a general rule or a universal truth, while in relativist epistemologies, it is solely embedded in particular cases without the possibility of generalization. The result is that such either/or epistemologies do not respond to the Aristotelian question of 'what is good or bad for man?'. They are particularly weak when confronted with issues of power and inequality because they cannot tell the difference between news narratives that block spectators' capacities to engage with suffering – such as the accident in India or the floods in Bangladesh – from those that cultivate this capacity, such as the news about the Nigerian woman who has been sentenced to death by stoning. They cannot address questions of how hierarchies of human life are reproduced in the news narratives of television or how a more egalitarian representation of the 'other' can take place in these narratives. Foundationalism and relativism cannot, in other words, adequately serve as critical epistemologies.

The phronetic perspective, in contrast, can. This is because it avoids both types of '-isms' and considers every particular action to be informed by a 'universal' principle of what is the right thing and the wrong thing to do. Far from being an ahistorical constant, the principle that informs particular action represents nothing more than those public values and norms that, at a particular moment in time, happen to be dominant in social life – hence their 'universal' status. As Flyvbjerg puts it, phronetic researchers 'realize that our sociality and history is the only foundation we have, the only solid ground under our feet' (2001: 130).

The critical spirit of phronetic research comes, then, from the study of how everyday news texts in television's output mundanely enact ethical values that, ultimately, come to shape our present as a particular historical moment. In asking how news texts participate in shaping the ethical norms of the present, the phronetic perspective is fully harmonious with contemporary poststructuralist enquiry. In fact, the 'how' question, as Foucault poses it, not only addresses Aristotle's concern with 'what is good or bad for man' but also pushes this concern further in order to find out under which conditions a particular practice may turn out to be 'good or bad' for a specific category of human beings. This is the focus of Foucault's concern with power.

The term *analytics* of power – which Foucault borrows from Aristotle to distinguish his approach from a *theory* of power – aims at describing in detail the complexities of practice and discourse that place human beings in certain relationships of power to one another within a specific social field, such as the field of media and mediation.[15] The 'how' question opens up the study of news discourse to a mode of inductive reasoning that uses the example in order to demonstrate its properties in detail and reach a new conclusion as to why this example possesses these properties and which effects of power these properties might have on people.[16]

How are certain scenes of suffering construed as being of no concern to Western spectators or capable of arousing the spectators' emotions? Do visual properties – such as the absence or presence of moving images – play a role in the construal of these scenes? How can we differentiate between representations of suffering that may simply bring a tear to a spectator's eye and those that may actually make a difference in the sufferers' lives? Is the presence or absence of public opinion and expert deliberation in the news important in rendering distant suffering a moral cause for the media public? The question of how, in other words, engages with news discourse in order to define the choices made that mean distant suffering is presented as worthy or unworthy of the spectators' attention.

However, the analytics of power do more that this. Rather than just seeing suffering on television as a reality of our times, connected exclusively to the technological possibilities of mediation, the analytics of power also demonstrate how news discourse draws on historical themes and genres that have come to define our collective imaginary of the 'other'. This element of historicity is important because it connects the question of how with the question as to why news discourse today shapes the ways in which we see the world via television in a fundamentally biased way. It is this element of historicity that many contemporary accounts of media and mediation lack. According to Boltanski (1999), however, the aestheticization of human pain and the portrayal of the scene of suffering as populated by benefactors or evil-doers are crucial effects of discourse that originate in Hellenic and post-Enlightenment genres of public representation. In their reappropriation by electronic media, these historical effects of discourse do not cease to operate as strategies of power but still continue to produce and reproduce hierarchies of place and human life.

In Chapter 4 I develop, as the title 'The analytics of mediation' suggests, a method of studying each news text that uses three categories inherent in the public exposition of suffering:

- *multimodality* – the properties of language and image that construe the spectacle of suffering on screen
- *space–time* – the representation of proximity/distance to the scene of suffering
- *agency* – the representation of action on the sufferer's misfortune.

Through the grid of the analytics, I identify three *regimes of pity* – that is, three distinct fields of meaning that cluster around three groups of news texts, which, as I will explain shortly, are *adventure*, *emergency* and *ecstatic news*. All the regimes of pity construe suffering as an aesthetic spectacle, but each offers the spectator a different quality of emotional and practical engagement with the distant sufferer. Hierarchical as these regimes of pity may be, they are, nevertheless, neither fixed nor immutable – they have certain conditions of possibility that can be reflexively revised and changed.

The contribution of the analytics of mediation to the debate on public norms today is that it demonstrates in a practical way the contingency of these regimes of pity, their human-made nature, and so offers us the language we need to revise them, to make them 'good for man'.

The merit of example

The idea that hierarchies of place and human life are reproduced in Western news is not new in social research. Nevertheless, no language of description has been developed so far to show us just how specific regimes of pity are actually shaped by news discourse and how they may begin to change. This is, again, a consequence of the either/or divisions in epistemology. Just as the study of ethics as a field of knowledge hovers between foundationalist truth and relativist doubt, so, in nomothetic science, the choice of example as a methodological tool is too context-dependent to yield generalizable results or, in idiograph science, too unique and idiosyncratic to require validity.[17] Against these unproductive either/ors, phronesis reminds us that the example bears the power of particular knowledge that always articulates with theoretical insight, with a 'universal' claim.

Phronesis, Aristotle says, produces knowledge that goes beyond the individual case, but it is not simply about 'universals'. Rather, phronesis 'must also take cognizance of particulars, because it is concerned with conduct, and conduct has its sphere in particular circumstances' (Flyvbjerg, 2001: 70).

The nine broadcasts in this book constitute, in the phronetic sense, a strategic group of *particular circumstances*. They consist of ordinary and extraordinary pieces of news that fall into the genres of scheduled broadcast and live footage.[18] The category of live footage consists of three different extracts from the 24/7 coverage of the September 11th attacks. The scheduled news items cluster around short-duration and medium-duration pieces of news. The killings and floods in India, Indonesia and Bangladesh constitute the cluster of short pieces, whereas the rescuing of illegal African immigrants in the Mediterranean or the 'death by stoning' sentence for a Nigerian mother make up the cluster of relatively longer pieces of news.[19]

All the broadcasts come from European television, but as they draw on two national television networks – from Denmark and Greece – and on a global but UK-based broadcasting service, BBC World, they simultaneously reflect different national and cultural trends within Europe.[20] All the pieces of news, with the exception of two BBC World items, consist of moving images received via satellite and local voiceovers, which work to domesticate the satellite image to the national broadcast. The decision to include examples from BBC World news that have no moving images is not to be taken as representative of the network's broadcasting ethos but, rather, as illustrative of the possibility of a global network reporting on suffering without visualizing the scene of suffering. The BBC, in fact, regularly includes on-location reports from scenes of suffering and often accommodates the demand for action in its news stories.[21] As a whole, these nine news items are representative of a transnational flow of instances of suffering that are subsequently articulated in various local contexts of transmission.

Important as local differences may be to understanding how news discourse works, it is not difference that I am interested in here. Rather, it is similarity that concerns me. If transnational news flows do not unify but redivide the world into hierarchies of place and human life, then the point is to show how patterns of media discourse participate in this symbolic work of division and classification. To this end, I extend the argument that television construes the nation as an 'imagined' community by homogenizing differences internal to the nation state and, similarly, I argue that transnational news flows construe a 'beyond the nation' community by establishing a sense of a broader 'we'.[22] This 'we', I assume, is the 'imagined' community of the West, which inhabits the transnational zone of safety and construes human life in the zone of suffering as the West's 'other'.

It is obvious that these examples of news discourse are not pure particulars but stand in a relationship of tension to theory. They do not claim to articulate an eternal truth nor to have 'universal' applicability, but neither are they random. They demonstrate a regularity in their features that, nationally grounded as it may be, comes to construe a broader repertoire of public identities for Western spectators vis-à-vis distant sufferers. These examples also demonstrate a systematicity in their effects, in so far as their features contribute to reproducing the Western equilibrium of viewing between zones of safety and suffering.

The three clusters of news in this study, then, constitute paradigmatic cases of research, in so far as they highlight more general characteristics of the societies they come from and, when subjected to principled analysis – the analytics of mediation – yield a redescription of the public values of these societies as ones that watch the rest of the world suffer.[23] It is on the basis of these paradigmatic clusters that I develop the typology of Western news discourse in this book as adventure, emergency and ecstatic news. Chapters 5 to 7 provide the 'thick descriptions'[24] of these three types of news, with adventure and ecstatic news occupying the two ends of the hierarchy of pity in this typology.

'Adventure' news, covered in Chapter 5, is news of suffering without pity – for example the instances of news from India, Bangladesh and Indonesia. The lack of pity in these news texts is related to the fact that they consist of only short reports accompanied by maps – a very simple multimodality. This leads to singular space–times, which maximize the distance between spectator and the scene of suffering, and a void of agency – that is, the absence of benefactors or persecutors acting in the scene of suffering. As a consequence of these features, the sufferer of adventure news is an Other, with a capital 'o': there is no possibility of human contact between the other and the spectator.

'Emergency' news, the focus of Chapter 6, is news of suffering with pity – the news about the illegal African immigrants, Argentinean famine victims and a Nigerian woman falling into this category. The presence of pity as emergency in these pieces of news is related to their multimodal texts, which articulate image and language in various forms of aesthetic realism. This means that the space–time dimensions of these news pieces also become progressively complicated and their agency options involve the spectator in increasing possibilities of action on the suffering. The sufferers of emergency news, then, may still be 'others' but now lie within the spectators' horizons of relevance and their capacity to act.

'Ecstatic' news, the subject of Chapter 7, is news such as that of the September 11th attacks, where the politics of pity is played out in a multimodal text with incredible complexities and representational possibilities. As a consequence, each of the three news stories explored in this chapter entails its own distinct aesthetic qualities – sentimental empathy, political denunciation and reflexive contemplation – but the space–time and agency possibilities in each extract bring the United States' sufferers as close to the European spectators as possible. The 'we are all Americans' headline (front page of *Le Monde*, 12 September 2001) is an act of identification made possible by the fact that these attacks were mediated as attacks in what is normally a zone of safety.

The concept of the 'public'

In begging the question of how the spectacle of suffering reaches our living rooms, phronesis also takes the relationship between spectator and sufferer as the paradigmatic relationship by means of which our public values are instantiated. Around these two figures, the description of news discourse becomes, at the same time, a description of acts of identity. The spectators of the news are themselves part of the news narrative, in so far as it puts spectators in the position of voyeurs of the pain of the 'other', philanthropists or activists who exercise some form of effective speech vis-à-vis the suffering they watch. Similarly, sufferers enter the news narrative in various forms of identity, ranging from a number without further specification to a human being almost like 'us'.

It is these acts of identity, engaging the spectators and sufferers in various relationships of proximity and agency to one another, that ultimately construe some sufferings as being worthy of our pity and others as unworthy of it. The concept of regimes of pity suggests, then, that spectators do not possess 'pure' emotions vis-à-vis the sufferers, but their emotions are, in fact, shaped by the values embedded in news narratives about who the 'others' are and how we should relate to them. Pity, by this token, is not a natural sentiment of love and care but a socially constructed disposition to feeling that, in Boltanski's words, aims to produce 'a generalized concern for the "other"' (1999: xx).[25]

By this token, the concept of the public is not a 'pure' concept that preexists our stories and narratives of it. This is because scientific discourse, just like media discourse, is implicated in the process of creating the public at the moment of referring to it – either by numerical evidence or ethnographic stories. Deciding to conceptualize the public as national or transnational and political or cultural, is a matter of perspective as well as historical reality.[26] In this sense, every research perspective chosen is, at once, a bias against the study of certain aspects of the historical world and a privileging of the study of others. To put it in Aristotle's terminology, every particular choice of research brings with it its own 'universal' of theoretical context and explanation. Inevitably, which news texts are chosen as examples of a Western discourse on suffering may reduce the value of differences across national news that play on the formation of a cosmopolitan public.[27] However, at the same time, what has been chosen gives us access to the symbolic conditions of cosmopolitan identity in the Western world as the moral mechanism of pity.

In this respect, the category of 'nation' in comparative research is less relevant when the focus of study is similarity, as is the case here, rather than difference. As Hannertz claims, even if the nation has been, in the past, a major resource for cultural resonance, the question today is whether or not we are being confronted with alternative resources that construe 'beyond the nation' modes of resonance and homogenize new configurations of people: 'How does the "new supranational restructuring" affect the generation and distribution of cultural resonance in the world?' (Hannertz, 1996: 83).

If we take this question seriously, which I believe we should, we also need to take into account that a new collective resonance – the 'we' of a transnational spectatorship, particular as it may appear on national television – maps itself on to a more general repertoire of existing public identities across Western societies.

The crisis of pity today, I would strongly argue, is inextricably linked with the history of Western public life and, specifically, with the narrow repertoire of participatory positions that this public life makes available for the ordinary citizen.[28] As we shall see, the spectator of ordinary television news can be, at worst, an indifferent listener of distant suffering and, at best, a potential activist, subtly encouraged to relate to the cause of the suffering. It is this relatively weak potential for public identifications in Western media that raises the key question of how transnational flows of visibility actually cultivate a 'beyond the nation' cultural resonance among Western audiences.

We need, therefore, to see the 'public' not as an empirical entity, corresponding to linguistically homogeneous populations or national borders, but, primarily, as a symbolic act of cultural identity. As Warner argues, 'When we understand images and texts as public, we do not gesture to a statistically measurable series of others, we make a necessarily imaginary reference to the public as opposed to other individuals' (1993: xviii).[29] This study makes its 'imaginary reference to the public' in the textual practices of news, which, in telling stories about the suffering 'other', always carve their own sense of 'we' out of a collection of watching individuals. The phronetic assumption here is that the ethical values of our public life become more amenable to critical evaluation when we study how the humanity of the sufferer emerges in the subtleties of image and fleeting wordings of voiceovers rather than when we look for the universal pragmatics of television. Far from implying that theories of the public sphere, such as Habermas's that the media are responsible for its 'refedalization', are not useful in the debate on public action, my point is this: we may better understand the conditions for ethical reflexivity in our societies if we turn our analytical attention away from the abstract rationalities of the public sphere and towards how television shapes the norms of the present by means of staging our relationship to the far away 'other'.

If my conception of public life is closer to Arendt's and Sennett's than Habermas's, this is because I take aesthetic spectacle, private emotion and public action to be constitutive elements of contemporary sociality, that are always already articulated with one another in situated practices but need to be tactically separated in order to be analysed.[30] Talking about public identity and cosmopolitanism in analytical rather than 'grand' theoretical language has an impact on our current conceptions of the 'paradoxes' of mediation. These 'paradoxes' cease to be seen as static impossibilities of modernity and become instead creative tensions of the present that always find a temporary resolution in contexts of situated practice.

In Chapters 8 and 9 – 'Mediation and action' and 'The cosmopolitan public' – I address some of these creative tensions of the present. I argue that cosmopolitanism today cannot be associated with physical proximity, embodied action or virtuous character. All of these are attributes of a public life that thrives on copresence, the Athenian polis, and must no longer haunt our political and cultural imaginaries. Under conditions of mediation, we should think of cosmopolitanism as a generalized sensibility that acts on suffering without controlling the outcomes or experiencing the effects of such action. Cosmopolitanism is now more than ever a radically undecidable regime of emotion and action. Yet, cosmopolitanism is possible.

The symbolic conditions for cosmopolitanism lie, first and foremost, in a break with the current politics of pity on television. This is because pity produces narcissistic emotions about the suffering 'other' that cannot move the spectator beyond the reflex of caring only for those like 'us'. Instead of global care, therefore, pity produces a form of global intimacy.[31] The emphasis on pity and emotion, I propose, should be combined with an emphasis on detached reflection, on the question of why *this* suffering is important and what we can do about it.

This is difficult.[32] We live in a society where our own private feelings are the measure against which we perceive and evaluate the world and others.[33] The media reflect this. They are almost obsessively preoccupied with our 'interiorities' – our intimate relationships, fears and desires, homes, bodies and appearance. Reality television is one obvious manifestation of a public culture that takes intense narcissistic pleasure in staging the private for all to see. The news genre, formal and detached from emotion as it often appears to be, becomes part of this culture of intimacy in so far as it, implicitly, reserves the potential for us to pity 'our' own suffering and leaves the far away 'other' outside our horizon of care and responsibility. In contrast to this, public discourse that combines the emotionality of pity with the concern for justice comes to remind spectators of this simple fact: our actions may be more relevant and effective when they are orientated towards those whose human needs have been neglected precisely because they do not share 'our' own humanity, rather than towards others like 'us'.[34]

It is controversial to be normative about the public ethos that television should promote, but it is necessary. In so far as the world is divided by the radical asymmetry of distant sufferers and the spectators who watch them, the question of 'what is good or bad for man' is still dramatically timely. At the same time, normative is not the same as prescriptive. As Aristotle reminds us, the 'what should be' already lies in 'what there is'. It is thus in the particulars of existing media discourse that the 'universal' ethos of cosmopolitanism already resides.

Let us recall the UN Secretary General Kofi Annan's, explanation of the international response to the Asian tsunami disaster: global visibility and global relevance. Indeed, if this response teaches us anything, it is not that the global public exists somewhere out there ready to show its willingness to act. Rather, it shows us that who we care for is a matter of whether or not their suffering is presented as relevant and worthy of our response.

It is, no doubt, good to celebrate global unity when it makes its rare appearances, but it is more useful to examine how and why the sufferings we watch almost always evoke pity for those like 'us'. In this critical examination, we may find a way of being public that avoids the narcissistic emotion of modern humanism, but does not abandon respect for the irreducible value of every human life.

Notes

1   Kofi Annan interview, BBC World, 9 January 2005.
2   I draw on a broad definition of cosmopolitanism as 'an orientation, a willingness to relate with the Other' (Hannertz, 1996: 103) that I subsequently elaborate on, in the contexts of social and political theory. See Tomlinson (1999) for a comprehensive discussion of the concept of cosmopolitanism in social theory of the media and Archibugi (2003) for a political theory approach to cosmopolitanism.
3   Notably Habermas (1989), Alexander and Jakobs (1998), Keane (1991), Dahlgren (1995).
4   See Schudson (1982), Silverstone (1984, 1999), Scannel (1991), Bondebjerg (2000, 2002), Schroeder (2002) for a similar argument from a media studies

perspective; Fowler (1991), Bell (1991), Fairclough (1995), Wodak (1996), Scollon (1998) for similar arguments from a critical discourse analysis perspective; Kress and van Leeuwen (1996), van Leeuwen and Jewitt (2001) who write from a visual semiotics perspective.

5   If the political economy of the media highlights how the concentration of power in specific media networks privileges the selection and presentation of news, media institutionalism highlights the complicated transformations of public service broadcasting by market forces. Both perspectives, covering a vast literature, capture crucial components of the constitution of the present as an economic, political and institutional reality that shapes both global flows and local news. For overviews, see Hjarvard (2002: 91–7). See also Golding and Murdoch (1991), Thussu (2000), Volkmer (1999, 2002).

6   Livingstone and van Belle (2005), Livingstone and Bennett (2003), and Higgins (1999) for research on the impact of breaking news that shows novel technologies of transmission, such as mobile satellite uplinks, mobile phones and the Internet, have indeed increased the number of reports on distant suffering on US television. Yet, the question remains, does this lead to an increase in spectators' sense of responsibility and care for distant sufferers?

7   Notably, Castells (1996, 1997), Bauman (1998), also Appadurai (1996), Featherstone (1990), Hannertz (1996), Morley and Robins (1995).

8   See Hall (1996: 1–17; 1997: 223–90) on the concept of difference and the 'other', Calhoun (1995: 231–82) on difference and national identity, Silverstone (1999) and Butler (2004) in relation to media and the 'other'.

9   See Said (1978) and, among others, Bhabha (1983, 1994), Hannertz (1996), Bauman (1996), Morley (2000).

10   See Derrida and Stiegler (2002) among others.

11   See Silverstone (2004b: 440–9) and Peters (1999) for this critical point.

12   See Silverstone (1999) for the concepts of *annihilation*, Peters (1999) for the use of Adorno's term *pathic projection*, Butler (2004) for the concept of *radical exclusion*. All these terms refer to the reduction of the humanness of the 'other' in the media.

13   See Aristotle (1976), *The Nicomachean Ethics* 1140a24–1140b12, 1144b33–1145a11.

14   See Flyvbjerg (2001: 110–28) for a powerful appropriation of Aristotle's work in poststructuralist epistemology and Ross (1995: 31–49) for Aristotle's inductive methods and analytics.

15   See Foucault (1980: 199), Flyvbjerg (2001: 131–8).

16   See Ross (1923/1995: 52–4) for Aristotle's *demonstration* and *definition* in scientific enquiry.

17   See Bourdieu (1990) and Bourdieu and Wacquant (1992) on the distinction between nomothetic and idiographic science, Chouliaraki and Fairclough (1999: 29–36) for further criticisms of this duality and Laclau (1996) for the productive overcoming of the duality by means of the concepts of the *universal* and the *particular*.

18   This is the strategy of *maximum variation* in the selection of the material (Flyvbjerg 2001: 79–81). Maximum variation makes it possible to identify two extreme ends in the news narratives on suffering – namely, a group of news pieces that say very little about an instance of suffering and the rare piece of news that replaces the programme flow with live footage from the scene of action. By this token, the *maximum variation strategy* also makes possible the delineation of a middle space occupied by pieces of news that establish some form of connectivity with the distant sufferer while avoiding the minimalism

and maximalism of the other two categories. In turn, these three positions – the two extremes and the middle one – make possible the construction of a news *typology* – that is, a grid of three classes of news that differ from one another in terms of how they employ the categories of multimodality, spacetime and agency in order to stage the spectacle of distant suffering on our television screens.

19   This is the strategy of *critical cases* in the selection of the material (Flyvbjerg, 2001: 79–81). The critical case – here defined in terms of news piece duration – makes it possible to study how differences in the length of the news piece have an impact on the staging of suffering and, hence, on the representation of the spectator–sufferer relationship in each news narrative. In this respect, each group of news pieces that clusters around similar-length variations constitutes a *critical case* in this study, with each case illustrating a particular regime of pity in the hierarchical typology of news.

20   As well as reflecting diversity across media cultures, the decision as to which networks were chosen was further informed by the claim that the study of discourse requires a solid linguistic and cultural background for the texts under study. As a Greek who has lived long in Britain and now lives in Denmark, I am able to bring to the analysis of each example that intimate knowledge of culture and language deemed crucial in intensive qualitative research (Barry, 2001: 22–3; Flyvbjerg, 2001: 81–7; Fairclough, 1992).

21   Gowing (2004), BBC Worlds main presenter and news analyst, makes a strong case for the study of how the changing technological conditions of remote disaster broadcasting bear on today's information landscape – including the conditions of journalistic work and military action in danger zones. Gowing argues for the need to identify the ethical, political and practical implications of the new 'real time tensions' that arise because the instantaneous transmission of information by anyone anywhere makes today's reports on distant events more frequent and intense than ever before.

22   See Anderson (1983), Giddens (1990, 1991), Hannertz (1996). For media studies, see Schlesinger (1991), Carey (1998) and Dayan (1998).

23   See Flyvbjerg (2001: 80–1).

24   See Geertz (1973: 6).

25   See Nussbaum (2001: 297–400) for a powerful argument on the relationship between emotion and public deliberation and (2001: 401–54) for compassion and the good of public life. See also Gilligan (1993) for the connection between emotion and the gender bias in social action and Tester (2001: 66–71) for the relevance of Gilligan's position on the relationship between emotion and humanitarian action.

26   See Hannertz (1996), Beck (2002), and Ekecrantz (in press), among others, for reservations about the category 'nation' as the key criterion in the study of the media on the grounds that global processes gradually erode the distinctiveness of the nation as a solid point of departure for comparisons. Such reservations, Ekecrantz claims, should be used as a tool for methodological reflection rather than as a cause for ignoring the 'nation' in comparisons of differences across media cultures. As I argue below, the use of 'nation' is more relevant when research focuses on difference and less so when it focuses on similarity across media cultures.

27   For example, public identity may be enacted differently in national cultures where care for the 'other' is institutionalized and incorporated into state

governance as 'foreign aid' and in national cultures where there are no institutionalized agencies or ministries to organize humanitarian action. For a discussion of the systematic correlations between national political cultures and foreign aid policy see Noel and Therien (1995).

28 See Boltanski (1999: 170–92) for a similar argument.

29 This perspective informed my use of examples in the typology of news in Chapters 5–7. It is not according to the criterion of the 'nation', but that of the 'most illustrative example' that meant I eventually selected the cases I did out of a rich body of empirical material. If adventure news consists of two BBC World pieces and one Greek television one, this is because my purpose is to talk about key features in the semiotic make-up of this class of news and these examples illustrate these best, not to point to obvious national media differences. Similarly, if ecstatic news consists of Danish television's footage of the September 11th attacks, this is in order to study in detail the alternation of radically different regimes of pity in the live flow, which constantly engages the spectator of this footage with various emotions and dispositions to action – hence the term 'ecstatic' for this class of news. Finally, in emergency news, my intention is to show that the demand for action on distant suffering may take different forms, creating an internal hierarchy of pity within this class of news. The demand for action is a historical–generic feature of the public representation of suffering that cuts across emergency pieces of news from all three media contexts under study. Yet, the examples from Greek television fit my purpose best as they progressively propel the argument away from news that engages spectators in the position of voyeur of sufferers' misfortunes towards news that invites them to join an Amnesty International protest. I, elsewhere, discuss in detail the demand for action in BBC and DR news (Chouliaraki, 2005b; forthcoming).

30 See Barnett (2003: 60–80) on the distinction between 'cultural' and 'political' publics and Robins (1994: vii–xxvi) for a useful discussion of distinct models of public life along the lines that I argue here. For the distinction with respect to the media, see Alexander and Jakobs (1998) Schudson (1992) and Scannel (1989).

31 Grisprud (1992: 89) formulates this pervasive tendency when he claims that 'what the world [news] is really about, is *emotions*, fundamental and strong: love, hate, grief, joy, lust, disgust […]. If the world looks incomprehensibly chaotic, it is only on the surface. Underneath, it's the same old story.'

32 See Morley (1998: 136–56) in his, tellingly entitled, 'Finding out about the world from television news. Some difficulties.'

33 See Sennett (1974/1992).

34 See Silverstone (1999: 135–6; 2004a and b: 776–7), Peters (1999: 230) and Cohen (2001: 168–73).

1

MEDIATION AND PUBLIC LIFE

Confronting Western spectators with distant suffering is often regarded as the very essence of the power of television. This is the power to make spectators witnesses of human pain by bringing home disturbing images and experiences from faraway places. The spectators see and hear about children dying in the refugee camps of the Sudan, the school siege of Beslan or the streets of Gaza, Baghdad and Kabul. 'You cannot say you didn't know': this is television's mode of address to spectators safely watching the news in their own living rooms.[1] No, we cannot say we didn't know, but can we *act* on what we now know? What are we supposed to do with our knowledge of suffering? This tension between a knowing yet incapable witness at a distance is the most profound moral demand that television makes on Western spectators today.

This demand also places television's role as an agent of ethical responsibility at the centre of current debates in media and social theory. The ethical role of television is indeed a controversial matter. On the one hand, there is optimism. The sheer exposure to the suffering of the world, which television has made possible to an unprecedented degree, brings about a new sensibility. It brings about an awareness and a responsibility towards the world 'out there' that has previously been impossible to create. On the other hand, there is pessimism.[2] The overexposure to human suffering has unaestheticizing, numbing effects. Rather than cultivating a sensibility, the spectacle of suffering becomes domesticated by the experience of watching it on television. As 'yet another spectacle' too, suffering is met with indifference or discomfort, with viewers switching off or zapping to another channel. Ultimately, the debate is polarized into ungrounded optimism – spectators' involvement in distant suffering *is* possible – and unnecessary pessimism – this involvement is, de facto, *impossible*.

I now take as my point of departure for this debate on media and social theory a discussion of the two competing narratives on the ethical role of television in social life – the optimistic and pessimistic ones. The main concept in this debate is mediation. The question is how we can study mediation as a public–political process, a process that sets up norms of public conduct and shapes the spectator as a citizen of the world. My own argument is that the potential of mediation to cultivate a cosmopolitan sensibility is neither de facto possible nor a priori impossible – it has its own historical and social conditions of possibility. In order to investigate these conditions, I propose to investigate empirically how television creates sentiments of pity in its news reports on human suffering.

I approach the notion of pity not as the natural sentiment of human empathy but, rather, as a sociological category that is constituted in discourse. Pity is a product of the manner in which television signifies the relationship between spectators and distant sufferers. Pity, therefore, draws attention to the meaning-making operations by means of which sufferers are strategically, though not necessarily consciously, constituted so as to engage spectators in multiple forms of emotion and dispositions to action. 'In order to generalize', Boltanski writes, 'pity becomes eloquent, recognizing and discovering itself as emotion and feeling' (1999: 6). As the discursive mechanism that establishes a generalized concern for the 'other', pity is central to contemporary conceptions of Western public life and indispensable to the constitution of modern democratic societies.[3]

I propose two particular dimensions of the spectator–sufferer relationship that enable us to analyse the 'eloquence' of pity, its production in meaning. These are the dimensions of *proximity–distance* and *watching–acting*. How close or how far away are spectators placed vis-à-vis sufferers? How are spectators 'imagined' as reacting vis-à-vis sufferers' misfortunes – look at it, feel for it, act on it?

Using these questions to investigate the ethical impact of mediation helps us break with dominant perspectives on how television should or should not moralize the spectator and allows us to examine how television actually produces its own ethical norms and standards for public conduct. The research practice I am exercising is *phronesis* – an Aristotelian practice that approaches ethics as the situated enactment of values, rather than abstract principles of conduct.

Mediation

The concept of mediation is often defined in relation to its ethical implications – that is, in relation to the capacity of the media to involve us emotionally and culturally with distant 'others'. Tomlinson (1999: 154) provides two distinct definitions of mediation, the combination of which highlights the ethical underpinnings of the concept. In the first definition, mediation is about 'overcoming distance in communication'. As such, it is responsible for the deep cultural transformations of our times. Mediation is responsible for deterritorialization, the overcoming of geographical distance, as well as the compression of space and time and the real-time witnessing of faraway events. Mediation, in this definition, is not only about overcoming geographical distance, but also 'the closing of moral distance' between people who live far away from one another.

At the same time, wishing to avoid a naive determinism that celebrates mediation as the happy bringing together of the world, Tomlinson also cares to emphasize the role that the medium plays in closing the distance between disparate locales. His second definition of mediation, then, is about the act of 'passing through the medium'. This definition draws attention to the fact that everything we watch on screen is subject to the interventions of technology and the semiotic modes that the technology of the medium puts to use. Satellite transmission, strategies of camera work, television's narratives and genres are some of the techno-semiotic affordances of television that affect the manner in which the closing of the distance between spectator and spectacle occurs.[4]

These two definitions of mediation – concerning distance and the medium – are brought together because they serve the ultimate purpose, or the *telos*, of mediation. To connect:

> one way of thinking about the development of modern media and communi-
> cation technologies is as the constant attempt to deliver the promise of the
> first definition [closing distance, LC] by reducing the problems of the second
> [refining the medium, LC].
>
> (Tomlinson, 1999: 155)

Tomlinson provides us with a teleology of mediation – a story of progress constantly striving for connectivity. How can the promise of connectivity between places and people be fulfilled? For Tomlinson, mediation connects us by delivering immediacy – one that is qualitatively distinct from face-to-face interaction. Specifically, mediation is about putting *technical* immediacy – the high fidelity of transmission – at the service of *socio-cultural* immediacy – the sense of copresence with faraway others. The ethical capacity of mediation rests on immediacy as a certain sense of togetherness or 'modality of connectivity' in Tomlinson's words (1999: 157).

Let us take an example. The European spectator is, in theory, unable to share the same emotional and cultural experience as a Nigerian woman who has been given a death sentence under the sharia law (the case of Amina Lawal in summer 2002). Yet, television's shocking images of collective violence, showing street scenes of an African woman being mobbed by an enraged crowd of men, facilitate *modal* imagination. Modal imagination is the ability of spectators to imagine something that they have not experienced themselves as being possible for others to experi-ence. It is not simply impossible or unreal.[5] This may sound simple, yet the capacity of television to mediate events from far away as possible and thus factual rather than render them imaginary and fictional is, as we shall see, highly debatable. For now, let me insist that the visual immedi-acy of such television scenes makes it possible for spectators to perform an 'as if' operation. Instead of orienating spectators towards the news on death by stoning simply as an object of their thoughts – a 'thinking of' stoning, to use Boltanski's words, 'without considering this object to be possible in the real world' – this 'as if' operation triggered by the image permits the spectator to think that stoning is an actual possibility for a woman out there in the world. Boltanski claims:

> Thinking that, assumes that one considers [objects of thought] to be possible in a real universe by putting oneself in the state of mind of someone who makes judgements concerning them.

> (Boltanski, 1999: 51)

I return to the highly suggestive 'thinking of' – 'thinking that' distinction and its implications for the moralization of the spectator below. For now, the news about the Nigerian woman suggests that mediated immediacy is about construing proximity – a sense of 'being there' that, albeit different from face-to-face contact, evokes feelings and dispositions to act 'as if' the spectator were on location.

Mediation, intimacy and politics

Is the involvement of the spectator with a distant other a new theme in the study of mediation? No, it is not. The emotional and practical involvement of the spectator with the distant other has already been studied as the theme of *intimacy at a distance*.[6] This is the spectator's non-reciprocal feeling of closeness to public personalities. Princess Diana's appeal for global audiences and the unprecedented reaction to her death are the standard examples given in the relevant literature. For my purposes, using Diana as an example raises the question of how spectators are able to sustain a certain emotional orientation towards a person unknown to them and suggests that such an emotional orientation involves a constant tension in the spectator–celebrity relationship. This is the tension between spectators feeling close to their idols while, simultaneously, knowing that it is impossible to establish physical contact with them. In this sense, intimacy at a distance expresses both tensions of mediation. It expresses the tension between proximity and distance – feeling close but unable to approach the person – and between watching and acting – seeing the idol on screen, but being unable to do something with or for that person.

The theme of intimacy at a distance, however, cannot conceive of these tensions of mediation as fundamentally ethical ones, because the spectator – celebrity relationship does not entail the same radical asymmetry as the spectator – sufferer relationship. Tester describes this asymmetry as 'an imbalance in the material relationship between the audience which reads the newspaper or watches the television and the suffering and miserable other on the page or the screen. [Whereas] the audience is in a position of relative leisure and safety, the suffering other is in a position of frequently absolute destitution' (2001: 78).

My focus on the spectator–sufferer relationship rests on the assumption, implicit in Tester's quote, that we must examine mediation as the most important ethical power of contemporary public life. Ethics has to do with the norms according to which television represents the spectators' relationship to the distant 'other', to somebody the spectator does not experientially or culturally identify with and cannot, in principle, share the misfortune of. How does this difference between spectators and sufferers become meaningful on television? Can distant 'others' be endowed with humanness or will they always remain radical and irrevocable alterities?

Such questions are never purely ethical. They are also political. The mediation between spectator and sufferer is a crucial political space because the relationship between the two of them maps on to distinct geopolitical territories that reflect the global distribution of power. As Cohen rightly notes, it is always 'audiences in North America or Western Europe [that] react to knowledge of atrocities in East Timor, Uganda or Guatemala', rather than the other way round.[7]

What happens when the roles are reversed and the West suddenly becomes the sufferer, as in the September 11th attacks? What happens, in other words, when a shift occurs from a *hypothetical* thinking of the USA as a sufferer to thinking that the suffering of the superpower is now a historical *fact*? The shock of those attacks, Chomsky (2001) reminds us, lies 'not in their scale and character but in the target'. Indeed, rapid changes in the management of the world order after September 11th show only too clearly that any attempt to shift the dominant sufferer–spectator position belongs to the political as much as the ethical order.

It is this close articulation of ethics with politics in the mediation of suffering that raises the question of public action. What kind of public demands do sufferers make on spectators, if at all? Are spectators supposed to forget about the suffering or stand up and take sides? At this point, we can clearly see the equivalence that the theme of intimacy at a distance establishes between the celebrity and the sufferer. Both figures, the celebrity and the sufferer, enable us to examine mediation as the public space that reorganizes relationships in the private space. However, in suffering, intimacy takes on a different nuance. The sentiment of pity, which the sufferer may evoke, raises questions of political power and cultural difference. In so doing, it organizes the disposition of the spectator not (at least not only) around the identity of the cultural consumer or the celebrity fan, but mainly around the public figure of the citizen of the world, the cosmopolitan.

What we need to examine, then, is the conditions of possibility under which the figure of the cosmopolitan may come into being in the process of mediation. In what follows, I examine the degree to which social theory on media and mediation conceptualizes the cosmopolitan spectator as a public actor. I do so in two moves. In the next section under the heading 'Mediation and Cosmopolitanism', I discuss the two key narratives on the ethics of mediation – pessimistic and optimistic. I argue that neither leaves conceptual space for the question of how the spectator's connectivity to the distant 'other' is symbolically achieved. The idea of cosmopolitanism may be inseparably connected to the media, yet much theory on the media takes the idea of cosmopolitanism for granted.

In the section after this, 'The public realm and cosmopolitanism', I evaluate the two models of the public realm that the debate on mediation presupposes – the dialogue and dissemination models (Peters, 1999). I argue that, for different reasons, each of these models of the public realm fails to conceptualize it as a space where dispositions to action at a distance may be effectively forged. Again, current transformations in public life are seen as connected to the media, yet much theory on the media takes the idea of public life for granted.

If the conditions for cosmopolitanism and the public realm are not objects of investigation, what, is then, the main object of theory on the media? The main object, I claim, is technology. Once more, however, the two most pressing ambivalences that technology has introduced into public life today – proximity–distance and watching–acting – are treated as static either/ors or irresolvable paradoxes. This does not help us assess the role that the media play in public life today. It does not help us to understand how, in 'closing the moral distance' between us and the 'other', the media may provide the conditions for a cosmopolitan public.

In Chapter 2 – 'The paradoxes of mediation' – I propose that we stop debating the paradoxes of mediation in the abstract. I argue that the ethics of the public realm can be more effectively studied if we begin with examples of technologically disseminated discourse and the 'universal' norms of public conduct these examples enact. It is in the course of putting the spectator – sufferer relationship into discourse that television resolves the tensions of mediation between proximity–distance and watching–acting. In so doing, it also shows us how far the cosmopolitan spectator is possible in Western media discourse.

Mediation and cosmopolitanism

In social theory of the media, as mentioned above, there are two narratives about how the process of mediation may shape the cosmopolitan spectator: the pessimistic and optimistic ones. Both narratives emphasize the fact that television creates a new connectivity between spectators and distant 'others'. Both also stress the role of the medium in 'manipulating' the spectators' sense of proximity to and, hence, their ability to connect with the spectacle of suffering. However, they differ in the ways in which they understand the impact that television has upon the quality of the connectivity between spectators and sufferers. As a consequence, the two narratives reach different conclusions as to the ability of television to engage spectators with sufferers' misfortunes. This ongoing debate between a pessimistic and an optimistic narrative of the ethical role of television is not new. The controversy can be traced back to Adorno's criticism of the culture industry for creating the illusion of collectivity when it really cultivates individualism and Merton's belief in the mass media as creators of rituals that forge new forms of social cohesion.[8]

The pessimistic narrative

Robins's eloquent paradox of *intimate detachment* echoes the pessimism of Adorno.[9] The pessimistic narrative maintains that television appears to create proximity, but, in fact, fosters distance.

This narrative is deeply suspicious of technology – not because technology turns audiences into passive dupes, as simplistic accounts have it, but because technology entertains the illusion that audiences participate in public life when they are simply, in Adorno's words, 'regressing in listening' or watching (1938/1982: 270). The reason for this regression is that the very technological form of the medium 'sanitizes' reality – that is, it cuts real life off from its raw sensations. The medium's sense of immediacy may be due to an ever-enhanced technical perfection, but, ultimately, it is these same technical determinants that deprive on-screen suffering of its compelling physicality and shift the fact of suffering into pixel fiction.

We can identify two versions of pessimism. The first maintains that technology distorts the authenticity of the represented event, so we may call it the *intervention of technology* version of pessimism. The second version maintains that it is the conditions of people's homes, where spectators watch television, that interrupt their connectivity with distant sufferers. Thus, we may call it the *domesticity of reception* version of pessimism.

The intervention of technology

The first remove from the scene of suffering occurs because the technology of television is unable to mediate a broad spectrum of physical senses and bodily sensations, such as smell, touch, heat or discomfort. Television lacks the compelling testimony of the body, of embodied presence and, hence, it can never fully claim to represent the body's reality.[10] Even if the beautiful body easily lends itself to the aesthetic requirements of the screen, the suffering body resists such 'easy' inscriptions. Let us remember the taboo surrounding visuals of warfare casualties on Western television during the Iraq war and the controversy over Al Jazeera's graphic images of death and destruction. Crucial, then, as it may be in triggering modal imagination, the visual also severs suffering from its physical context and weakens its moral appeal.

Robins, for instance, challenges the moral force of television precisely by challenging the capacity of its spectacles to evoke authenticity. Spectators' reactions to violent television spectacles demonstrate that they have the capacity to domesticate terror and contain the urgent appeal for compassion. 'How is it', Robins wonders, 'that such realities [of violence] can be diffused?' (1994: 458). It is the medium itself that bears anaesthetizing effects on the spectator. Visual editing, soundtrack, repetition or fast tracking help spectators to create a sense of distance from the spectacle, while the zapping and switching off options strengthen spectators' sense of control over what they watch. The ethical appeal of television images disappears because, as a consequence of this distance, the distinction between reality and fiction loses its relevance for the spectator.[11] In other words, in the technological intervention version of pessimism, suffering on television presents us with the spectacularity of human misfortune, but not its authenticity.[12] As a consequence, suffering becomes a thing to watch just as any other and human pain turns into what Peters calls 'an exercise in Pavlovian compassion', (2005: 227) as we are freshly torn by the day's allotment of collapsing buildings, fires, floods, and terror.

The domesticity of reception
The second remove from the scene of suffering has to do with the fact that spectators receive the spectacle of suffering in the safety of their own living rooms. This occurs because the image of suffering, already fictionalized, is further contained within the material frame of a television, 'this rectangle of bulging glass', rendering the scene of suffering as small as the television screen itself.[13] It is miniaturized, so to speak, and made equal to other objects within the physical viewing environment – the spectators' living rooms. This embeddedness of the scene of suffering in the materiality of technology and the domestic milieu not only severs the reality of suffering from its *own* nexus of sensations, as we just saw, but also reinserts suffering into *another* nexus of sensations – the spectators' own immediate physical states and moods. Because this latter nexus of sensations and feelings has existential priority over on-screen events, theorists claim, it is bound to always background the spectators' concern for the distant 'others' in favour of those who live 'at home'.

This is not a new thought. Smith, as early as in 1761, writes that the hypothetical impact an earthquake in China might bear on a 'man of humanity in Europe' would be nothing more than some sober reflections on the vanity of life. Yet, even though *'he* [the man of humanity in Europe] *will snore with the most profound security over the ruin of a hundred millions of his brethen'*, Smith remarks, *'if he was to lose his little finger tomorrow, he would not sleep tonight'* (1759/2000: 192–3). Similarly today, as Tomlinson echoing Marx says, it is 'the dull compulsion of the quotidian' that constitutes the individual's relevant horizon of feelings and actions. No matter how compelling suffering on television is, it remains – by virtue of its mediation – a distanced and discontinuous experience that presses less demandingly on the spectators' moral sensibilities than events within their own immediate sphere (1999: 178).

Summary
The pessimistic narrative, in both its versions, clearly illustrates the paradox of technology. The *capacity* of technology to deliver immediacy is simultaneously the *failure* of technology to establish connectivity. Whereas some theorists seek to work around the ethical impasses of this paradox, others remain resolutely negative. The most radical version of pessimism on the role of the media in social life is Baudrillard's thesis, in which the media are considered to be responsible for the disappearance of the real into a *simulacrum* – a mirror image of reality that is nowadays the only authentic reality for spectators. This position entails a nihilism that leaves no space for us to consider the ethical content of mediation, let alone the demand for public action that the television spectacle of suffering may provoke.

From mild defeatism to nihilism, from the belief that only an ethics of proximity is possible to the belief that no system of ethics is possible at all, the pessimistic narrative on the ethical role of television is undercut by suspicion. This is the suspicion of the promise of technology to produce authenticity. As this promise is undelivered, the purpose of mediation – to connect – also fails. This has dire consequences for contemporary ethical life, as spectators live the illusion of a collective existence that is simply not there; they inhabit an inauthentic reality.

The optimistic narrative

In the optimistic narrative, the immediacy of television's images and stories brings the world closer together. Part of the broad communitarian tradition of Durkheim and Merton, this narrative rests on the anthropological premise that the media work as symbols that generate authentic sociability. How so? In two respects.

In the *celebration of communitarianism* version of optimism, television introduces the spectator to a broad community of fellow spectators simply by engaging each in the act of simultaneous viewing. In the *democratization of responsibility* version of optimism, television's flow of messages from around the world increases each spectator's awareness of the distant 'other' and, thereby, also increases their concern for the misfortunes of these sufferers.

The celebration of communitarianism
In this version of optimism, the possibility of a cosmopolitan consciousness rests on the capacity of television to establish an imaginary 'we' that brings all spectators together in the act of watching. This vision of the

mass media stems from as early on as McLuhan's idea of the 'global village'. 'Global village' is a metaphor for the world being a place where all can be connected in a single community by means of the coordination of viewing action rather than the message of communication itself (1964).

This argument is also present in current accounts of mediation that claim that television establishes a spectatorial 'feeling in common' based more on the activity of viewing and less on the content of the spectacle. In this account, Eco says, television *'speaks less and less of the exterior world ... it speaks of itself and of the context it establishes with its audience'* (Eco, 1985, in Maffesoli, 1996: 66). This self-referential quality of television evidently comes about due to the capacity of this medium to have us all watching the same images at the same time. Yet, unlike the pessimistic thesis, where images may ultimately erode our sense of the real, here, the dissemination of images has the positive effect of bringing spectators together, in new forms of sociality and emotional connectivity. How, then, does the question of ethics figure in the celebration of communitar-ianism version of optimism?

Ethical questions are largely cast in terms of the style of their visualiza-tion. The question of violence, for example, is seen primarily as one of screen management. As Maffesoli claims, even if violence is an inevitable part of social life, the media 'war of images' always seeks to fit violence into the spectacular logic of television. The consequence, he says, is that violence may *'become ritualized and hence experienced at less cost or, as in ancient tournaments, only to the first blood drawn'* (1996: 140).

Although his argument has some truth – television does every so often stylize and sensationalize images of violence – Maffesoli goes too far in allowing the logic of the spectacle to replace a logic of explanation and action. The point is not so much that such an argument sidelines the historical and political relationships that lead to or can end violence but that the argument ignores the content of violence as a dramatically urgent reality for some people and only talks about the aesthetic appreciation of violence on television as a visual ritual form.

What this ethical–aesthetic view of mediation misses out is an orienta-tion towards the 'other'. It is not the connectivity to the 'other' seen on the screen that counts as the purpose of mediated experience, but the con-nectivity to fellow spectators. In this self-referential loop, the question of authenticity also becomes irrelevant. Who cares if what we watch is authentic or not if the purpose of watching is to keep us together. In this argument, technological immediacy – the images that bring the sufferer close to our homes – does not act as testimony of the sufferer's pain, but as a guarantee of the copresence of spectators.

At this point, we can see that the 'communitarian' version of optimism stands behind the 'intimacy at a distance' argument I examined earlier. It is now clear that events such as Princess Diana's death belong to this particular account, which celebrates the therapeutic effects of television on its audiences and the new 'emotional' publicness that television brings about. Tomlinson explains the unique expression of mass sociality that Princess Diana's funeral triggered off by resorting to this argument:

> The apparently strong desire of the mourners to share their grief in public could be read as ... the cultural desire to escape from the privacy of routine local life into wider, more fulfilling communities of experience.
>
> (Tomlinson, 1999: 168)

The democratization of responsibility

Not all versions of optimism for the ethical role of television are concerned with the experience of watching television as 'jouissance', in Maffesoli's words. The 'democratization of responsibility' version of optimism takes as its point of departure the reflexive organization of the self in late modernity and begs the question how can the mediated experience of the spectator translate into public–political consciousness?[14]

The concern here is with how a collectivity of television spectators can take the shape of the public and how such a collectivity can sustain a sense of responsibility towards the distant 'other'. The constant flow of images and information on our screens, the argument has it, inevitably opens up the local world of the spectator to the sight of the 'other' and, broadly, to non-local experiences. This contact further enables the reflexive process by means of which the spectator begins to think or talk about non-local experiences and may do something about them. It is the interplay between the visibility of the 'other' and the reflexive action of the spectator in response to the 'other' that contains the promise of cosmopolitanism.

This optimistic account of the ethical force of mediation goes so far as to consider the media as changing democracy today towards a deliberative model. Deliberative democracy, as opposed to representative democracy, is a non-localized, non-dialogical model of democracy that comes about when audiences use media information to form judgements about distant events and undertake public action in the local contexts of their everyday life. In the face of the crisis of representative forms of public participation via political parties and social movements, deliberative processes contain the hope for new practices of politicization and collective action.[15]

How, though, is this hope for a new public life to be realized? Thompson's response – the most influential articulation of the democratization of responsibility argument – simply reiterates its faith in the power of mediation. According to him, it is 'the increasing diffusion of information and images through the media that help to stimulate and deepen a sense of responsibility' (1995: 264). Yet, rather than asking how exactly this might happen, the democratization of responsibility version of optimism ultimately turns to wishful thinking. Audiences, we are told, must turn their sense of responsibility 'into a form of moral–practical reflection' because this is 'the best – the only option we have '(1995: 265). The dream of deliberative democracy is asserted, but the question of how we get there is essentially ignored.

Summary
The two optimistic versions of the ethics of mediation debate understand cosmopolitanism as the formation of a certain relationship between the spectator and the distant 'other'. In the 'celebration of communitarianism', this relationship connects the spectator with other spectators in the viewing communities of television. In the 'democratization of responsibility', this relationship carries a sense of responsibility towards the distant 'other'.

Although there is truth in both views, neither exhausts the ethical potential of mediation. On the one hand, to reduce mediation to its aesthetic effects – as the 'celebration of communitarianism' version does – does not help us to understand how the spectator can move beyond sensuous delight and develop a reflexive understanding regarding distant 'others'. On the other hand, to reduce mediation to a flow of images that can, by the sheer force of reiteration, generate sensibilities of global citizenship is equally simplistic.[16]

The paradox of technology, I would argue, haunts the optimistic narrative of mediation just as much as the pessimistic one. Technology connects, but how and who connects with whom remain unaccounted for. As the pessimistic narrative reminds us, however, the idea of cosmopolitanism does not emerge automatically out of the miracle of technological bonding because technology itself is thoroughly implicated in the production of the relationship between spectators and their distant and nearby 'others'. If there is a lesson to be learned from the pessimistic account, it is not so much that technology is to blame for failing to connect, but that technological contact with the imagery of the 'other' does not necessarily link to ethical responsibility; nor does the act of simultaneous witnessing, by definition, cultivate democratic 'publics'.[17]

In order to understand how cosmopolitanism is shaped as a mutual feeling of togetherness with fellow spectators or as responsibility to the distant 'other', we need to keep separate the conceptual space between watching and acting. This is the space of mediation as a public–political space and it is to a discussion of the qualities of this space that I now turn.

The public realm and cosmopolitanism

The rivalry between the pessimistic and optimistic narratives on the role of mediation in ethical life is one between two distinct models for the conduct of public life: the *dialogue* and *dissemination* models.[18] Both models agree that mediation is indispensible in today's public life. How else could we hear or see what is going on in the world at any moment without the radio, television or the Internet? The two models also agree on the ways in which mediation comes to shape public life. Mediation makes the world visible and audible to spectators and invites them to engage with it. Mediation, they say, is about those practices of viewing that lift people from the realm of their idiosyncratic interests, their 'particularity', towards the realm of common interests, the 'universal' values that join them together and define a collectivity of spectators as precisely a 'public'.[19]

Cosmopolitanism in both models, then, is about those practices of mediation that represent sufferers to spectators using an array of 'universal' values, each of which motivates the spectators to take a public stance vis-à-vis the sufferers' misfortunes. Be these 'universal' values humanitarian charity (sending aid to the Sudan's refugee camps), political denunciation (protesting against the war in Iraq) or the sublimation of terror (being shocked by the sight of planes crashing into the World Trade Centre), the point is that these practices of mediation seek to act on the spectator as moralizing forces. They seek to take the spectators out of their homes and present them with the necessity for action orientated towards the conditions of the historical world. This is the case even if, in the absence of a proper terrain for immediate action, the response of the powerless spectators is just a whisper in their own minds. As Boltanski puts it:

> It is by speaking up that the spectator can maintain his [sic] integrity when, brought face to face with suffering, he is called upon to act in a situation in which direct action is difficult or impossible. Now even if this speech is initially no more than an internal whisper to himself [...], none the less in principle it contains a requirement of publicity. It is in some way already public speech addressed to an indefinite number of partners whose status is undefined.
>
> (1999: 20)

Boltanski sets a minimal requirement for public life as internal speech. Even though it may appear too little to account as effective action, the 'internal whisper to oneself' is strategic in my discussion. This is because this minimal requirement allows me to investigate the relationship between mediation and public conduct as a relationship of degree. Public conduct, it suggests, is not only the openly public act – the street demonstration or the party political manifesto – but also any mundane act that addresses suffering as a cause that deserves to be seen and heard by other people, even if the other people's 'status is undefined'. At the same time, in insisting that the public space is an undefined entity, Boltanski further implies that the relationship between mediation and public action is one of mutual constitution. It suggests, in other words, that the spectators' responses to suffering on television do not directly call on a pre-existing public but they (partly, at least) constitute this public at the moment of addressing it.

What follows from this is that each model of the public realm – dialogue or dissemination – presupposes a different conception of mediation as appropriate for engaging spectators in public conduct. In turn, what counts as public conduct crucially depends on the conception of mediation each model of the public presupposes and promotes.

Which conception of mediation informs the dialogic model and the pessimistic narrative on ethics that this model entails? Which conception of mediation lies behind the dissemination model and its optimistic ethics of mediation? I address these questions respectively in the sections 'Pessimism and the dialogic model' and 'Optimism and the dissemination model' that follow each other below. It is the inadequacies of these two models of public life to conceive of mediation as a properly ethical force that make me look for an alternative. The study of the ethics of mediation, I propose, should abandon ideal models of the public and turn towards the phronetic study of concrete practices of mediation as a politics of pity.

Pessimism and the dialogic model

The dialogic model of public life assumes that mediation should be like face-to-face communication. Reminiscent of the 'polis' – the ancient Athenian public life – the idea of being physically close and connecting directly with the 'other' is the norm for public conduct in this model. In a similar manner, the pessimistic narrative understands the ethical problem of mediation – the spectator's incapacity to connect with the distant 'other' – as a problem of the lack of face-to-face contact. The fact that these two figures – the spectator and the sufferer – do not share the same space, nor the same temporality, makes it impossible for the spectator to assume an ethical responsibility towards the misfortune of the 'other'. Central, then, to both versions of pessimism – intervention of technology and domesticity of reception – is the view that passing from the intimacy of the home to the public realm needs to overcome the obstacle of non-presence – namely, the physical separation of the spectator from the sufferer.

Both versions of pessimism blame the nature of the medium for not being able to fulfil the ideal of copresence. In the domesticity of reception argument, we saw that television is to blame for being monologic and, therefore, out of tune with the spectator's lifeworld. In the intervention of technology argument, television is to blame for being unreliable. Television, the argument has it, is unable to deliver 'the' truth of suffering because it cannot offer us direct access to it – it can only deliver *evidence* of this truth.

The inability of the medium to evoke a sense of face-to-face contact is a problem that each version of pessimism addresses in a different way. In the domesticity of reception version, the idea is that television must itself compensate for its one-way flow and, therefore, must make up for the loss of continuity that characterizes its spectacles. It must do so, theorists say, by incorporating some degree of face-to face dialogicality within itself. That is, television must anticipate what the situation of reception is and stage the spectacle of distant suffering in ways that are relevant to the spectators' lifeworlds:

> the 'stories' that frame issues of distant moral concern need to be told in ways which render them congruent with local horizons – indeed which translate these concerns into the realm of the personal and the intimate.

> (Tomlinson, 1999: 179)

Tomlinson's proposal seeks to evoke a sense of copresence by translating the 'otherness' of distant misfortune into the terms of the spectators' lifeworlds. The moral proposal of the dialogic model, then, formulates the demand for publicness, for spectators' rising beyond intimacy, using the very rules of intimacy. This has consequences for the figure of the cosmopolitan. If spectators encounter the world out there only in terms of their own local horizons, their own lifeworlds, how would they ever get a glimpse of the irreducible difference of 'others'? Which measure of the personal and the public is required so that the representation of suffering opens up the horizons of spectators and helps cultivate a cosmopolitan sensibility?

Even if the cosmopolitan is a possibility, albeit a problematic one, in the domesticity of reception argument, the intervention of technology argument leaves no space at all for this figure. In this version of pessimism, connectivity between spectator and sufferer is impossible because technology, by definition, renders distant suffering a spectacle to watch and encourages spectators to think of suffering as an object of the imagination rather than a reality for those who live outside the zone of safety.

In conclusion, even though the dialogic model of the public realm acknowledges that the media play a central role in contemporary life, it holds media responsible for a considerable decrease in people's engagement with public life. The problem lies, particularly, in the fact that the media have today brought about doubt concerning the authenticity of distant realities. It is this doubt – threatening to turn the reality of suffering into fiction for spectators – that increasingly corrodes the cohesion of public life.

For the dialogic model, then, the place in which spectators' ethical relationships with distant sufferers begins is not the space of mediation itself, but the face-to face at home – the domestic context of reception. Herein lies the contradiction of the dialogic model. It cannot imagine public actors outside the premises of intimacy.

Does the dissemination model of public life deal with the possibility of cosmopolitanism under conditions of mediation in a more effective way?

Optimism and the dissemination model

In the *dissemination* model, it is not any more the polis, but, rather, the globalized world that informs the norms of public life. Rather than insisting on the ideal of copresence, the dissemination model feels comfortable with the disjunction of experience that mediation has brought about in public life. As a consequence, its norm of public conduct is broadcasting – that is, the dispersion of messages and the possibilities for connectivity that these messages generate in the absence of a sender or a receiver. This is evident in the two versions of the optimistic narrative of mediation, both of which regard mediation as a space of appearance, not as a space of copresence.

Both versions of the dissemination model of public life praise the capacity of mediation to disclose the world to us because this capacity can create a new ethics of public life. Whereas in the 'celebration of communitarianism' version, mediation establishes a publicness that is about people indulging in the euphoria of collective belonging, in the 'democratization of responsibility' version, mediation establishes a publicness that is about each individual's responsibility for non-local issues. Both versions of optimism, then, can be described in terms of what Maffesoli calls (speaking only of the former) 'a transfiguration of the political' (1996). The term refers to the decline of the public realm as a single sphere of conduct and the rise of a publicness consisting of instantaneous experiences, fragmented encounters and local communications among people. In breaking free from the guilt relating to the loss of authentic public life, dissemination is a promising model of the public realm. In this model, it is fine that mediation is monologic or technological because it is not about speaking to the one next to us; it is about 'speaking into the air', to use Peters' words. Nevertheless, dissemination fails to consider important ethical issues that arise in the process of speaking into the air. What is spoken into the air and how do we respond to it?

It is hard to find answers to these questions in the dissemination model of public life. By holding a view of mediation as the constant flow of images, both optimistic versions of mediation ignore the distinct weight that technologically disseminated discourse carries. In democratization of responsibility, the emphasis on television as a medium of dissemination ignores the fact that the sheer flow of images and talk often fails to create coherence and continuity. The seriality and reiteration of images may result not in establishing coherence but, on the contrary, in interrupting the coherence of mediation. This is what Giddens has called the 'collage effect' of television (1990). Too much information simply becomes too much.

The consequence of the collage effect for the spectator may well be less responsibility towards the sufferer and more apathy vis-à-vis the world. Suffering, it tells us, occurs all the time everywhere and it has become all too common to raise an eyebrow. It becomes banal. This means that the spectacle of suffering is not doubted in terms of its veracity, but, on the contrary, passively accepted as the truth of television and, indeed, of life. As McQuire puts it, talking about evil, 'resistance to believing has been overrun by the perception that such evil is "human all too human"' (1999: 153).

In this resigned acceptance of the banality of suffering – intensely debated under the name 'compassion fatigue' – lies the question of the apathetic spectator. The apathetic spectator is reconciled with the presence of evil and regards the injustice of suffering as an inevitable condition of life. This is an issue that, as I argued earlier, the democratization of responsibility thesis only wishes away rather than systematically addresses.

In the second version of optimism – the celebration of communitarianism – the emphasis on the dissemination of images completely ignores the content of mediation. Yet, isn't it just this question of *what* makes people get together that makes the difference between a group of spectators connected by simultaneous watching and a group of spectators connected by common values and action?[20] Attending to the 'what' of mediation means that we attend to a *cause*, a political and ethical discourse that presents the demand for action and, thereby, turns a mass of individual spectators into a public.

The cause is one of the constitutive properties of the public realm because it signals precisely that moment when spectators shift from the particularity of their domestic existence to the 'universal' values that motivate action for the 'other' – to protest against Amina Lawal's death by stoning sentence or the Iraq war. This 'swing to commitment' as Boltanski calls the ethical drive for common action, is 'the grand moment par excellence' of the public realm (1999: 30). Yet, in the communitarian version, the idea of cause does not refer to the suffering 'other' but the spectators belonging to their own collectivity. By closing off the theme of the 'other', the celebration of communitarianism version keeps the key issues of the cause and public action outside the debate on the ethics of mediation.

In conclusion, the dissemination model of the public realm moves from a view of mediation as *information exchange* to mediation as *world disclosing* (Peters, 1999). In disclosing or opening up the world to the spectator, mediation may democratize responsibility and create new collective bonds among spectators. The drawback of the dissemination model, however, lies in assuming that *technological* immediacy leads automatically to *sociocultural* immediacy. In my view, what is missing from the dissemination model is attention to the content and texture of mediation – the 'what' is being represented and the 'how'.

Conclusion

Social theory of the media concentrates on the role that technology plays in transforming the ethics of public life. Whereas the pessimistic narrative accuses technology of eroding traditional public collectivities, the optimistic narrative capitalizes on the promise of technology to cultivate new collective sensibilities among media publics.

Pessimism and optimism reflect two different norms of public life. Pessimism reflects the dialogic model and its public norm is the ethics of proximity, acting on those who are close to us or, at best, translating distant events into our own lifeworld.

Optimism reflects the dissemination model and its public norm is action at a distance. Cosmopolitanism is closer to the disseminative conception of public life, yet this narrative also fails to tell us how television connects us with the 'other' and how it may engage with distant suffering as a cause of action.

Haunted by the presence of technology, these two narratives provide us with an either/or way of understanding the ethics of public life, which does not address the question of how practices of mediation may turn the random collectivities of spectators into cosmopolitan publics.

Notes

1 See Ellis (2000: 1).
2 See Tester (2001) for a similar classification.
3 See Boltanski (1999) and Arendt (1963/1990: 58–114, 'The social question') for a seminal critique of the conception of post-Enlightenment European public life around the question of pity and McGowan (1998: 81–95) for a discussion.
4 Tomlinson draws on dictionary definitions of mediation. First, mediation as 'the means by which something is communicated', which refers to the facilitating aspect of mediation in connecting people, and, second, mediation as 'the intervening substance through which impressions are conveyed to the senses', which refers to the impact of the medium on communication, as it qualitatively changes the experience of the thing communicated (1999: 154).
5 Boltanski (1999: 50) draws on Piper's *Impartiality, Compassion and Modal Imagination* (1991: 726–57). For the same claim, see Smith's *The Theory of Moral Sentiments* (part I, section 1, 1761/2000: 8) for this point:

> The compassion of the spectator must arise altogether from the consideration of what he himself [sic] would feel if he was reduced to the same unhappy situation, and, what perhaps is impossible, was at the same time able to regard it with his present reason and judgement.

6 See Tomlinson (1999: 171–80) for a discussion relating to the 'closing of moral distance'. See also Giddens (1990, 1991, 1992), Thompson (1995, 2000), Morley and Robins (1995), Silverstone (1999, 2002a and b), and Misztal (2000).
7 See Cohen (2001: vii). See also, among others, Tester (2001: 7–8) on 'the media coverage of famine, misery and suffering' that 'serves to isolate the world of the audience from the world in which it seems that violence and brutality run amok'.
8 See Adorno (1938/1982) and Merton (1946). At the same time, as Peters reminds us, the core controversy in social and media theory reflects a deeper rivalry between Marx's conflictual view of society and Durkheim's consensual view of the social body (Peters, 1999: 223).

9   See Robins (1994: 461).

10 See Scannell (1996) and Peters (2001).

11 See Tester (2001: 1–9) and Miller (1971: 183).

12 Peters' historical perspective broadens up the conditions of doubt over the testimony of the body to include more than technologies of mediation such as television. For Peters, doubt is a condition inherent in the function of witnessing itself and has always left its mark on a range of public practices that use the body as a site of authentication:

> The whole apparatus of trying to assure truthfulness, from torture to martyrdom to courtroom only testifies to the strange lack of its core. Witnessing is necessary but not sufficient [and] a witness is never conclusive or final despite the most militant attempts of martyrs and torturers to make it so.
>
> (2001: 713)

13 See Miller (1971: 126).

14 See Giddens (1990, 1991), Thompson (1990, 1995) and Tomlinson (1999).

15 See Thompson (1995: 114–16) for examples of such possibilities and Alexander and Jakobs (1998: 22–41) on American civil society.

16 See Chouliaraki (2000: 293–314) for a criticism of the 'democratization of responsibility' position.

17 See Silverstone (1999, 2002a and b) and Derrida and Stiegler (2002).

18 See Peters (1999: 33–62) for the distinction at the level of communication models. From a historical perspective, Peters associates the two models of communication with the archetypal figures of Socrates – for *dialogue* – and Jesus – for *dissemination*. By making this move, he manages to add conceptual nuance and historical depth to a whole host of twentieth-century traditions of thought on the public realm. Peters' distinction has the further advantage of talking about the possibility of communication as a public act with heavy ethical implications and, in this sense, it fits the purposes of my own discussion.

19 See Barnett (2003: 100–7), Chartier (1999: 161–8) and Robbins (1999: xii–xxvi).

20 Relevant here is Sartre's distinction between a collectivity connected to an externality – the *series* – versus a collectivity connected by mutual praxis – the *group* (1976) – discussed in both Tomlinson (1999: 202–3) and Derrida and Stiegler (2002).

2

THE PARADOXES OF MEDIATION

The discussion on the subject of the two models of public life in the previous chapter shows that cosmopolitanism is a blindspot in current theories on the media and public life. Cosmopolitanism is either impossible (in the dialogic model) or possible (in the dissemination model). Together, these either/or positions ultimately present us with a view of mediation as a series of irresolvable dilemmas, as paradoxes. A more effective assessment of the possibility of cosmopolitanism today should begin, I believe, from an analytical position that examines how the paradoxes of mediation appear as temporarily resolved in concrete representations of suffering on television.

In the Aristotelian spirit of phronesis, I describe this shift as one from high theory to an analytics of mediation. I discuss the concept of analytics in Chapter 4, so, for now, it is enough to say that analytics is a research strategy that approaches the paradoxes of mediation by means of the study of examples. Analytics, thus, asks the question how do specific television texts make an ethical demand on the spectator by construing the distant sufferer as a reality that requires the spectator's response?

Three paradoxes of mediation traverse the debate on the ethics of public life. The first is clearly the paradox of technology, which thematizes the role of the media in simultaneously establishing and undermining the immediacy of suffering for the spectator. The second paradox is about mediation as face-to-face contact or as speaking into the air and thematizes the role of proximity and distance in the representation of suffering. The third paradox is about mediation as world disclosure or information exchange and thematizes the spectator as an onlooker or actor on the spectacle of suffering. Let me discuss each of these paradoxes in turn.

The paradox of technology

Technology closes the moral distance between spectators and sufferers and so cultivates a cosmopolitan disposition in public life, yet, at the same time, it fictionalizes suffering and leads spectators to indifference. This is the paradox of technology. If looking *through* the screen immerses spectators in suffering as authentic reality, as social theory tells us, looking *at* the screen reminds them of the reality of the medium that disseminates suffering as spectacle and fiction.[1]

However, we might ask, is this ambivalent condition of technology new? Far from it. As Boltanski reminds us, the practices of representation characteristic to public life, such as political manifestos but also literary or artistic genres, have always implicated their media in the act of representation and, therefore, have always had to account for the tension in technology between delivering and manufacturing the truth (1999: xv).

Even though television rearticulates and reforms these old genres, it still operates decisively within their premises. The medium of television appropriates other media (from photographs to radio and from painting to website layouts) and, in the process, reformulates the content of eternal ethical dilemmas in new ways, throwing into relief both their continuities with the past and their distinctly contemporary character. The appropriation of other media and their genres is, then, crucial to understanding the tension in technology not as a failure of mediation to construe authenticity but as an inherent element of mediation as *re*-mediation.[2]

The theme of suffering entails its own media and genres of representation that, when adapted to television's own technological apparatus, create an array of possible spectator–sufferer relationships. Specifically, Boltanski's historical typology of suffering genres encompasses the novel, the political manifesto and painting.[3] Each of these three genres gives rise to distinct potentials for emotion and options for action on suffering, by using a distinct medium. The *novel* organizes the spectator's affective potential around empathy with the sufferer and is prototypically carried via the medium of the book (1999: 85–95). The *manifesto* organizes this affective potential around denunciation of the evil-doer and is prototypically articulated via the medium of the political pamphlet (1999: 59–67). Finally, the *tableau vivant* directs the spectator away from specific emotional states and towards a distantiated contemplation of the aesthetics of suffering in the medium of the painting (1999: 114–30).

Each genre seeks to represent suffering as if the medium were absent from the scene of action, drawing on the conventions of objectivity in literary language, political discourse or visual aesthetics. Simultaneously, each genre also seeks to represent suffering by capitalizing on the very presence of the medium and its specific capacity to arouse emotion – in the book, street pamphlet or the tableau. It is these possibilities for representing the scene of suffering – by at once concealing and acknowledging the meaning affordance of each medium – that the politics of pity comes to define.

At this point, let me formulate the concept of the politics of pity to fit better the context of contemporary mediation. The politics of pity is the symbolic mechanism of television news by means of which various media and their genres construe the spectator–sufferer relationship via emotions of empathy and denunciation or aesthetic contemplation while also seeking to present this relationship as transparent and objective.

From the bias of technology to the politics of pity

The politics of pity seeks to study the mediation of suffering as remediation. To put it in Bolter and Grusin's terminology, the politics of pity approaches the mediation of suffering both as *hypermediacy* – suffering passing through media – and *immediacy* – suffering as if it were happening in front of our eyes.[4] Let me now briefly discuss how these two dimensions inform the analysis of suffering on television.

Hypermediacy seeks to assess how technology participates in the social process of mediation and how, in so doing, it shapes the encounter between spectator and sufferer. Rather than deploring the intervention of technology in public life, the analytical concern with hypermediacy asks specific 'How?' questions. How does television bring digital visual technology and historical literary genres together in particular news on suffering? How do the techniques of visual editing or slow motion manage to trigger off spectators' emotions in various spectacles of human pain?

Such questions have a strong aesthetic orientation because they raise the issue of how media and their semiotic modes stage not the spectacle of suffering, but suffering as a spectacle. The majority of media and social theorists reserve the term 'aesthetic' for pictorial representation only – sometimes with unfortunate consequences. I use the term 'aesthetic' more broadly, however, to refer to television's systematic articulation of semiotic resources – linguistic and pictorial – that aim at cultivating specific dispositions of emotion and action towards distant 'others'. In this sense, aesthetic considerations do not stand on their own but, rather, connect with the problematic of the public realm and its conditions for action. I believe that the formation of publics is an aesthetic operation, in so far as this formation entails its own active authoring process or, in a more theatrical language, its own mise en scène of collective identities. The mise en scène (a concept I return to in Chapter 4) is the process by which discursive resources and historical genres are brought together to stage suffering as an on-screen spectacle that touches the spectator's heart and mind.[5]

Immediacy seeks to assess how television establishes specific emotional states and modes of action as natural and objective for the spectator. Unlike the dissemination model, which ignores the semantic content of mediation, this analytical perspective asks what the spectacle of suffering is about and how it makes us feel. Does the spectacle of suffering appear factual and urgent or fictional and irrelevant to spectators? Does the spectacle engage spectators in empathy or indignation with what they are watching or does it leave no trace in their memories?

These questions draw attention to how suffering becomes an immediate reality for spectators and acknowledge that content is crucial for the analysis of power in mediation. Simultaneously, these questions presuppose a thorough understanding of the category of mise en scène and, thereby, indicate that our attention to immediacy cannot be separated from our analytical attention to hypermediacy.

Current theories on mediation systematically privilege the image over language and, as a consequence, simplify the processes of the symbolic formation of spectators into a public. In the vocabulary of the politics of pity, this is because such theories fail to integrate the focus on hypermediacy, the semiotic work of television, with the focus on immediacy, the social relationships of power that seek to moralize the spectator in the process of mediation. Chapter 3 addresses this shortcoming by developing a view of mediation that attends to both the meaning affordances of television media and the power relationships of media discourse.

Mediation as immediacy and hypermediacy makes it possible to consider the two subsequent paradoxes of mediation proximity–distance and watching–acting in a new light. I begin with the paradox of distance.

The paradox of distance

In the pessimistic thesis, the management of *geographical* distance fails to close the *moral* distance between spectators and the sufferers. However, even in the optimistic thesis – where the dissemination of images is believed to make an ethical demand on the spectator – distance is a thorny question. This is because the optimistic thesis proves to be a halfway house between the dissemination and dialogic models, in that it regards, simultaneously, broadcasting as instrumental in the new democratic sensibility but sees such sensibility as ultimately originating in the spectators' lifeworlds.

Let me emphasize that to open up the issue of the management of distance is not to challenge the fact that the spectators' experiences of television spectacles are anchored in their lifeworlds.[6] It is, rather, to challenge the idea that this anchoring of television experience in their lifeworlds is the only advantageous position from which to study how our responses to the 'other' are shaped by television. Even though I take both spectators' lifeworlds and the texts of mediation to be crucial sites for the construal of suffering, to privilege the study of lifeworlds over the texts may result in misleading views as to who bears responsibility for the audience's 'compassion fatigue'.

Tomlinson's suggestion to 'throw the moral responsibility back upon the media' (1999: 179) acknowledges that the process of mediation itself may be an advantageous analytical position from which to consider the management of distance. Yet, Tomlinson lacks the language to analyse the mediation of suffering. For him, the representation of suffering should be personal, so that it establishes a certain degree of congruence with the spectator's moral lifeworld. However, is the personal an appropriate norm by which to measure how the public disposition of the spectator may develop?

Silverstone offers a more adequate response when he argues that the issue is not the media's capacity to get personal, but, rather, their 'capacity to bring people together while simultaneously keeping them apart' (2003: 259). It is this ambivalence of mediation – constantly hovering between closeness and distance – that lies at the core of the ethics of mediation. The politics of pity seeks to address this ambivalence, too:

> Distance is a fundamental dimension of a politics [of pity] which has the specific task of unification [...] needed to establish equivalence between spatially and temporally local situations.
>
> (Boltanski, 1999: 7)

Boltanski talks here about the politics of pity in a manner reminiscent of Tomlinson's view of mediation as the closing of moral distance, but he goes further than this. Boltanski suggests that the mediation of suffering is a *politics* that establishes *equivalence* between places and times, strategically recombining them so as to create new senses of proximity and connectivity.

There is, in this approach to space and time, a recognition of the autonomous power of mediation to shape our sense of distance and proximity vis-à-vis the scene of suffering we are watching. In a similar spirit, Butler suggests that the medium's 'structure of address' has a crucial moralizing effect on spectators' experiences. In her words: 'What binds us morally has to do with how we are addressed by others in ways that *we cannot avert or avoid*' (2004: 130 – emphasis added).

Far from depriving spectators of the reflexive agency to decide if and how to respond to suffering, Butler points to the fact that they are always already addressed as ethical subjects before their moment of decision. The address by the 'other' happens, as Butler says, by virtue of being confronted with the spectacle of suffering itself, unexpected and unplanned in the monologic flow of television. This structure of address consists of those practices of discourse – linguistic and visual – via which television construes the scene of suffering as a spectacle to be watched and invites spectators to feel for and engage with sufferers' misfortunes.

From distance to the politics of space–time

In the analytical language of pity, the management of distance in media discourse appertains again to both dimensions of mediation – hypermediacy and immediacy.

Hypermediacy refers to those television practices, such as camera work and linguistic narrative, that regulate the various degrees of proximity to spectators that the suffering may take, thereby offering to them a vantage point from which to witness the suffering. For example, the visualization of suffering is an instrumental semiotic choice in bridging the distance between spectators and sufferers because visualization facilitates modal imagination. Visualization facilitates the move from thinking of Amina Lawal's condition as a story in our heads towards thinking that her imminent stoning is an urgent and horrific reality for a young mother out there in the world. Although not a guarantee that there will be a closing of the moral distance between the two, the visualization of the sufferer is nevertheless a mode of address with a strong moral appeal to the spectator.

Immediacy refers not to suffering as a mise en scène, as theatrical spectacle, but, rather, as an emotional and practical reality in itself. The topics of empathy, denunciation and aesthetic contemplation are key discursive devices in the construal of suffering as suffering because each topic entails, implicitly or explicitly, an emotional proposal for the spectator to reach towards or stay clear from the sufferer. Feelings themselves introduce a measure of proximity or distance from spectacles of suffering.[7] For example, war footage may use interviews with medical doctors and hospitalized civilians, especially mothers and children, in order to bring spectators into close proximity with the sufferers or it may film a scene of warfare from afar and above, offering spectators the position of an onlooker to military action.

These examples tell us something else, too. They tell us that the topics of pity present us with suffering not only as a 'purely' *personal* reality of feelings, but also as a *public* reality, in so far as these personal feelings are inevitably informed by 'universal' values of what it is conventionally right to think and do vis-à-vis the scene of suffering. The proximity to a hospital easily evokes the sentiment of empathy with individual war victims, whereas the panorama of bombing operations minimizes emotional identification with sufferers and reflexively engages spectators with the condition of warfare via the aesthetic register of Hollywood cinematography.[8] Whether it is empathy without contemplation about the causes of the war or the aestheticization of military action without a human touch, both perspectives are ways in which to represent war on television as an ethical spectacle, inherently depending on the politics of space–time.

Proximity and distance are, in this respect, not only vantage points from which to witness the scene of suffering but also analytical nodal points that bring together and fuse the dual character of pity as both a personal and public process – a discussion I take up in Chapters 8 and 9. For now, let me insist on this point. To look on pity as an outcome of mediation that combines particular circumstance and explanatory context suggests that neither proximity nor distance, in themselves, have to do with the closing of moral distance. Indeed, if we consider these two to be 'pure' categories, we may easily misunderstand proximity as *always* leading to intimacy and private emotion. Equally, we may also misconstrue distance as *always* leading to depersonalization and indifference.[9] The symbolic construal of suffering, as any news text would indicate, involves more complicated space – time articulations.

What is the implication of looking into the paradox of distance as a politics of space–time? The main implication for our pursuit of the cosmopolitan disposition is this. Rather than seeking to moralize spectators by bringing the suffering of 'others' as close as possible to spectators' life-worlds, we should ask instead which is the *proper* distance from which television should invite us to contemplate the humanness of sufferers and the historicity of their suffering (Silverstone, 2003: 469)?[10] The humanness of sufferers demands that we neither zoom too close up to assume that they are like 'us' nor zoom too far out, reducing them to dots on the map. The demand for historicity requires that each instance of suffering is placed in a meaningful (though not tiresomely exhaustive) context of explanation and understanding that addresses the question of why this suffering is important and what there is to do about it.

The paradox of in/action

The final paradox that I wish to address sets up mediation as information exchange against mediation as world disclosure or appearance. Mediation as information exchange undercuts the pessimistic narrative of mediation, where the medium of television turns suffering into pure spectacle and reduces spectators to being passive voyeurs of the pain of 'others'. Mediation as world disclosure informs the optimistic narrative, where the image of suffering has a moralizing impact on spectators, making it possible to imagine them as public actors who respond to the demands of 'others'.

Does the sheer visibility of sufferers on our screens present us with a new ethical dilemma specific only to our own mediated times? The response is no. Despite the unprecedented expansion in the visibility of suffering nowadays, Boltanski rightly reminds us that the unease that the spectacle of suffering provokes is not a consequence of the media: 'The problems posed to the spectator (should he continue his meal, as if it was nothing?) emerged at the same time as pity was introduced into politics' (1999: 12).

Rather than a radical discontinuity between a past without mass media and the present times of mediation then, there is instead a suggestive historical continuity. It is the problem of action at a distance that provides this continuity: people have always been confronted with the moral dilemma of knowing that suffering occurs out there but not being able to do something about it. It is the theme of pity that provides a solution to the problem of powerlessness because pity offers to spectators two different options for action that transcend their own local space and time.

Each type of action draws on a distinct historical practice of public life: the *agora* and the *theatre*. Originating in the Athenian polis, both the agora and the theatre acknowledge the inability of spectators to act directly on the suffering because of the problem of the distance separating the spectators from the sufferers. They are, however, metaphors of agency, in the sense that each conception of action entails its own specific discursive procedures that facilitate action at a distance.[11] Each metaphor, that is, puts forward its own proposal as to how action could be undertaken had the spectator the capacity to undertake such action.

The *agora* is a metaphor of agency as people gather to gaze and reflect upon – precisely to contemplate – a theme of common interest by means of dialogue and argumentation. The *theatre* is also a metaphor of agency as people gather to gaze and identify with – or feel for – the spectacle of suffering by means of drama and theatrical expression. In both conceptions of agency, the citizen is imagined to be primarily a disinterested spectator.[12] This a priori dispassionate observer comes to join the public realm of 'universal' values by the force of argument in agora and by identification in theatre.

The reference to the agora and the theatre is important because, in both metaphors, agency does not inhere in the spectators' cognitive or emotional capacities to think or feel but resides in the distinct discursive practices of the public realm itself – in practices of mediation. The politics of pity is this symbolic mechanism of mediation that seeks to motivate the spectators' move from dispassionate observation to agency, to public conduct. This is why, as I mentioned earlier under the heading 'The paradox of technology', the representation of suffering needs to skillfully navigate between objective observation and emotion, be this empathy, anger or shock and awe. Whereas impartiality gestures towards the necessity for a dispassionate and rational predisposition on the part of spectators, emotionality is necessary for their 'swing to commitment' to a moral cause.

From in/action to the politics of agency

The duality of agency – simultaneously theatrical emotion and agoraic deliberation – again manifests itself in mediation as immediacy and hypermediacy.

Immediacy comes across in the theatrical dimension of the public realm. This is because immediacy foregrounds the spectacle through the screen and focuses on suffering as a scene of emotion, where dispassionate observers are invited to feel for and identify with characters already active in the scene of suffering. Whereas empathy orientates the spectators' feeling potential towards the benefactors, the figures who alleviate suffering, denunciation orientates their feeling towards the persecutors, the figures who commit the evil, and, finally, the aestheticization of suffering invites the spectators to indulge in their own feelings of awe and sublimation vis-à-vis the sufferers' misfortunes.

Hypermediacy foregrounds the spectacle on the screen and focuses on suffering as the staging of a performance, where the dispassionate observers are invited to join the deliberative processes of the agora and engage in rational argumentation on the 'universal' values of the spectacle that they are watching. Part of this hypermediated engagement is the spectators' awareness that their act of connecting with the medium simultaneously connects them with others and with their own possible arguments about this same spectacle. The process of deliberation – celebrated in the optimistic version of mediation – stems precisely from this awareness by the spectators that they are always part of an ongoing conversation, even if this conversation takes place in the confines of their own homes – indeed, 'as a whisper'.

The whisper is a sign of agency in so far as, in the absence of a physical public space, it stands for speech that the spectators intend for others. The whisper qualifies as public speech because it evokes a scene of appearance, theatrical or agoraic, where the spectators' action is assumed to be visible, audible and subject to judgment by all. It is a space populated by an undefined entity that shares with them the same principles of conduct.

In assuming the space of appearance, agency further presupposes another thing. It presupposes a certain reflexive ability – namely 'the spectator's ability to consider himself as a speaker' (Boltanski, 1999: 40). How else could the spectators utter the whisper unless they were able to monitor themselves as if others were around? Agency, then, refers at once to two spectatorial positions that correspond to the duality of mediation. The ordinary spectator who acts as if she were in the scene of action (the condition of immediacy and identification) and the reflexive spectator, who acts as if she were heard and judged by others (the condition of hypermediacy and deliberation).

Although both positions are as if or imaginary positions (let us not forget that pity resolves the problem of action at a distance), they nevertheless point to a crucial but neglected property of mediation. This is that the structure of address by means of which television 'speaks' to spectators not only moralizes them by managing distance and proximity vis-à-vis the suffering but it also moralizes the spectators by managing personal feeling and public opinion.

Cosmopolitan agency is an emotionally motivated response but one that is strictly based on the condition that a suffering has been impartially assessed as worthy of being a 'universal' cause for action. This means that pure immediacy is not a sufficient condition for the production of the cosmopolitan disposition. The reason for immediacy alone being inadequate to produce pity lies in the risk – inherent in any exaggerated particularity, such as the stories of heroic soldiers in the battlefield – of ultimately exhausting the spectators' response by easy sentimentalism without an overview of the causes and effects of war suffering.[13] However, connectivity cannot be achieved by too much generality either. This is because talking only about strategic plans and casualty statistics evacuates suffering of its dramatic urgency and removes it from the order of reality for spectators. By presenting, for example, the Iraq war from an operational point of view – embedded journalists using military talk, with terms such as 'collateral damage' or 'precision strikes', and no images of death – British television footage was accused of giving to the war a fictional quality.[14]

Instead, cosmopolitanism is about articulating the two elements in a single position of *reflexive identification*. As we shall see in the case of *ecstatic news*, when I discuss the live footage of September 11th, cosmopolitanism as reflexive identification is the discursive practice that facilitates television spectators incorporating in to their private responses to suffering 'the demand for public speech and the anticipation of an active attitude' (Boltanski, 1999: 23). Even if this speech is nothing but a whisper to themselves, public speech differentiates itself from other responses to suffering in that it seeks to cast the spectacle of suffering in some 'universal' ethical norm and thereby to join a broader community of judgement and action.

Conclusion

In the spirit of phronetic research, I suggest that the search for cosmopolitanism should be grounded in the study of how television signifies the relationship between the spectator and the distant sufferer.

I propose three dimensions of mediation that constitute the spectator as a public subject. First, the politics of pity – that is, the ways in which various media and their semiotic resources produce meaning about the spectator–sufferer relationship in television. Second, the management of space–time – that is, the ways in which mediation manages spectators' distance from or proximity to the scene of suffering. Third, the management of agency – that is, the ways in which mediation manages to resolve the spectators' incapacity to act on distant suffering.

The assumption behind this approach is that the moral horizon of the spectator resides in media discourse and, thus, has a thoroughly textual form before it becomes part of the spectator's consciousness and her or his will to act. In this sense, cosmopolitanism is less an empirical identity that pre-exists the texts of television and more 'a mode of managing meaning' on and off the television screen, as Hannertz puts it (1996: 238). The main reason for social theory on the media having so far failed to adequately address the question of the cosmopolitan spectator, I argue in the next chapter, is precisely because of its inability to think of media texts as something more than an image.

Notes

1   See Bolter and Grusin (2000: 41) for the distinction.
2   Bolter and Grusin (2000: 45) draw on McLuhan's remark that 'the content of any medium is always another medium' to define *remediation* as 'the representation of one medium in another'. They argue that 'What might seem at first to be an esoteric practice', appearing unique to a specific medium, 'is so widespread that we can identify a spectrum of different ways in which digital media remediate their predecessors'. Even though the authors' interest lies in digital media, in fact, they are keen to emphasize that it is not only digital but all media, including seventeenth-century Dutch painting, that remediate others' media.
3   See Boltanski (1999: 57–146) for a detailed exposition and thorough critique of the three topics of suffering – 'the topic of denunciation', the 'topic of sentiment' and the 'aesthetic topic'.
4   See Bolter and Grusin (2000: 70–1).
5   See Yudice (1993) for the link between aesthetics and the public realm. Corner (1995: 94–5) uses the concept of mise en scène to describe the way in which different representational elements are put together to create a certain aesthetic effect at the level of the shot. Mise en scène, as Bordwell and Thompson (2001: 156–7) also suggest, can describe a finite sequence of shots, that make up a coherent filmic text.
6   See Scannell (1988), Silverstone (1994; 1999) and Livingstone and Lunt (1994). For an overview, see Jensen (2002: 156–170).
7   For a comprehensive discussion of relationships of proximity, intimacy and sociality, see Misztal (2000: 130–47). See also Nussbaum (2001: 297–327) for a discussion on emotions, values and the cognition of compassion.
8   See Chouliaraki (2005b).
9   See Silverstone (2002a; 2003). See also Chapter 9 for a more comprehensive critical discussion of the culture of intimacy.
10 See Peters (1999: 230) for the idea of defining humanness as the key question for contemporary communication theory. Drawing on Adorno (1974: 105), he argues that the key question:

> – a question at once philosophical, moral and political – is how wide and deep our empathy for otherness can reach, how ready we are to see 'the human as precisely what is different'.

11 See Arendt (1958), Sennett (1976: 259), Villa (1999: 128–154) and Alexander (2001: 6) for a similar conception of public action that is not instrumental but theatrical – in the sense of connecting action to society as a scene; action as performance.
12 See Boltanski (1999: 35–8) for more on the disinterested spectator. It is from the perspective of the disinterested spectator that we can now appreciate the importance of authenticity so prominent in the pessimistic narrative of mediation. The question of authenticity is precisely the question of how suffering on television comes to be represented as free from a particular perspective – that is, how it manages to count as evidence of objective reality and, thereby, carrying a 'universal' norm that everyone agrees on. It is only on the condition that the particular suffering appears to be reported objectively to the

disinterested spectator – that is, free from the bias of mediation – that the suffering may become the carrier of a 'universal' value and invite the spectator to respond to the suffering in public. For a discursive perspective on the 'universal' and the particular, see Laclau (1996). For an analysis of universal and particular meanings in media discourse, see Chouliaraki (2005a).

13 Lewis (2004) comments extensively on the complicated role of embedded journalists in the Iraq war (March–April 2003), including their role (successful to a degree) in establishing the authentic aura of 'being there' with the soldiers. On the whole, however, he argues that:

> what the embed system [...] did was to get journalists to focus on the progress of the war at the expense of broader contextual issues. The absence, for obvious reasons, of embeds with Iraqi forces combined with traditions of taste and decency that made it difficult to show the ugly side of war, created a stream of footage that humanized the US-led forces and dehumanized the Iraqis.
>
> (Lewis, 2004: 308)

14 See Brooks et al. (2003), Lewis (2004) and Chouliaraki (2005b).

3

MEDIATION, MEANING AND POWER

The pessimistic and optimistic narratives on the ethics of public life explored in the previous two chapters are informed by a view of mediation as image. In pessimistic narrative, the image fails to provide reliable evidence of suffering for spectators. In the optimistic narrative, it is the image that triggers off the spectators' connectivity with distant 'others'.

In a similar way, the failure of these narratives to 'imagine' the cosmopolitan spectator has to do with their difficulty in evaluating the impact that television has on the image. In the pessimistic narrative, the impact of the medium on the image is detrimental because it turns the reality of suffering into fiction. In the optimistic narrative, this impact leads to connectivity because television constantly confronts spectators with the image of the 'other'. Why are images so central in these assessments of mediation? Why have these image-based assessments failed to adequately address the question of public action?

I shall now look into these questions by examining two influential narratives on the meaning-making processes of mediation: the *post-aesthetics* narrative connected to the pessimistic thesis and the *aesthetic reflexivity* narrative connected to the optimistic thesis of mediation. My argument is that the emphasis of these narratives on aesthetics and visuality tends to oversimplify the work of television to produce ethical dispositions and shape public life today.

In a manner reminiscent of the theories of public life in Chapter 1, there is here again a preoccupation with technology as a paradox – as connectivity that fails to deliver its promise. The difference now is that the paradox of technology reappears as a paradox of the image. The omnipresence of images, these narratives tell us, both constitutes social relationships today and, simultaneously, undermines the meaningfulness of political and ethical relationships. As a consequence of their view of image, these narratives fail to tell us just how the scene of suffering is translated into meaning and tend to overestimate the power of television over spectators, denying them the options of critical thinking and collective action.

My alternative is to propose a view of discourse and power inspired by Foucault that moves away from mediation as a relay of ideological meanings and towards mediation as a double economy of freedom and constraint. In this account, mediation is a technology of discourse that construes spectators as free agents, people who may act on the spectacle of suffering in their own wish or will, but always within the premises of ethical action already defined in the contexts of historical and political power relationships of viewing.

The post-aesthetics thesis of mediation

In the pessimistic narrative on mediation, the image of suffering fails to represent human pain – it aestheticizes human pain. This means that the image tends to bring forth the formal properties of suffering as a spectacle on the screen (the blood, the flesh, the tears) and take attention away from the content of suffering as a painful reality for somebody out there in the world. Image, in the pessimistic narrative, blocks modal imagination – that is, the capacity of spectators to think about suffering as fact rather than fiction – and stops the promise of engagement that such imagination entails. Image favours, instead, what McQuire calls 'the soft murder of voyeurism' (1999: 151).

Does the emphasis on the image suggest that aesthetic representation is necessarily deprived of meaning, though? No it does not. In modernity, the aesthetic has been precisely a search in meaning for a higher form of knowledge, for what truly counts in life. It is in postmodern times that the aesthetic becomes divorced from content and sacrifices the 'depth' of meaning for 'surface' appearance.[1] It is only under contemporary conditions of mediation that visual form is perceived to be, at once, a testimony of distant suffering and an inadequate carrier of the meaning of suffering.

This gap between aesthetic representation and discourse, in the present time, is again a consequence of the technology of the mass media. The catalyst is the camera and its photographic devices. By manipulating the photorealistic effects of images, media technologies bring about new visual experiences that tend to take precedence over coherent narratives of language and image over meaning. This is captured in McLuhan's dictum 'the medium is the message', which refers to the cultural transformations brought about by television. It doesn't matter *what* we see, it is the new fascination with *seeing* that counts.[2]

The catalytic role of mediation on aesthetic experience is elaborated in Baudrillard's work on mediation as *simulation*. Simulation is mediation without a referent. Let us think of the September 11th plane crashes at the World Trade Center. Its television image, Baudrillard claims, refers less to an actual planes crashing and more to pervasive cultural icons that we all know about via other mediations:

> in this Manhattan disaster movie, the two 20th-century elements of mass fascination are intertwined to the greatest degree: the white magic of cinema and the black magic of terror. The white light of the image and the black light of violence.[3]

Simulation, Baudrillard tells us, is not a representation of something other than itself – that is, the planes – but, rather, a representation of already existing spectacles of mass fascination that refer to themselves as the 'real'. In this self-referential act, simulation cancels any claim to reality, the violence of terror, except for the reality of the spectacle itself – the terror attacks become 'this Manhattan disaster movie'.

The technology of the camera is key to simulation. It is the capacity of the camera to both represent by analogy, in perfect image copies, and dissociate the image from a reference source, by means of montage or decoupage, that turns mediation into simulation. These possibilities of manipulation turn the television image into a floating element in a network of relationships that continually recombine and circulate it.[4] More than that, Baudrillard claims, it strives to perfect it. Indeed, according to him, this capacity of the medium to both depict photographically and modulate its depictions creates not a quasi-real, faded representation of an external reality, but a *hyperreal* – an accentuated or perfected sense of the real. For Baudrillard, what defines contemporary culture as the 'age of the simulacra' is that there is no distinction between mediated image and reality. What takes the place of reality is 'the implosion of the medium and the real in a sort of nebulous hyperreality where even the definition and distinct action of the medium are no longer distinguishable' (1983: 44).

Our age, then, marks an end point to traditional aesthetics, where images had meaning. The present is the age of post-aesthetics, where images become surfaces for the play of a sensuous hype, a frenzied reception of visual stimuli. In them, 'we look for the giddiness of their superficiality, for the artifice of their detail, the intimacy of their technique' (Baudrillard, 1988: 43–4).[5]

Where does this leave spectators of contemporary television? Can they still be regarded as reflexive subjects? No, spectators today are not required to call on their capacities to create and interpret meaning. They only watch; they are voyeurs. At the same time, even if simulation breaks with meaning making and obstructs the potential of spectators for reflexivity, it nevertheless introduces a new relationship between them and the medium: seduction.

By 'seduction', Baudrillard means two things. First of all, it is a certain reception mode – a 'brute fascination' of spectators with television's pornographic transparency, where everything is displayable and on constant display.[6] As a consequence of this total visibility, no space is left for strong emotions – for surprise, challenge, shock. Indeed, for Baudrillard, brute fascination not only weakens the spectators' reflexive engagement with television, but it also debilitates their basic sociability, turning home 'into a kind of archaic, closed-off cell, into a vestige of human relations whose survival is highly questionable' (1988: 17–18). Yet, survival is possible because seduction is not only brute fascination but also (perhaps by the same token) the only possible political force in contemporary societies. Seduction is the only force that can challenge authority. The brute fascination of spectators with television may leave no space for rational criticism, but it has some potential for resistance: the potential of resisting all principles of reality. Seduction is a politics of pleasure that rests on the spectators' desire to indulge in pure appearances, take delight in the floating of images, resist the truths and certainties of systems of power and social control.

Do brute fascination and seduction offer the possibility of ethical relationships developing via television? Is there space for connectivity between spectators and sufferers in Baudrillard's thesis? Only partially. By drawing our attention to the seductive force of the spectacle and the pleasure of images, the post-aesthetic thesis opens up a domain of enquiry that defies easy acknowledgement. Fantasy and the pleasure of watching indeed play a key role in shaping the spectators' potential for action in television's spectacles of suffering. Theatricality and aestheticization intrinsically belong to television's symbolic mechanism of pity. This advantage granted, however, the post-aesthetic thesis is unable to shed light on the political and ethical dilemmas that the sufferers' presence on screen confronts spectators with.

This is because post-aesthetics simplifies both the operations of power and the operations of discourse in mediation. First, the post-aesthetics thesis takes one cultural mode – the aesthetic of 'appearance' – to be the only condition of contemporary social life. As a consequence of the primacy it gives to appearance and visuality, the post-aesthetic thesis cannot tell us much about how relationships of power operate in our societies. The hegemonic distribution of viewing relationships, the systematic mapping of zones of safety and suffering on to zones of political and economic domination and the problematic of sufferers as the 'others' are not part of the post-aesthetics discussion. If they do enter the discussion, it is as part of the spectators' 'seductive' resistance to authoritative systems of power.[7]

Second, the post-aesthetic thesis talks about aesthetics only as image and surface. The image, however, is not exhausted in its surface form, nor does it exhaust television's capacities for aestheticization. Language, with its multiple narrative types and their combination with the visual, complicates the aesthetic landscape of television in ways that the post-aesthetic view cannot begin to capture.

In sum, post-aesthetics makes us aware that mediation combines a politics of pity with seduction and pleasure, but tells us little about how these two regimes are brought together. It does not tell us how ethics and aesthetics shape the spectacle of suffering and how, in so doing, they may be able to shift the disposition of spectators from voyeurism to cosmopolitanism. Post-aesthetics tells us even less about the discursive work of mediation – how images and language combine on screen in order to make complicated representations of suffering possible.

The 'aesthetic reflexivity' thesis of mediation

Aesthetic reflexivity, the second narrative of mediation I examine in this chapter, also begins with the dominance of technology in our culture, but goes some way to addressing the impasses of the post-aesthetic narrative. If post-aesthetics talks about contemporary culture as the 'age of the simulacra' – an age where knowledge (content) is disconnected from technological image (form) – the thesis of aesthetic reflexivity seeks to return aesthetics to the realm of meaning – to reconnect content with form. The optimistic account of the ethical role of television, in the 'democratization of responsibility' thesis, rests precisely on the capacity of the image to present suffering to spectators as a meaningful reality out there in the world.

How does aesthetic reflexivity reflect this optimism? It begins by taking one step back from the totalizing, almost apocalyptic, gaze of the post-aesthetic position. It looks on mediation not as the end point of representation, but as a historical phase in the trajectory of representation itself. The present phase of mediation, the thesis argues, is not a complete rupture with the past, but differs from it because it has its own social relationships and reorganizes older forms of knowledge and subjectivity into new formations. Poster (1990/1996: 6) uses the expression 'the mode of information' to talk about contemporary mediation in these terms. Adapting Marx's description of capitalist societies as defined by their mode of production, Poster's mode of information describes contemporary societies in terms of the ways in which electronic media are changing the structures of signification:

> By mode of information I similarly [to Marx and Althusser, LC] suggest that history may be periodized by variations in the structure, in this case of symbolic exchange, but also that the current culture gives a certain fetishistic importance to 'information'. (1990/1996: 6)

It is now not the break with meaning making but the variations in meaning making, in the structure of symbolic exchange, that define the age of mediation. The emphasis on variations draws attention to continuities as well as discontinuities between past and present forms of mediation and the ways in which these reconfigure the semiotic resources of different media in new and unpredictable ways.

Technology, once again, is a catalyst in the new mode of information. The technological capacity of television to instantaneously spread information across space not only breaks with the locales of face-to-face interaction but also changes the relatively expanded space–times of print media. As in Baudrillard, the aesthetic reflexivity thesis argues that technology produces signs without referential anchorage, which changes the ways in which we process these signs into meaning. However, in contrast to Baudrillard, aesthetic reflexivity emphasizes that signs do not necessarily change in the direction of simulation and hyperreality. Rather, aesthetic reflexivity insists that the relationship between image and its reference points to something else that lies outside the world of the media. Thus, attention now shifts from describing how the world 'implodes' into the media to analysing how the discursive resources of television are employed in different ways and different genres in order to shape the consciousness of spectators in new ways. 'What is at stake,' Poster adds, 'are new language formations that alter significantly the network of social relations [and] that restructure those relations and the subjects they constitute' (1990/1996: 8).

This type of critical discourse on meaning making in television is associated with a broad body of social theory that shares the post-aesthetic diagnosis that the media construe a 'depthless' world but does not abandon the idea that meaning is an inherent, though suppressed, element of contemporary culture.[8] According to Lash (2001), the linguistic and the visual are two distinct but coexisting 'regimes of signification', the relative prominence of which differentiates modern from postmodern aesthetics. Each regime privileges certain modes of mediation. Text, coherence and interpretation are characteristic of modern mediation, whereas image, collage and fragmentation are characteristic of postmodern mediation. Contemporary mediation is postmodern in that it is characterized by an intense preoccupation with the image and a focus on the strategic intervention of visual aspects of our culture. In short, it is characterized by aesthetic reflexivity.[9] Television plays a major role in this aesthetic reflexive process by mediating image patchworks, 'collages' or 'pastiches' that momentarily flash on to the screen, only to disappear again in amnesia, in forgetfulness.

Yet, unlike Baudrillard – for whom this diagnosis of the present time becomes 'the' condition of contemporary experience (a 'metaphysics of appearance') – for aesthetic reflexivity theorists, the emphasis on appearance is understood as a historical condition.[10] The mode of information, they argue, is part of the broader dynamic of advanced capitalism and the spin of globalization. Although commodity design has always been a concern of capitalist markets, the heightening of aesthetic reflexivity today suggests that increasingly more aspects of our culture are becoming aestheticized and commercialized, including lifestyles and interpersonal relationships. However, this is not taken to be the one and only account of contemporary culture. Aesthetic reflexivity, theorists say, is a particular dimension in the reflexive project of modernity, whereby questions of 'how things should *look*' seem to be more important today than questions of 'how things *are*' (cognitive reflexivity on rules of social action) or 'how things *should* be' (normative reflexivity on rules of ethical action).[11]

These different dimensions of social life, however, coexist with one another and it is not a matter of the one winning over the other, once and for all. In fact, age-old questions about ethics and politics assume increasingly vital importance. It is this dialectic between the simulacrum and an ethics of cosmopolitanism that Baudrillard himself tries to capture when he is confronted with the September 11th spectacle, but is unsuccessful. As Harvey argues, the quest for ethical norms may appear to withdraw at the level of a hyperreal spin, but it re-emerges precisely through that spin, seeking to re-anchor social experience, to recentre the self. In postmodernity, as Harvey claims, 'the greater the ephemerality, the more pressing the need to discover or manufacture some kind of eternal truth that might lie therein' (1989: 292).

Aesthetic reflexivity, in sum, sets back on the agenda the problematic of ethics in mediation. This is important because we need to be able to study how television mediates the world to the world – especially how the Western spectator is put in contact with floods in Bangladesh or death by stoning in Nigeria. What is at stake in the analysis of news on suffering is precisely the tension between Lash's two regimes of signification – language and image – but also their rearticulations on the screen. In my view, it is precisely the focus on the tensions and discontinuities of media texts that open up the study of mediation to the pressing ethical and political questions of our times.

Visuality: an impoverished logic of mediation

Post-aesthetics and aesthetic reflexivity are the two key narratives that inform the debate on the role of the media in public life. Both of them understand mediation as a technologically driven practice and take visuality to be the main semiotic code of media discourse. In this sense, both narratives give primacy to mediation as an aesthetic process. However, each thesis understands the power of visuality in different ways. Their differences have considerable implications when it comes to analysing television news as a politics of pity.

The post-aesthetic account heightens our sensibilities towards image as seduction, as a politics of pleasure, but does not provide us with tools to analyse how visual staging produces meaning about suffering. This problem is related to Baudrillard's view that contemporary mediation is a breaking off of form from content; a breakdown in semiosis, in meaning making.

The connection between this view and the pessimism about the role of television as an ethical force in today's world is rather straightforward. Technology, in both accounts, transforms the nature of media discourse in ways that thoroughly fictionalize reality and cancel the demand for action on the world. Indeed, if sufferers are only part of a chain of depthless signifiers, it is difficult to imagine how their presence can possibly make spectators care about them. The pessimism about television's role in cultivating a cosmopolitan disposition is inseparable from the view that technological mediation is essentially representation without reference – a hyperreal without reality.

In contrast, the aesthetic reflexivity thesis regards mediation as discourse that has today shifted from one semiotic mode – the printed word – to another – the screen. This shift, however, is not a breaking off of form from content, but, rather, a shift from one form/content to another form/content. This makes television a more complicated medium of discourse than post-aesthetics assumes as it makes television a *polysemantic text*, where 'information and entertainment, education and propaganda, relaxation and hypnosis are all blurred' (Castells, 1996: 336). In introducing the idea of television as a polysemantic text, aesthetic reflexivity enables a different set of questions to be asked about television representations and brings us closer to the concerns of this volume with how mediation may enable the disposition of cosmopolitanism.

Nevertheless, I would argue that there are problems with the view of visuality in the thesis of aesthetic reflexivity. The image may now be recognized as being a semiotic sign, but the function of the image is reduced to the 'signal'. The image as a signal is present in Castells' argument that 'the media tend to work on consciousness and behaviour as real experience works on dreams, providing the raw material out of which our brain works.' Distant suffering is the example he chooses to carry this idea through. The normalization of images of death and war in our everyday experience, Castells says, stems from the fact that we are watching these images in the safety of the home and, thereby, we come to absorb them as a part of our broader cinematic experience, as 'part of action movies'. This, he concludes, ultimately results in reducing all television content to the spectators' own repertoires of media images (1996: 337).

Lash elaborates on this argument of television image functioning as a signal.[12] Our age, the 'age of information', marks a peak in this visual regime because of the speed with which mass and new media operate today. The unprecedented velocity of mediation turns the image into a particular type of mimetic sign – the *signal*. The signal is an indexical sign that only stands for what it 'flashes'. For example, the Greek letter gamma (Γ) is used as a street signal that stands for 'right turn'. The image then becomes a signal when, instead of allowing time for contemplation on its family resemblance, it takes on a most immediate relationship to its referent, which is when it becomes indexical and, thus, 'highly motivated' by the object it signifies:

The sports, the news on television, the sending of electronic messages, playing computer games, is signification via signal and may be more or less indexical [...] the sort of signification that is going on is neither predominantly symbolic nor iconic, but instead indexical through the signal.

(Lash, 2001: xx)

Lash is careful to point out that the dominance of the signal in television does not imply that the technological image erases reality, as Baudrillard does. Nevertheless, he holds the signal function of television responsible for bringing about a new semiotic economy – 'an entire other economy of signs in space' – and, with it, a novel type of sociality: *informationality* (2001).

The social relationships and moral engagements of the age of informationality are triggered by this new visual economy of the media, which makes the world more visible than ever before and brings the various parts of the globe closer together. Doesn't this account remind us of the optimism of the 'democratization of responsibility' thesis, which I discussed in Chapter 1? Isn't, in both accounts, global visibility a promise for a cosmopolitan public? Perhaps so, but there is also a difference between them.

For Lash, unlike Thompson (1995), the short-term and elliptical function of the signal never achieves an adequate depth of meaning and, therefore, never enables these social engagements to develop into projects of public action organized around a cause. The core of publicness still exists today, but the public character of collective engagements is fragmented and dispersed, occuring via the particular pursuits of ephemeral and shifting collectivities. Even though this description is not far from a model of public life that may sustain the cosmopolitan ideal, as I argue in the conclusion, informationality lacks the ethical dimension that is crucial for conceiving of public action as action that makes a difference to the 'other'.

In my opinion, the thesis of aesthetic reflexivity seeks to be affirmative about the present, avoiding both nihilism and a celebration of technology, but fails to do so. This is because, despite the faith of the thesis in new collectivities, its reductive view of the image as a signal seriously undermines the capacity of the theory to consider television as an ethical force in public life today.

What is missing from aesthetic reflexivity, I believe, is a view of signification as *remediation*. Rather than talking about signification in terms of distinct periods, relating the image to the era of the mass media, as Lash does, we need to talk about signification in terms of the simultaneous coexistence of images with language across different media, as well as across contexts and times. This means that the television image has a potential for multiple signification that can be activated simultaneously, depending on its semiotic environment. It may be called to signify as an index and as a signal, but also as an icon and/or a symbol. The visualization of the Nigerian woman given the death by stoning sentence in one of my news examples illustrates this point. It is precisely because the picture of Amina Lawal, a young mother holding her baby, functions at once as an index of herself, an icon of a 'Madonna'-type motherhood and a symbol of women's oppression under the sharia law, that this piece of news can enter into an urgent politics of pity and signify the spectator–sufferer relationship in terms of a complicated regime of emotion and action.

In summary, despite the fact that the thesis of aesthetic reflexivity recognizes the relationship between mediation, meaning and power, it does not have the tools to analyse how this relationship is established and which effect its content may bear on the spectator. As a result, and from an interest in social criticism rather than seduction, the aesthetic reflexivity narrative ends up in absolutist assessments of mediation that are similar to those of post-aesthetics. For post-aesthetics, mediation obeys a logic of simulacra, while for aesthetic reflexivity, mediation obeys a logic of informationality. Neither of the two can convincingly gesture towards the problematic of the ethics of suffering on television.

Aesthetic narratives and the question of power

Why do these aesthetic theories insist on mediation as form? This question, I believe, takes us back to the suspicion vis-à-vis technology that haunts the sociological and artistic imagination of the twentieth century. Drawing on the legacy of the early militant criticism of the visual arts (notably expressed in the radical modernism of the European avant-garde), both aesthetic narratives ultimately express a similar disillusionment with the promise of technology to liberate society.

At that time, art was considered to be the privileged field of social change and artistic form was the privileged locus for the articulation of new social meanings. By asserting the autonomy of form – that is, the capacity of the image to break free from the authoritative conventions of art – radical modernism also asserted the power of the image to challenge the social status quo and signify social life in a new way. Visual form entailed the political promise of producing a more equalitarian vision for society than had existed up until then. This was the case, for example, in the anti-representationalist art of the surrealists and futurists. Culture and society, aesthetics and politics, were thus linked by the modernist belief that art, 'though autonomous, could offer a symbolic transformation of social content by the aesthetic form' (Delanty, 2000: 134).

Yet, this radical promise failed to bring about social change. As Adorno and the Frankfurt theorists have argued, this failure is inextricably linked to the spread of the mass media and the eventual colonization of art by the culture industries and their market interests. The rise of mass media spectacles meant the decline of public life – hence Habermas's view of the media as responsible for the 'refeudalization of the public sphere' (1989).

In my opinion, it is to the historical failure of this radical project that the aesthetic narratives on television are responding. In the shadow of the Adornian critique, let us recall, the pessimistic narrative uses television as an exemplary case of how the power of mediation erodes public life and social solidarity. The optimistic thesis may retain its faith in the politicization of form, but still remains deeply suspicious about the disempowerment of civil life by technology. Neither seduction nor information machines leave space for a politics of critical resistance and social change.

The lesson that we should learn from this brief genealogical excursion is, I believe, not that the focus on image is an inadequate one with which to address the ethics of mediation debate. We should not share, that is, the disillusionment of critical social theory with the radical project of modernity. Rather, our lesson should be that the inadequacy of the image as a means of answering the question of power relationships and public action today is a consequence of a broader epistemological mistake in these narratives.

Post-aesthetics and aesthetic reflexivity alike take up a historically specific description of contemporary culture, which is that media technologies privilege form and suppress content, and use this as a model to tell us about how mediation creates the world in meaning. The simulacrum and the signal are, in this sense, categories of description that provide a diagnosis of the conditions of mediation today and simultaneously categories of analysis that explain how meaning and power produce stories on the television screen.

My own position is that, although technology has indeed intensified the role of visuality in our culture, we must nevertheless maintain a phronetic distinction between the questions of how we believe that the world looks today and how we study it. The implication of this point is the following. We should provisionally bracket out narratives of hyperreality or information-ality and seek to develop an analytical language about how television produces the scene of distant suffering as a meaningful reality for spectators.

The key idea here is remembering that the stories on television have always been in a relationship of tenuous complicity with the medium that represents them. There is no proximity to the sufferer without the image from a camera. In the language of remediation, there is no immediacy to distant suffering without the technology that represents, or hypermedi-ates, suffering. The image, it follows, is neither simulacrum nor signal. In articulating form with content, the image participates in the dual logic of hypermediacy and immediacy.

Remediation theorists, in fact, argue that the spectator's awareness of hypermediacy – the 'looking at' the screen – is not a reminder of television's technological manipulation, but it crucially contributes to the spectator's 'looking through' the screen as a window to reality.[13] The CNN layout, for example, testifies to the fact that immediacy in television does not require the transparent visual plenitude that spectators enjoy in their ordinary vision, but it may be achieved via the hypermediacy of split screens, graphic bars and logos. Does anyone seriously challenge the authenticity of CNN news on the basis of what its screen layout looks like?

Immediacy, in this case, does not seek to fool the spectator into an 'as if' proximity by erasing the medium of its representation. Rather, immediacy reveals itself precisely as an effect of this medium and its semiotic modes, image and language, claiming both the authenticity of proximity and the illusion of 'as if'. Immediacy, in this account, cannot work without the hypermediacy of technological form and, thereby, without the spectator's sense that 'the experience of the medium is itself an experience of the real'(Bolter and Grusin, 2000: 71)[14].

The main implication of this view of mediation is that people are neither dupes of technology nor ideological subjects of media discourse unable to take a critical stance. The power of television does not reduce spectators to complete powerlessness, nor does it block their capacity to feel for and relate to the causes of distant suffering. Instead of lamenting the loss of critical discourse or public life today, we should look for the ways in which the technological conditions of mediation make critical consciousness and cosmopolitan citizenship possible in the everyday texts of television.

Towards an analytics of mediation

The shift towards an analytical perspective on mediation is, simultaneously, a shift towards a poststructuralist view of the power of mediation. This is because, in line with the ethos of phronesis, poststructuralism prioritizes the explanatory question of how mediation produces ethical norms of public action over the prescriptive question of which ethics we practise or should practise in the age of mediation.

The term 'analytics', originally an Aristotelian term, is associated with the poststructuralist turn in political theory, which replaces the traditional study of the State as a structure of authoritative rule with the study of local rationalities of government – the study of governmentality.[15] The main implication of this turn is that the object of analysis (the State), ceases to be conceived of as a totality of functions and ideologies of domination and becomes the study of specific regimes of practice with local power effects on people. These regimes of practice are not homogeneous, but are composed of minor activities, technologies and forms of meaning that stand in complicated relationships with one another and result in multiple and ambivalent effects of power – effects of freedom as well as subjectification.

The mediation of meaning on television must also be understood and analysed as a technology of contemporary rule.[16] This is because mediation is about the (re-)production of the social relationships of viewing and so it begs for an analysis of power that focuses specifically on the articulation of the medium with its visual and linguistic texts. Mediation, then, is a fully textual technology of governmentality. In its governmental capacity, mediation mobilizes meaning in order to shape the conduct of particular spectatorships in terms of who connects with whom and who cares about whom. In this respect, it is important not to think of mediation as a coherent and intentional form of power that regulates the flow of news across zones of influence. Rather, the power of mediation takes the form of 'a generalized resource of symbolic definition' that is characterized by an inherently programmatic character (Silverstone, 2003: 8).

As a resource of symbolic definition, the power of mediation works by selecting and staging the events it reports and, simultaneously, by promoting its own norms about how we should feel, think and act on the world that this selection and staging entails. Such utopian goals of mediation – the implicit emotional and ethical dispositions towards suffering – are carried via television's explicit ends: its ambition is to provide a dynamic and global informational service. What does this mean? It means that it is precisely at the moment when CNN or the BBC addresses the spectator as a global citizen of the 'be the first to know' or 'putting news first' type that their news broadcasts also reproduce a certain version of world order, defined by space–times of safety and danger and hierarchies of human life. In this sense, mediation as a governmental technology is neither purely regulatory nor purely benign. Rather, mediation combines the exercise of rule on spectators by promoting modes of conduct that may be positive and even desirable for them, such as being a philanthropist or political activist, for example.

The analytics of mediation, I wish to argue, opens up the question of how power operates in television in two respects. First, it asks how television texts participate in the production of hierarchies of power. How, in other words, news texts help shape global viewing relationships in terms of the political classifications of 'us' and 'them', safe spectators and distant sufferers. This refers to the concern of analytics to problematize the seeming stability and taken-for-grantedness of the spaces and temporalities of global television, by showing that these spaces and temporalities are, in fact, constituted in inherently historical and contingent ways. I discuss this concern in the next section, – 'Mediation as a "history of the present"'.

Second, the analytics of mediation asks how television texts shape the agency of spectators by establishing local relationships of pity between spectators and sufferers. This refers to the concern of analytics to show us that the agency of the spectator does not automatically come from some cosmopolitan values inherent in transnational information flows, but is the result of practices of power that affect on the actions of spectators. I discuss this concern in the final section of this chapter, under the heading 'Mediation as the "conduct of conduct"'.

Mediation as a 'history of the present'

The analytics of mediation mistrusts narratives that treat the present as history, so to speak, by telling us what the nature of the present is or should be. Analytics begins with the concrete relationship of Western spectators with distant sufferers and works on the assumption that the news stories about suffering tell us a bigger story about our own times, about how our public life today is shaped by means of television's proposals of where, when and how to act on distant 'others'.[17] It is this reversal of order that takes us from narratives of the 'present as history' to narratives of the 'history of the present'.

Two methodological principles follow from this analytical project. The first is the principle of *normativity*.[18] How can we tell right from wrong in the representations of suffering in television news and, more generally, how can we arrive at judgements on the norms of our present with the help of the analytics of mediation?

The second principle of analytics is the principle of *historicity*. Which type of context does the analytics of mediation evoke to make sense of the television text and, more generally, how can we explain the representation of suffering in the news in the light of the broader sociocultural tendencies of our times?

Normativity
This takes the study of spectators' engagement with suffering, the study of proximity and action, as a barometer of the ethical norms of the present. The space–time and agency choices of the news are, in this sense, indicators of the moral values that are available in television and define the norms of public conduct in our times. The appeal to sign the petition for saving Amina Lawal's life in Nigeria, for example, or even the coverage of the Baghdad 'shock and awe' bombardment are informed by such a normative element, by some form of utopian goal – a more responsible way of relating to the 'other' or a more efficient way of acting on the 'other'. Yet, not all spectacles of suffering articulate this normative element in the same way. How each piece of news establishes its own norm on suffering and how, in so doing, it seeks to moralize the spectator are the first normative steps of the analytics of mediation.

The second normative step is to study a variety of news texts on suffering across television networks. Studying them without the 'pressure' of applying to them some a priori judgement, raises the counter-intuitive, but pertinent, question of why the September 11th sufferer and the Bangladeshi sufferer occupy the two poles of the hierarchy of Western news. The normative 'moment' proper of analytics then is the comparative perspective, which connects seemingly unrelated news pieces on suffering in a pattern of potential forms of engagement for spectators. What emerges, as a consequence of this comparison, is a hierarchy of spectatorial subjectivities from no involvement to total involvement with distant 'others'. It is clear, at this point, that attending to every single piece of news bears a weight that is not only analytical but also moral. This is because each piece confronts us with human pain in its irreducibility, in its 'taking place', rather than as an abstraction of history or statistics.[19]

It is this question of how a certain 'fact' of suffering reaches us in the immediate form that it does that demands an analytical orientation towards television as text and towards the comparative perspective across news texts in the study of mediation.

Historicity

At the same time, paying attention to singularity alone bears a risk. It is that of reducing the news to a 'now' moment containing the reported event in a vacuum. This risk calls for the second methodological principle of the analytics of mediation. The present is not to be seen as a pre-existing reality that simply contains the event, as an ontological a priori, in Foucault's words. Rather, the present is to be seen as a historical a priori – an analytical construction that identifies a certain action as a 'significant' event within a particular juncture of other potential events. The event, then, that television mediates as an unfolding flow of 'now's is impregnated with multiple potential outcomes, but, ultimately, is only described in terms of one.[20]

What this view of historicity tells us is that what an event is, the definition of an event, always emerges in the context of a certain flow of action – a context that we can only understand as historical. Thus, we need to keep a reflexive balance between the single case and its context and treat each piece of news in both its singularity and historicity.[21] I would like to discuss two versions of historicity that are relevant to the analytics of mediation. These are historicity as *social explanation* and historicity as *chronotopic analysis*.

If the analysis of a singular piece of news tells us how this piece happens to appear in the form that it does, historicity as social explanation is about why this turned out in this way. In its historicity, then, we approach the news text with the purpose of illustrating how a relatively stabilized arrangement of power relationships – the historical a priori – contextualizes a singular report on suffering in a broader pattern of social and political relationships – that of who watches whom suffer. Any piece of news in cultural or geographical proximity to the West has priority over news from afar, often independently of the latter's magnitude. This hierarchy of viewing depends on the concentration of the economic and political powers of broadcasting in the West, which renders the sufferings of Western people relevant and urgent to global spectatorship and places the sufferings of those far away low on the news agenda.[22] It is not possible to understand the politics of pity in Western broadcasts and make sense of their hierarchy of suffering without putting forward a view of power as something that systemically constrains the flow of information at the same time as it enables and globalizes it. Indeed, I believe that the analysis of mediation becomes misleading without this basic premise of historicity – that is, without a view of how power already organizes and activates broader regimes of meaning and text, of how it 'authors' suffering.

Social explanation, however, can never be a sum total. The present may not be random or infinitely open, but neither should we regard it as completely ordered. Rather, the present is only partially and unstably structured – that is, it is structured in a manner that leaves room for unpredictability and change. This Bakhtinian view suggests that the present is not a solid reality on which we can safely rationalize our predictions for the future or accurately reconstruct our knowledge of the past.[23] If we read the present as one single and solid narrative, this is because we read into it only the potentiality that was ultimately actualized. We read the present anachronistically rather than historically.

This insight into the nature of the present points to the second dimension of historicity that I wish to discuss – historicity as the specific horizon of space and time that contextualizes the singular event. This sense of historicity refers to the function of news text to create proximity and temporal dynamism in the event it reports. This sense of historicity as a local and contextual property of the singular event is what Bakhtin calls the 'chronotopic' universe of the event.[24] Historicity as chronotopic analysis, then, refers to the work that each news text performs in order to manage the unfinalizability of the present and 'contain the event within a specific context of place and time'.

The textual understanding of historicity as chronotopic analysis is closely connected to the first version of historicity as social explanation. This is because social explanation implies that power relationships not only keep patterns of viewing in place but, by the same token, also privilege certain narratives about suffering over others across news texts. This historical context of power conditions the sense of historicity that each piece of news enacts as chronotope. Part of the task of the analytics of mediation is that of identifying how variations in the historical sense of each piece of news (chronotopicity) are related to a social hierarchy that distributes pity unequally across parts of the world (social explanation).

For instance, the historicity of *adventure* news – that is, news on suffering without pity – is minimal as events in India and Bangladesh are placed in a logic of appearances without the depth of 'How come?' or 'Where will this end?' questions. In contrast, the historicity of *ecstatic* news – the September 11th live footage, for example – entails an intense and multiplied sense of time that passes through recurrent logics of appearance and explanation, emotion and action.

I consider, therefore, the demand for historicity – both as social explanation and as chronotopic analysis – to be a crucial diagnostic tool in the study of the moral mechanism of mediation. It is by extracting the element of historicity embedded in each piece of news that we better come to comprehend the nature of our present as a historical moment with its own ethical norms and possibilities for acting on itself.

Mediation as the spectator's 'conduct of conduct'

The question of how to act on suffering draws attention to the forms of the self and the ethos of viewing that television produces and reproduces in its news stories. By this, I do not mean to say that these forms of the self directly interpellate the spectators as social agents as they are not the definite endpoints of practices of mediation. What I wish to suggest, rather, is that the television text has a certain programmatic character and such forms of the self are part of this, largely utopian, programmatic project of television to propose some dispositions for action and not others as desirable for spectators. It is in this respect that I take mediation to be a governmental technology for the *conduct of conduct*.

According to Foucault, the shaping of conduct is a technology of rule that, instead of the direct exercise of authority, relies on indirect action – that is, action on the actions of individuals. Instrumental in this narrative of power is that individuals are already conceptualized as actors because it is only on their relative capacity for action, their agency, that power can come to bear its effects. This is obvious in the news, where spectators are not addressed en masse, but as an abstract singularity or individual. This person is, for example, an informed citizen or a caring philanthropist.[25]

No doubt, news on suffering encompasses a broad spectrum of proposals for spectators to relate to the distant suffering. These range from ticking off the facts to watching a high–adrenaline spectacle or engaging empathetically with the agony of an individual to contemplating the scene of action as a tableau vivant. This repertoire of attributes suggests that the regulative function of television is not based on a single and monolithic apparatus of institutional control but that it capitalizes on a set of potential capabilities that television both 'imagines' on behalf of spectators and enables them to enact as 'free' subjects. The figure of a spectator, then, is part of the governmental pedagogy of television, in so far as who the spectators should become is encoded in the multiple news stories of human pain and the modes of relating to the 'other' that these stories propose.

It is the fact that moral action on television is always action at a distance that most forcefully thematizes the dimension of mediation as a technology of governmentality. Because of the practical impossibility of acting directly on the suffering 'other', the forms of engagement and action that television proposes to spectators have less to do with immediate, practical intervention and more to do with patterns of imaginary or projected action on the part of spectators.[26] Such patterns belong to two historical modes of action at a distance, which are feeling for the sufferer and contemplating the suffering objectively. Feeling for the sufferer is associated with the ancient public of the theatre, whereas contemplating the suffering is associated with the public of the agora.

How else could pity work as an emotional reality for spectators unless it builds on and enacts the historical roles that have always shaped our structure of feeling – the tender-heartedness of the philanthropist, the indignation of the activist or even the social and aesthetic sensibilities of the voyeur? At the same time, how could pity work as public discourse unless it incorporates the historical figure that has always shaped our structure of political thinking: the citizen, the impartial deliberator? What emerges, then, out of television's proposals for action at a distance is an array of public roles that makes spectators feel that they act freely on their own, with 'spontaneous' humanitarian and civil sensibilities vis-à-vis the spectacle of suffering.

The view of power as governmentality, exercised indirectly over the actions of spectators, moves us away from mediation as an ideological mechanism in the sense that critical studies of the media often suggest.[27] Equally, it challenges the view that the consciousness of spectators is the only active location of critical resistance, as audience studies often have it.[28] Rather, the analytics of mediation formulates the relationship between television news and spectators as a relationship of conditional freedom. I use the term conditional freedom to refer to the function of the television text to regulate, but by no means determine, spectators' capacities for pity by opening up multiple ethical positions for them to engage with. This multiple economy of identification is inherently ambivalent. It is positive because we can only relate to the 'other' on the condition that we are already constituted as free subjects drawing selectively on an existing repertoire of identity resources. It is also negative because the systemic 'bias' in the resources for identification across types of news ultimately reproduces an exclusively Western sensibility towards 'our' own suffering at the expense of sufferings of the distant 'other'. It is this ambivalence in television's economy of identification that makes the relationship between television text and audience a political relationship par excellence and a crucial stake in the shaping of the cosmopolitan subjectivity.

Conclusion

Post-aesthetics and the aesthetic reflexivity thesis understand mediation as technology and can, therefore, only grasp the content of mediation as aesthetic form. The inability of these narratives to address the content of mediation as political and ethical is a result of their impoverished view of media discourse as image. Their intense preoccupation with aesthetic form both intensifies and impoverishes the role of discourse in their accounts of contemporary social life. On the one hand, mediation as form intensifies the role of semiotic practice in these accounts because it understands contemporary social life predominantly as a proliferation of images. On the other hand, mediation as form impoverishes the role of semiotic practice in these accounts because it reduces contemporary meaning exchange to either simulacrum or the signal.

These reductions lead to totalitarian views of power, which only reluctantly (if at all), endow the spectator with critical capabilities and public agency. I propose, instead, a different view of discourse and power as governmentality. This view defines mediation as a symbolic technology of power that operates via the news stories of television and endows spectators with conditional freedom – the option to be an agent in the world watched on television and bring about social change. How can we analyse mediation as a symbolic technology of power that both enables and constrains spectators as public actors? This is the topic of Chapter 4, 'The analytics of mediation'.

Notes

1   This claim is associated with the postmodern position, which today defines culture, society and politics predominantly in aesthetic terms. What Delanty calls the 'aestheticization of the social' (2000: 131–2) refers to the contemporary fusion of the cognitive, normative and aesthetic dimensions of the social that, separated as they were in modernity, now fuse together in an aesthetic view of social life and political relationships. The postmodern aestheticization of the social, Delanty claims, can be seen as bringing together two distinct modernist characteristics:

> on the one side, the avant-gardist negation of form and the autonomy of art, and, on the other, the reluctance to engage in politics [...] Postmodernism allows the aesthetic to enter everyday life without political implications.

> (2000: 136)

2   I take Baudrillard (1983, 1988, 1994) to be a prototypical figure of this strand of theory, but figures such as Mafessoli (1993, 1996), Virilio (1991, 1994) and Vattimo (1992) also belong here. From a sociological perspective, the works of network society theorists, such as Castells (1996, 1997), constitute an affirmative version of the postmodern account of the dissolution of traditional social and political formations, now replaced by new communities and forms of communication. In this chapter, I take Lash (1990, 2001 and Beck et al., 1994) as the prototypical figure of affirmative sociology because of his consistent focus on signification, the image and discourse. Other theorists of the postmodern, critical of postmodern cultural and sociological studies, with an interest in signification and discourse, are Harvey (1989, 1996) and Jameson (1981, 1991). See also Delanty (2000: 142) for a similar categorization and McQuire (1999) and Armitage (2000).

3   As Baudrillard wrote in *Le Monde*, after the September 11th attacks:

> After the fact, one seeks to assign any given meaning to it, to find any interpretation for it. But there is none and that is the radicalism of the spectacle, the brutality of the spectacle that alone is original and irreducible. The spectacle of terrorism necessarily brings with it the terrorism of the spectacle. And against this immoral fascination (even if it triggers a universal moral reaction) the political order is powerless against it. It is our own theatre of cruelty, the only one we have left – extraordinary in that it unites the highest point of the spectacular and the highest point of challenge – a sacrificial model that pits the purest symbolic form of challenge against the historical and political order.

> ('The mind of terrorism', 2 November, 2001)

4   See McQuire (1999: 92–104; 132–50) for a discussion, among others.
5   See Delanty (2000: 8–31) for a relevant discussion on modernity and post-modernity.
6   See Baudrillard (1988: 33).
7   For an illustration of this point, see Minc's response to Baudrillard's 'The mind of terrorism' article on the September 11th terrorist attacks. Minc, entitling his article 'Terrorism of the mind', argues that:

> from the holder of a 'Master in Variations', one might have expected another analysis on the geminate nature of the real and virtual, of the image and of substance, of the media and reality. The collapse of the Twin Towers could only signal, in his eyes, the definite triumph of the virtual, the moment when he deafeningly snatches up the real ...

From this perspective, Minc attacks Baudrillard for his incapacity 'to recognize that there exists a hierarchy of values and that referring to morality is not incident' ('Terrorism of the mind', *Le Monde*, 6 November 2001).
8   Affirmative postmodernists Lash (1990, 1994, 2001) and Castells (1996, 1997) – see note 2 – meet here with the post-Marxism of Jameson (1981, 1991) and Harvey (1989, 1996). Despite their differences, they are all inspired by the critical spirit of the Frankfurt school and the situationists' denunciation of the society of the spectacle and commodification of social experience by the media (Plant, 1992). In fact, the young Baudrillard (1968) also belonged to this Marxist-inspired tradition.
9   See Beck et al. (1994) – a key reference for aesthetic reflexivity.
10 See Castells' (1996) seminal account of the 'network society', Lash (1994) – particularly his 'critique of information' – and Jameson (1991: 86–7), who understands postmodernism as the 'cultural logic of capitalism' (1991).
11 See Beck (1986) and Beck et al. (1994).
12 Mediation, Lash (1994, 2001) rightly argues, creates particular regimes of signification – linguistic or visual – that depend on which medium articulates particular sign values at any moment in time. In his periodization of mediation, language dominates the age of printing and is inscribed in media such as the book or the newspaper. Linguistic meaning is primarily symbolic. It works by evoking an abstraction, a referent graspable either via denotation (language establishing correspondence with it) or connotation (language establishing associations with it). The visual, in contrast, dominates the age of the mass media and is associated with photography and cinema. This visual regime of signification privileges iconic representation. Iconic representation does not occur via symbolic abstraction but 'mimesis' – that is, in images that look like the referent they evoke (resemblance) or those that claim to stand for the referent itself (indexicality).
13 See Bolter and Grusin (2000: 190–1).
14 In the same spirit, Darley provides a historical argument for the spectator's astonishment with hypermediacy in her early encounter with the medium – an astonishment, however, that does not seem to recede as cinematic technology became increasingly established and familiar, but continues to be present today in the spectator's delight with television's visual illusion:

> The spectator does not get lost in a fictional world and its drama, but remains aware of the act of looking, the excitement of curiosity and its fulfillment.
>
> (Gunning, 1989: 36, in Darley, 2000: 46)

15 See Foucault (1991: 87–104). In relation to the media, see Barnett (2003: 33–54). In relation to discourse and discursive practice, Bennett (2002: 47–67), as well as Rose (1999), Flyvbjerg (2001) and Dean (1999).

16 This definition of mediation as a technology of governmentality capitalizes on the felicitous semantic ambiguity of the term 'technology' as something that enables both the process of mediation – that is, its form or materiality – and the exercise of power – which is the reproduction of the social relationships of viewing. Although most governmentality studies do not focus on meaning making and text, see Bennett (2003: 47–67) for an exception.

17 See Foucault (1984b: 87–8) and Flyvbjerg (2001: 112–16).

18 See Chouliaraki (2002) for this idea of normativity in discourse analysis and Chouliaraki (2004) for media discourse.

19 Derrida and Stiegler (2002: 77) make this point when they say that 'Attention to process should not efface the event … Each time, there is a singularity to murder. It happens, and no process, no logic of the simulacrum can make us forget this. For, along with process, we must also think singularity.'

20 See Morson and Emerson (1990: 36–52) for this Bakhtinian view of the event and time and Badiou (1988, in Barker, 2002: 74–82).

21 See Bourdieu and Wacquant (1992) for this dual perspective in sociology. See Chouliaraki and Fairclough (1999) and Chouliaraki (2002) for this perspective in discourse analysis.

22 See Tester (2001), Cohen (2001) and Cambell (2004).

23 See Morson and Emerson (1991: 43–9).

24 See Bakhtin (1981: 84–5, 243–58) in M. Holquist (ed.) 'The dialogic imagination. Four essays by M. M. Bakhtin'.

25 See Scannel (1991 and 1993: 9–24).

26 See Barnett (2003: 102).

27 See Barnett (2003: 81–107), Thompson (1997: 10–49) and Hall (1997: 208–36) for this critical perspective.

28 Hall's 'encoding–decoding' thesis, which grants audiences the privilege of a relative autonomy of interpretation over the ideologies encoded in television text (1973/1980), differs from the analytics of mediation in that the latter offers a view of the text as itself a double economy of autonomy and subjectification. For the analytics, unlike Hall's thesis of audience empowerment, the text is already a space of agency options for the spectator and works as an instrument of conditional freedom.

4

THE ANALYTICS OF MEDIATION

The analytics of mediation is an approach to the study of television that considers it as both a semiotic accomplishment (as text) and a technology embedded in existing power relationships of viewing. In this sense, the analytics of mediation seeks to keep the modernist legacy of social criticism and change alive and serve the project of the critical interpretation of the present. However, it does so by avoiding the theoretical abstractions of the public ethics narratives of Chapter 1 and the aesthetic narratives of Chapter 2. Instead of using 'grand' theory about the ethics of deliberative democracy or postmodernity, the analytics of mediation turns to the local study of particular news texts in which suffering is represented. This preference for the particular follows the Aristotelian ethos of phronesis, whereby the study of ethics takes as its point of departure the ethical values already embedded in singular practices of discourse and seeks to problematize the ways in which these values become normative in these practices of discourse. The object of study in the analytics of mediation is thus the genre of television news as a *regime of meanings*.

The term regime of meanings refers to the bounded field of possible meaning relationships that obey a certain regularity in the ways in which they can be combined and circulated and, as a consequence, the possibilities they offer to constitute legitimate forms of knowledge about the world and of self for the spectator of television news. In the study of suffering, we speak of regimes of pity to refer to this array of semiotic practices that construe suffering as a meaningful spectacle with its own proposals for relating to the spectator. I referred to this concept in the previous chapters, but we can now better grasp the idea of a regime of pity in relation to the September 11th example.

What are we to feel when gazing at the Manhattan skyline enveloped in thick grey smoke? What are we to do when watching fire brigades and ambulances rushing to help victims just after the towers' collapse? Visualizing the event via a street camera places it in the temporality of emergency, of frantic and contingent activity, and endows it with the aesthetic quality of testimony, the first-hand knowledge of the eyewitness.

This regime of pity offers a sense of close proximity to the scene of suffering and organizes the spectacle of suffering around action that may alleviate the sufferers' misfortunes. This is different from the long shot of New York's grey skyline. Here, pity takes the form of aesthetic contemplation vis-à-vis the sublimity of the catastrophe and invites reflection on the event's causes and consequences. The long shot – as opposed to the 'involved' camera of the Manhattan streets – entails an interest in historicity and analysis rather than actuality and activity.

These two examples suggest that mediation as a regime of pity incorporates the problematic of governmentality, because it uses the meaning-making affordances of television in order to guide the spectators' conduct of conduct into specific ways of viewing, while it also makes them feel that they relate to suffering of their own free will, emotions and desires.

It is clear that the study of regimes of pity requires a language about the television text that moves away from descriptions of the simulacrum or the signal. It is precisely this language that the analytics of mediation proposes. Central to this analytical language is the distinction between *hypermediacy* and *immediacy* – a distinction that, as we already know, is constitutive of the process of mediation itself. The analytics of mediation takes both hypermediacy and immediacy to be semiotic categories – that is, categories that produce meaning in television by marking some form of *difference*.

As I argued in Chapter 2, meaning comes about by means of two types of difference that constitute the semiotic process. On the one hand, there is the difference inherent in the medium of meaning making, in the technologies of verbal and visual recording that turn the screen into a material reality of images and narratives. This is hypermediacy.

On the other hand, there is difference that lies outside the media of meaning making and is shown and enacted on screen in the asymmetrical relationship between the sufferer and the westerner who watches or acts on the suffering. An example of this is the relationship between the Nigerian woman sentenced to death by stoning and the European political activist who speaks in her name. This is immediacy. In this sense, the analytics of mediation integrates the critical interest in the production of meaning on television – in *difference within the semiotic* – with the regulative function of television to shape specific dispositions of viewing and acting – in *difference outside the semiotic*.

At the same time, the distinction between difference within the semiotic and difference outside the semiotic helps us separate two levels of analysis. On the one hand, it helps us focus on the analysis of how meaning making about suffering takes place on the television screen as a hypermediated accomplishment – what I refer to below as *multimodal analysis*. On the other hand, it helps us focus on the analysis of how the news brings forth emotions and wishes for engagement with the suffering as an immediate reality for the spectator – what I call below *critical discourse analysis*.

Critical discourse analysis consists of the analysis of the space–times within which each piece of news places the encounter between spectator and sufferer and the options for action that this piece makes available for spectators. The production of suffering as a barometer of the ethics of the present arises out of the interplay between these two dimensions of analysis – multimodal and critical discourse analysis.

Difference within the semiotic: the multimodality of mediation

Difference within the semiotic points to difference that lies inside the semiotic systems themselves. This point is well developed by Derrida. For Derrida, who pushed structuralist linguistics to its limit, the idea of difference is not a social category (difference among people), but a systemic category (difference within a sign system) that resides in the very organization of language.[1] Derrida's claim is that the sign, rather than being split into internal form (medium) and external content (representation), is seen as a *mark* that consists of both materialities:

> The possibility of repeating, and therefore of identifying, marks is implied *in every code*, making of it a communicable, transmittable, decipherable grid that is iterable for a third party, and thus for any user in general.
>
> (1982: 315)

By emphasizing that meaning operates as a 'mark in every code', Derrida tells us two things. First, following Saussure, the founder of structuralism, he tells us what the aesthetic narratives of mediation have ignored or suppressed. He tells us that the visual is internally differentiated into form and content and the visual is itself a semiotic code. As I argued in Chapter 3 when discussing the aesthetic reflexivity thesis, the implication of this claim is that the visual now becomes an object of semiotic study in its own right. It is not a simulacrum or signal, but has the 'potential' to produce content and a grammar for the realization of meaning. As van Leeuwen puts it, the visual is a semiotic mode that:

> can be conceived of as a loose collection of individual signs, a kind of lexicon, or a stratified system of rules that allow a limited number of elements to generate an infinite number of messages.
>
> (2001: 17)[2]

This means that, even when the content of television appears minimal – for example in fast, 'pastiche' images of advertisements – the screen still confronts spectators with a meaningful message that it is possible to systematize and to analyse.

At the same time, Derrida's understanding of meaning as a mark consisting of both form and content – as an *instituted trace* – pushes the point on visuality beyond the legacy of Saussure. Given that visuality is itself a code, Derrida argues, why is language prioritized over the visual? This is an ironic question, considering the contemporary privileging of *visuality* in our culture, as we saw in Chapters 1 and 3. Derrida's point, however, perceptively targets a deeper hierarchy, which assigns to language the role of conceptual and analytical thinking and relegates visuality to a secondary and simpler representational mode. This underprivileging of the visual also explains the poverty of theory on visuality in the two aesthetic accounts of mediation.[3]

Derrida claims, however, that orality and visuality are two distinct but equally complicated semiotic codes and the relationship between them is fundamental when describing the process of meaning making. Meaning making combines marks that are both oral and visual. Meaning, then, comes about as a result not of a positivity – a fixed presence that these marks carry around – but as a result of the difference between the media of such marks, pictorial or spoken, and the content potential of these media – what they 'say' or 'show'. Meaning is always an unfinished business because these marks constantly alter their relationship to other marks as they travel from context to context: 'traces of signs exhibit a minimal sameness in the different contexts in which they appear, yet are still modified in the new contexts in which they appear' (Howarth, 2000: 41). It is this capacity of the mark to both repeat itself – that is, to change context – and be identified – to be recognized as the same; the *iterability* of the mark, in Derrida's words – that lies at the heart of 'difference within the semiotic'.

Let us take, again, the news example of the boat accident in India. How could this piece of news be represented on television? Let us imagine two different ways. It could be represented by means of verbal text read by a studio anchor or on-location footage of the rescue operation of the boat's passengers.

These are two possible inscriptions of the 'boat accident', a single content, in different media, language and moving image. It is obvious that the semiotic code in which each medium inscribes the content of the event radically alters the meaning of suffering in it. Listening to a brief verbal report is different from witnessing the scene of the rescuing of the passengers. This difference, in turn, has a tremendous effect on the politics of pity around this instance of suffering. The brief verbal report renders the boat accident a piece of 'adventure' news, an instance of suffering without pity that makes no demand for a response from the spectator. On the contrary, the intense visualization of rescue action renders the boat accident an instance of suffering with pity, a piece of emergency news that incorporates the demand for action in the news story itself.

Iterability, in this context, helps us understand the hypermediated dimension of mediation. Iterability, in other words, shows that the use of different media transforms the meanings of suffering in ways that make it difficult to separate how these meanings both remain the same and become different. Wouldn't we react to the boat accident news in its two diverse presentations by saying 'it's the same and yet it's not'?[4]

Multimodal analysis

Multimodality is the study of the semiotic processes by means of which the hypermediated environment of television manages to create a coherent regime for the representation of suffering – a regime of pity that construes the event of suffering as the spectator's most immediate reality.[5] The methodological principle of multimodal analysis is that regimes of pity do not coincide with the specific image or language we watch on screen. Instead, the image and language of suffering follow a systematic pattern of co-appearance and combination, which organizes the potential for the representation of suffering into the generic conventions of the news broadcast. Because regimes of pity are patterns of co-appearance and combination rather than single pictures or sentences, they are best understood as analytical constructs that help us to describe the systematic semiotic choices by which the spectacle of suffering becomes meaningful to spectators in the genre of the news.

I take three aspects of this genre to be relevant in the construal of regimes of pity. These are the *mode of presentation* of the news text, the *correspondence between verbal narrative and image* in the news text and the *aesthetic quality* of the news text.

Mode of news presentation

The mode of presentation of the news refers to the locations from which the news story is told and the media used to tell the story. Modes of presentation may include a studio anchor, who secures the flow and continuity of the broadcast, usually accompanied by footage (video or live) and commentary in the form of a reporter's voiceover. Whereas studio presentation may include the commentary of invited experts, footage may include the oral testimony of witnesses from the scene of action. Choices made regarding the mode of news presentation have a considerable impact on the ways in which spectators get in touch with and come to evaluate the news on suffering. Although, as Lash says, there is indeed a sense of ephemerality and obsoleteness in the flow of the news, his insistence that all television viewing is ephemeral cannot capture the systematic variation in the types of engagement that each piece of news may offer to spectators. The mode of news presentation enables us to study the internal hierarchy in the ephemerality of the news and shows that, whereas some instances of suffering combine a wide range of presentation positions and ample time to discuss and reflect on the conditions of suffering, other news pieces close the suffering off in a brief oral report. Furthermore, live reportage creates a greater sense of proximity and urgency vis-à-vis the reported suffering for spectators than does a studio anchor presentation.

At the same time, despite this internal hierarchy, which decides just how immediate the reality of a particular suffering becomes on the television screen, suffering does appear as a reality in all pieces of news. Depending on how the visual presentation relates to anchors' pieces or voiceovers, each mode of news presentation offers spectators a distinct approach to the reality of the event, a distinct form of *'narrative "realism"'*.[6]

Narrative realism can evoke the tangible reality of facts based on the truth of what we see, on the power of visual perception. This is what we call *perceptual realism*.

Narrative realism can also bring about the reality of the heart, a reality evoked by strong feelings rather than facts, giving rise to a form of realism that we call *categorical realism*.

Finally, narrative realism can make use of the reality of the 'doxa' – a reality appealing to our deep-rooted certainties about what the world is or should be like. This is what we call *ideological realism*.

The realities of both the heart and doxa are versions of *psychological realism* – a way of knowing about reality that appeals to our emotional and moral sensibilities rather than our quest for facts.

News realism, then, is not about presenting spectators with the single reality of suffering but, rather, presenting them with different realities about suffering – different meanings through which suffering can be represented.

The mode of presentation of the news is, evidently, a major criterion of newsworthiness. The September 11th live footage, for example, hectically alternates modes of presentation and, in so doing, establishes multiple and unrelenting variations on engagement with this instance of suffering. These modes include on-location reports with witness interviews, which invest the presentation of the event in the 'this is how it is' factuality of perceptual realism, and long shots of Manhattan accompanied by studio panel talk, where the mode of presentation frames the event in ideological realism, knowledge and belief about the attacks that the experts reiterate for us. In contrast, the brief news on the Indian boat accident – which combines a descriptive report with a map of India only – employs minimal narrative conventions and, as a result, construes the suffering of the Indian people as something that is devoid of proximity, urgency or agency.

When we analyse a piece of news, then, questions concerning the mode of presentation include the following.

- Is the news introduced in the studio with presenter-to-camera speech and is it accompanied by illustrations or is there a reporter on location?
- Which sense of news realism is being evoked in the news?

  - Is the suffering shown at all or is it narrated, using language only?
  - If yes, is it shown in a manner that seeks to evoke a 'this is how it is' type of reality or does the emphasis fall more on a 'this is how we feel about it' or 'this is how sad/horrific/wrong the suffering is'? Does the emphasis of the narrative make an appeal to the spectators' sense of compassion, righteousness or justice? Alternatively, does it refrain from engaging spectators in a sustained emotional relationship with the piece of news?

Verbal–visual correspondence
The distinct sense of the reality of suffering that each news text attempts
to evoke for the spectator is not easy to identify simply by looking at the
mode of presentation. In order to be able to describe precisely how types
of realism emerge from the multimodal combinations of the news text, we
need to talk further about the work that language and image perform in
the text.

This distinction between language and image, let us recall, is based on
the assumption that each semiotic mode has its own logic of producing
meaning, its own meaning-making affordances, and, thus, its own mechanism for mediating suffering. The verbal entails three modes of *narrating* the
suffering – what I term below *descriptions, narrations proper* and *expositions*[7] –
whereas the image entails three modes of *portraying* suffering – as the
index, icon and *symbol*.[8] Let me focus on each of these two semiotic modes
in turn.

The visual   The impact of any news text is almost always a function of
its *visual referent*.[9] As Corner says, 'the offer of "seeing" is absolutely central to the project of television journalism' (1995: 59). As we saw in the
theories of Chapter 1, it is precisely the 'seeing it happen' that is
the power of the image and enables it to make the strongest claim to the
authenticity of suffering in television, 'burdening' spectators with the
moral role of the witness. At the same time, the image is also instrumental in helping spectators to remember the suffering. This is because it has
a stronger aesthetic impact than 'hearing it happen' and so makes a
stronger impression on spectators' memories. The image, in this respect,
participates in what Derrida calls a 'politics of memory' – a politics that
dictates which piece of suffering is worthy of retention and repetition by
the spectator and which is not. The shift from no visual towards an
increasingly intensive visualization of suffering is, in this sense, a shift
towards an increasingly intensive involvement with sufferers and, thus,
an invitation to spectators to remember and repeat the sufferers' misfortunes. For example, video images of human figures with their backs to
the camera places us in the scene of suffering but does not engage us
with the sufferers. In contrast, a quick and sharp sequence of suffering
children's close-ups, gazing at the camera, takes the form of a visual
bombardment and invites us to urgently respond to their tragedy. The
distinction between the former and the latter type of visualization is one
between adventure news, which we hardly register as such, and emergency news, which makes a demand on us to speak up or do something
about the misfortune we have seen.

At the same time, it is not the properties of the visual composition alone
that determine the claim to reality the image makes in the news. An image
may carry an indexical or iconic value, but, as we shall see below, it is
the participation of the image in the broader semiotic environment of

television that ultimately determines how the image functions as part of the news's regime of pity and participates in construing the form of realism that this piece of news evokes for the spectator. Because I discuss the visual–verbal correspondence of news texts below, the analytical questions about the visual that I am posing at this point do not address visual meaning in the news text as a whole, but are only about the image layout observable on screen. Such questions include the following.

- Which kind of visual representation does the suffering adopt in the news report? Is it is graphic (map, diagram), photographic, archive film or live transmission?
- If graphic, is the representation static and minimal or dynamic and multiple (computerized, as for example, in war maps of Iraq)?
- If there is written text, how does it interact with the image? Does the text add to the image (explicate, illustrate) or is it running simply in parallel to it?
- If video:

  - which point of view (above and afar or involved)
  - which angle (direct/gaze level oblique/profile or back filming)
  - which framing (actors' position, distance from camera, relationship to the overall visual composition)
  - which vectors of movement (between actors, towards the spectator, outside camera frame)?

The verbal   If visualization tells us something about the degree of authenticity and memorability that a piece of news is endowed with, it is the *verbal mode* that establishes the distinct form of the realism of the news. That is to say, the verbal establishes the sense of reality that the story evokes for the spectator. This is because it is 'words [that] carry the burden of naming and description, of interpretation and evaluation' (Corner, 1995: 61–2). It is therefore words that regulate the flow of edited images and create a meaningful story out of a usually unrelated series of images of places and people. In ordering and organizing the spaces and temporalities of events, the verbal narrative of the news performs fundamental classificatory activities. It includes and excludes, foregrounds and backgrounds, justifies and legitimizes. It separates 'us' from 'them'.

Three narrative functions of the news are responsible for this classificatory work, which are *descriptions*, *narrations* or storytelling proper and *expositions*. The hard facts of suffering are mainly evoked in *descriptive narratives* that tell us what we see and so they make the strongest claim to objectivity. For example, in the Indian boat accident news, a descriptive report sounds like this: 'Forty-four people drowned in River Baytarani'.

In *narration*, the factual reporting of events is replaced by elements of fictional storytelling, such as a chronological plot (with moments of deliberate tension or suspense), as well as generic conventions of opening and/or closure: 'It was the end of an ordinary school day, when the boat transporting the children on River Baytarani capsized; 44 people drowned'.

The term *exposition* refers to the verbal narrative that incorporates a point of view within the news and, in so doing, explicitly articulates ethical judgement vis-à-vis the reported suffering: 'Forty-four people feared drowned in River Baytarani'. Evaluation is here contained, in a suppressed form, in the use of the affective/impersonal process 'feared'.

Although there is an obvious analytical value to differentiating these three narrative types from one another, we should be aware of the fact that news texts often enact more than one narrative function at once. Just as the semiotic modes of language and the visual are multifunctional, narratives, too, coexist and complement one another. They are intertextual.[10] Concerning the role of the verbal mode in the news text, questions may include ones such as these.

- Is the verbal text of the news cast as a description of facts or does it also entail elements of exposition, with value judgements and normative proposals about the suffering? Could the news report be a narration of events with emphasis on drama and suspense and little consideration of the facts?
- If the report combines more than one of the narrative types, how do these relate to one another? Which one frames the rest? Which role do the lower-hierarchy narratives play in the development of the story?

This orientation towards the intertextuality of the texts – the mixing of narrative types – enables us to explore further certain hypotheses about the narrative impact of the news text.

- If the suffering is primarily cast as a description of hard facts rather than a dramatic narration of events, which is the realist narrative that organizes the representation of suffering in this news?
- If the suffering is primarily cast as dramatic narration rather than expository talk, does the realism of this news run the risk of sentimentalism or does it go beyond sentimentalism and invite a deeper contemplation of the conditions of suffering?
- If, alternatively, the suffering is reported as exposition, with elements of description and traces of narration, how does the realism of this news invite the spectators' reactions? Does it invite them to protest against the causes of suffering or care about alleviating the pain of the sufferers?

The relationship between the verbal and the visual   The verbal–visual relationship is often perceived as purely antithetical. The verbal is usually conflated with conceptuality and abstract thinking, whereas the visual is equated with spectacularity and aesthetic value. However, as we saw in the theories described in Chapter 3, the relationship between the verbal and the visual is more complicated than this. It is important that we pay close attention to this complexity because it takes our understanding of how the reality of suffering is construed in the news further, by means of the various forms of realism.

Indeed, each type of realism – perceptual, categorical and ideological – brings together its own combination of linguistic narrative with image and, in so doing, also establishes three distinct types of meaning relationship in the news text. These are *indexical, iconic* and *symbolic* meanings – terminology that we also encountered in Chapter 3, in the discussion on visuality. The realism of each news text, then, depends on the distinct claims to the reality of suffering that each of the three types of meaning makes:

- claim to the *facticity* of suffering in perceptual realism
- claim to the *emotion* of suffering in categorical realism
- claim to *justice* concerning the cause of suffering in ideological realism.[11]

The claim to facticity is the claim of perceptual realism and builds on an *indexical* relationship between the verbal and visual. This means that perceptual realism relies heavily on the image and uses descriptive language to tell us what we see on screen. *Indexical meaning* signifies precisely by employing language to establish some 'physical' or direct connection to the image. It is the reliance on the factual correspondence between 'what we see' and 'what we hear' that makes the news pieces based on perceptual realism appear as 'windows to the outside world', offering to the spectator an authenticity beyond doubt.[12] Although none of the news narratives in this volume relies exclusively on indexicality – not even the paradigmatic case of perceptual realism in Chapter 6 (the news of the rescuing of African refugees) – all these texts, inevitably, entail an element of indexicality that grounds them in the world out there.

The claims to emotion and, more explicitly, the ethics and politics of suffering inform *psychological realism* in its two manifestations – *categorical* and *ideological realism*. Claims to emotion and justice depart from the reliance on physical perception – the link between what we see and what we hear.

In the case of *categorical realism*, fact matters less and the welling up of the spectators' feelings towards the suffering matters most. In order to bring about emotions, categorical realism often relies on storytelling or narration proper, which frames the visual representation of suffering with dramatic urgency and sensationalism. In the news on famine in Argentina, for example, the relationship between image and narration gives rise to *iconic meaning* – meaning that is related to its referent not via some direct 'physical' connection, but via similarity or family resemblance. Iconicity, then, does not attach itself to a concrete reality. Iconicity, instead, represents an abstract reality by using image as the key signifier of whichever generic condition it seeks to capture. In the famine in Argentina news text included in this volume, images of emaciated children evoke the referent 'starvation' and function in a cumulative way to overwhelm spectators with the reality of children's imminent death by famine.

Ideological realism works similarly to categorical realism in that the image is associated with an abstraction. This time, though, the abstraction does not take the form of a generic category, such as famine, but that of a specific ideological dilemma – for example, whether we are for or against humanity – and urges spectators to take a public stance on it. Here, the relationship between the visual and verbal semiotic modes gives rise to *symbolic meaning*. Symbolic meaning is related to its referent neither by direct connection nor family resemblance, but by discursive associations based on conventional knowledge and value, such as the doxa of 'us' as humane and 'them' as savages. For example, in the news of the Nigerian woman, the visual contrast between a mother with her baby and an enraged crowd mobbing a woman evokes the widespread cultural belief that Islam is an 'inhumane' culture. Let us keep in mind that the function of symbolic meaning to dehumanize Islam already presupposes the doxa about Islam as an inhumane religion and, in embedding it within the news narrative, the television text further reproduces and disseminates this doxa.

In summary, it is the variation in the combinations of verbal narrative and visual flow that gives rise to forms of realism in the news on suffering. Each narrative–image combination makes a distinct claim to reality and, thus, activates a distinct emotional potential for the spectator. This analytical interest in the reality effects that the language and images in news texts bring about can be formulated in the following questions.

- Which role does each mode, language and image play in the news narrative? Do the verbal and visual modes unfold in parallel worlds with a minimal relationship between them or is there a substantial referential relationship between the two?
- If there are direct references between the visual and verbal, does the verbal mode 'accompany' the visual in a strictly factual narrative of depicted events or does it expand on the visuals?
- If the verbal mode expands on the visual, what is the 'transfer effect' of language on the visual mode? Which extra-pictorial meanings does the news narrative evoke by means of an 'over-interpreting' voiceover? Alternatively, does the voiceover stop to allow for the power of the visual or sound effects to come through? How does this type of verbal–visual combination impact on the processes of news meaning making?

It is important, at this point, to repeat that the three types of meaning (indexical, iconic and symbolic) are, in practice, not separated in a clear-cut manner. They often coexist with one another in single portrayals of suffering and it is this coexistence that gives to multimodal communication its inherent semantic indeterminacy. It is therefore a matter of empirical investigation to determine the cases in which a certain type of meaning takes over another and becomes the decisive one in organizing the narrative realism of a specific piece of news. When I claim, for instance, that the news about the Nigerian woman is constituted by virtue of symbolic meaning, we should be clear that relationships of indexicality and iconicity are already in place within this same piece of news. Yet, it is the symbolic element in the meaning relationships between the visual and the verbal that, ultimately, frames our overall engagement with this particular event.

In reverse, when I claim prominence for indexical or iconic meaning in other pieces of news, we should bear in mind that symbolic meaning always operates at some unarticulated level on the representation of suffering.[13] Indeed, one critical task of the analytics of mediation is to articulate this symbolic level at which suffering operates, independently of its dominant form of realism – perceptual or categorical. As I argue in Chapter 6, the 'symbolics of threat', which implicitly resides in many news items on suffering, is not only central in the 'othering' of every sufferer but is also decisive in proposing or blocking action on the suffering by the spectator.

Aesthetic quality
The aesthetic quality of the news is a consequence of both its mode of presentation and the relationship that the news text establishes between language and image. The aesthetic quality describes the overall semiotic effect of the news in terms of three historical tropes for the public staging of suffering. These are what we already encountered in Chapter 1 as Boltanski's topics of suffering. These historical topics for the representation of suffering are *pamphleteering, philanthropy* and *sublimation.* Pamphleteering is associated with the genre of political denunciation and aims to address the spectators' affective potential for anger vis-à-vis the evil-doer who inflicted the pain on the sufferer. Philanthropy is associated with genres of Christian care and aims to activate the spectators' affective potential of tender-heartedness towards the benefactor, who comforts the sufferers' pain. Finally, sublimation distances the spectators from the actuality of suffering and orientates them towards a reflexive contemplation of the conditions of human misery. The broadcasting genre may endow the reported event with a single aesthetic quality – say, philanthropic appeal for famine victims – or it may select and combine elements of many topics. In this latter case, the news casts suffering in more complicated regimes of pity and proposes a broader range of public values for spectators to engage with. For example, the aesthetic quality of the September 11th footage draws simultaneously on tender-hearted philanthropy in the scenes of emergency aid, indignation regarding the perpetrators of this evil in the public statements of witnesses and political figures and voyeuristic sentiments regarding the spectacular plane crashes into the Twin Towers. In so doing, the event invites the

spectators to at once denounce the attacks, empathize with the victims and indulge in a sublimated contemplation of the plane crashes.

The aesthetic quality of pity, however, is not only related to the emotional potential for identification with the sufferers that the news text may activate for the spectators. The aesthetic effect of the news is also related to the ways in which a regime of pity produces the spectacle of suffering as authentic for spectators. Against ideas that consider news broadcasts to be 'the' hard genre of factuality, we saw that the news actually construes the factuality of the event it reports by employing one or another version of narrative realism. The news is a kind of *fictional fashioning* and its factuality is, in fact, *artifactuality* (Derrida, 2002: 41). One of the aims of the analytics of mediation is to pinpoint how each of these types of realism resolves the question of the reality of suffering precisely by articulating media and meaning, aesthetic quality and universal moral values.

For example, the aesthetic quality of the news on how African refugees were rescued in the stormy Mediterranean is that of a high-adrenaline spectacle and draws on the spectators' cinematic experience, particularly of the action film genre. The political content of this aesthetics, I argue, is minimal. It exhausts the spectators' response to the suffering in the consumption of that spectacle and does not make them think about the causes behind the massive numbers of illegal refugees trying to get into Europe. In a rather different vein, the news of the famine in Argentina draws on an 'icons of starvation' aesthetic familiar to Western spectators who have in their memories a classic repertoire of African famine snapshots. The political content of this aesthetic, now orientated towards the spectator's heart rather than releasing adrenaline, can be summed up as the making of a humanitarian appeal or, to put it more broadly, cultivating a disposition for news spectators to be cosmopolitan philanthropists.

To conclude, the study of multimodality in the news seeks to identify what I referred to in Chapter 2 as the two elements of pity – pity as emotional engagement and objective deliberation. It is these two elements that give pity a different face, depending on the mise en scène that stages suffering in each piece of news. On the one hand, the multimodal analysis of topics of suffering reveals that a certain combination of language and image lies behind any emotional register of suffering that any specific piece of news manages to evoke. On the other hand, the multimodal analysis of realist narratives also reveals that certain forms of realism are behind any claim of the news to represent reality as an immediate and authentic experience for the spectator. It is, ultimately, the study of multimodality that enables us to trace down the process by which a singular representation of suffering comes to articulate a 'universal' value – the values that connect the feelings of the individual spectator with the objectivity of public action.

What are these values? How can spectators be guided to endorse them and articulate them as their own? In order to study the content of these 'universal' values, we must now turn to the study of the representations of suffering in television – that is, the ways in which the spectator–sufferer relationship takes on a specific ethical content on the screen. This is the concern with mediation as difference outside the semiotic.

Difference outside the semiotic: the multifunctionality of mediation

Difference outside the semiotic points to a kind of difference that lies outside meaning-making systems, even though we can only encounter it via texts. Difference outside the semiotic lies in the asymmetries of power that traverse the social world and the historical and political relationships within or between social groups.[14] The concern with mediation as difference outside the semiotic, then, is a concern with the social relationships of viewing that map out the world in terms of spectator zones and sufferer zones or in terms of space–times of safety and space–times of danger. Even though these are not clear-cut distinctions, there is a historically shaped topography of power, whereby it is the West that watches the rest of the world suffer. By the same token, the 'universal' values of the news broadcasts are those of the West. Denunciation, empathy and aesthetic contemplation – what I described above as manifestations of the aesthetic quality of the news – are simultaneously historically and culturally specific dispositions of the public life of Western societies.[15] The character of these values as specifically Western ones can also explain why the September 11th footage, shifting the West from the zone of safe spectatorship into dangerous spectacle, frantically alternates between the three topics and takes on the rare form of 'ecstatic news'.

Even if difference outside the semiotic draws attention to the macro-picture of power, the empirical focus in the study of mediation is the local semiotic practice of the news broadcast. It is the concept of discourse that connects these two components of the analytics of mediation – the macro-perspective of power and the micro-perspective of the television text.

The concept of discourse implies that the relationship between power and meaning is one of mutual constitution. As Foucault has argued, every attempt to put something in to meaning comes about from a position of power because power connects and organizes the social positions that cause meaning to come about.[16] Meaning, then, makes a claim to truth precisely because of the power position that enunciates it. This is not the truth but always a truth *effect* – a truth that seeks to reconstitute and re-establish power in meaning. In this light, the power asymmetry that is embedded in the social relationships of television viewing may not in itself bring about the economic and political divisions of our world, but it certainly reflects and consolidates them. Who watches whom suffer reflects the manner in which differences in economic resources, political regimes and everyday life enter the global landscape of information. Similarly, who acts on whose suffering reflects patterns of economic and political agency across global zones of influence and their historical divisions, North and South or East and West.

The study of contemporary rule as governmentality seeks to capture precisely this dual character of power as something 'bigger' than the present moment, as a 'historical a priori', to recall Foucault's vocabulary in Chapter 3, and simultaneously as something 'momentary', enacted and reproduced in the here-and-now practices of the news, in what Derrida calls *singularities*.

In the analytics of mediation, the relationship between singular practices of meaning making and the broader power relationships of meaning making is exemplified in the principle of the *multi functionality* of semiosis.[17] Multifunctionality assumes that every semiotic mode – language and visual – creates meaning that fulfils more than one function at once. These functions are performed by the semiotic system itself and, in this sense, are metafunctions of semiosis. However, they are simultaneously social functions because they serve the two fundamental communicative needs and relationships of society. The first is the social need to name and represent the world – the *ideational metafunction* of semiosis. The second is the social need to engage in interaction and relate to other people – the *interpersonal metafunction* of semiosis. There is also the *textual metafunction* of semiosis, which looks inwards to the text itself and serves the social purpose of creating meaning that is recognized as coherent and intelligible. In Jewitt and Oyama's words, the textual metafunction holds together 'the individual bits of representation–interaction' into coherent text wholes (2001: 140). In so far as it concerns itself with the combination of language and image in coherent texts, the textual metafunction obviously appertains to the multimodal analysis of television that I discussed earlier. It is part of mediation as difference within the semiotic. By the same token, in so far as the other two metafunctions concern themselves with the social effects of semiosis – that is, with naming and 'representation of reality' and interaction and 'orientation to the others' – they appertain to mediation as difference outside the semiotic.[18]

Critical discourse analysis

The analysis of mediation as difference outside the semiotic is called critical discourse analysis (CDA). CDA is a method of analysis of the television text that treats the linguistic and visual choices on the screen as subtle indicators of the power of television to mediate the world to the world. This is the power of television to classify the world into categories of 'us' and 'the other' and orientate (or not) the spectator towards this suffering 'other'.

In the analysis of *representations*, CDA looks into the construal of the scene of suffering within a specific space–time that separates safety from danger. Space–time, you will recall, is about the place and temporality of suffering. It tells us how close a specific instance of suffering is to the spectator and how urgent action on the suffering is. The analysis of space–time then focuses on the axes of proximity/distance or urgency/finality.

In the analysis of *orientations*, CDA looks into the category of *agency*. Agency is about who acts on whom in the scene of suffering. There are two dimensions of orientation that are relevant in establishing the social relationships of suffering. First, *agency* refers to how active sufferers themselves appear on screen and, second, it refers to how other actors present in the scene appear to engage with the sufferers. These two dimensions of agency come to shape how the spectators themselves are invited to relate to the suffering – that is, if they are supposed to simply watch, feel for or act in a practical way on the 'other's misfortune. Of course, those who live in poverty, destitution and war are, by definition, always 'others' for the safe spectators, yet there is a gradation in the 'othering' of sufferers in the news, ranging from those who deserve no pity to those whose misfortune we share as if it were our own. The study of agency, in this respect, focuses on the analytical axis of 'our own'/'other'.

I have so far described representations and orientations as two clearly separate categories of CDA. Again, at this point, we need a methodological caveat. This distinction between representation and orientation is a necessity that enables the analysis of television texts. In practice, representations and orientations are not separate parts of the television text. Following the multifunctionality principle of semiotic modes, representations and orientations coexist in one single news frame and the analytical perspective on discourse must therefore look at once into both metafunctions in order to determine how they are brought together in each news sequence.[19]

Space–time

The space–time of suffering is the category that analyses how the reality of the safe spectator encounters the reality of the distant sufferer in different degrees of intensity and involvement. In this sense, space–time is responsible for establishing a sense of immediacy for the scene of suffering and regulating the moral distance between spectator and sufferer. However, spatio-temporal immediacy is a fragile construction. This is the case not because most pieces of news come from faraway places, but mainly because issues such as famine mortality or death by stoning fall outside the spectators' lifeworlds, outside their structure of experience. They challenge the limits of the spectators' modal imagination – what safe spectators can imagine as real in the world out there. Yet, rather than lament the fact that connectivity between spectators and sufferers is impossible to achieve, as the pessimistic narratives do in Chapter 1, we simply need to acknowledge this inevitability.

According to Silverstone (2002a: 770), the acknowledgement that mediation cannot completely connect us with the 'other' should lead us to problematize the act of mediation itself and the manner in which mediation construes places as proximal or distant. His concept of 'proper distance', which, you may recall, I mentioned in Chapter 2, brings into focus the fact that the spatial dimension of suffering on television and the ethical positions implicated in it are context-specific and shifting. So they have to be determined case by case rather than once and for all. Just how effectively each piece of news articulates the spatial axis of proximity/distance or the temporal axis of urgency/finality in order to establish suffering as a reality for the spectator is the first of the two analytical priorities that I address in the study of pieces of news about suffering.

Concerning *space*, the analytics of mediation asks questions such as those listed below.[20]

- Is space actively shaping action or is it only a background to action?
- Is space replaceable or unique?
- Is space internally differentiated or is it presented as a homogeneous entity?
- Are the spaces of danger and safety in any form of interaction with one another or are they strictly separated?

In order to respond to these questions on the representation of space, I shall focus on the following semiotic choices made when presenting news:

- *visual editing* – for example, when a film cuts from street footage in Nigeria to video sequences from the EU headquarters in Brussels
- *camera position* – for example, filming from within the scene of action or from a location above or away
- *graphic specification* – such as a map, the presence of written text or split screen
- *linguistic reference* – such as the use of adverbs about space or geographical references.

Concerning *time*, the analytics of mediation asks questions such as these.

- Is the event taking place in the present or the past?
- Is time open, with multiple possibilities, or scripted in advance?
- How does the past impinge on the present?
- How does it impinge on possible futures?
- Which has the greatest value – the past, present or future?
- Which future, distant or immediate?

In order to respond to these questions on the representation of time, we focus on the following semiotic choices made when presenting news:

- *visual intertextuality* – for example, combining archive film and, hence, a reference to the past with on-location reports, thus shifting to 'right now' action
- *linguistic reference* – the use of temporal adverbials, such as 'simultaneously', 'previously' and so on, the use of tense, present or past, or modality/imperatives, such as 'no to death by stoning'.[21]

Depending on the broader, multimodal text in which these choices are embedded, the suffering may appear to be happening categorically in the 'right here, right now' temporality or the 'far away, in the indefinite past' temporality. If emaciated children are placed in the timeframe of a fait accompli, in the past tense, there is little to do about them, but, if they are represented in terms of an ongoing temporality, where coordinated action develops as we speak, famine becomes an emergency and acquires a radically different horizon of action. Suffering, however, may also be represented with a greater degree of ambivalence – it may appear to be happening simultaneously here and there, in the past and right now. Frontal close-ups of Argentinean children hit spectators right between the eyes and establish proximity with them, but zooming in on these children's emaciated body parts 'fetishizes' their fragile bodies, to use Hall's word, and maintains a radical distance between them and the spectators. Long shots across the smoke-enveloped Manhattan skyline establish a voyeuristic distance from the scene of action, but paradoxically, they also establish a sense of proximity based on the temporality of reflection as they give spectators the chance to ponder on the circumstances and consequences of the September 11th attacks.

We may say that the difference between categorical and ambivalent representations of space–time is a difference in the degree of spatiotemporal complexity in which the suffering is shown to occur. Although Bakhtin says that all events have their own *chronotopic universe*, I prefer to reserve the term chronotopicity for those events that involve more than one space–time. We can talk, therefore, of the chronotope of a news event as that regime of multiple spaces (danger and safety) and temporalities (present, past or future), through which the event 'moves' back and forth and, in so doing, presents spectators with not one single reality of suffering but multiple realities relevant to the suffering. In Chapter 6, I define the chronotope of suffering as that space–time which increasingly expands to encompass the following four elements:

- *concreteness*, which shows the concrete context of suffering as a physical space
- *multiplicity*, which moves spectators through the multiple physical contexts of suffering
- *specificity*, which shows the context of suffering as a singular space by elaborating on its unique properties or individualizes the sufferer as a unique person with an array of attributes
- *mobility*, which connects the contexts of safety and danger, suggesting a specific relationship of action between them.

The move from news defined by a minimum of these properties to news defined by increasing spatiotemporal complexity (chronotopes) is simultaneously a move from news with minimum potential for pity to news with maximum moral appeal and potential for engagement. The more complicated the space–time, the less the 'othering' of the sufferer. In this sense, the space–time forms part of our attention to the historicity of the news, not only in terms of chronotopic analysis but also in terms of the power of the news to establish a global hierarchy of human life – what in Chapter 3 I referred to as *social explanation*.

Agency

This is the analytical category that focuses on action on suffering in terms of the agency of the sufferers themselves and the system of other agents that operate in the scene of suffering. The type of action that these figures of pity play out on screen has an effect on the spectators' own orientations towards the sufferers. However, agency is as fragile a category as proximity and equally difficult to achieve. This is because, as we saw in Chapter 2, agency in television can only take the form of action at a distance – that is, action associated with the practices of the agora and the theatre. The first, the action of the agora, is contemplation and depends on the spectators' objective deliberation and judgement on the suffering. The second, the action of the theatre, is identification and depends on the spectators' participation in the psychological and emotional states of suffering.

The humane sufferer and the agora   In contemplation – the action of the agora – the spectator is expected to watch the sufferer's misfortune without bias and judge it objectively. However, the position of true impartiality is impossible. This is because, as long as there is a hierarchy of places of suffering that divides the world, there will, inevitably, also be a hierarchy of the human lives that inhabit these places. It follows from this that the spectators are more likely to speak out about the suffering they are watching if the sufferers are construed as being like 'us' and, in reverse, the spectators are more likely to switch off if the sufferers fail to appear to be like 'us'. The agency of spectators to engage in public speech about the suffering then depends on the humanization of the sufferers.

In the analytics of mediation, *humanization* is a process of identity construction that endows sufferers with the power to say or do something about their condition, even if this power is simply the power to evoke and receive the beneficiary action of others. The humane sufferer is the sufferer who acts. The difference, for example, between September 11th and the news on the devastating floods in Bangladesh is, at least partly, a difference in the sufferer's agency. The September 11th sufferers speak; the Bangladeshi sufferers do not.

The importance of voice in marking the sufferers' agency is thematized in Spivak's question 'can the subaltern speak?' (1988). Speech – initially formulated in Spivak's critique of colonial discourse – does not refer strictly to talk, but, more generally, to the capacity of suffering others to call attention to their unfortunate condition and engage their addressees with this condition. In a similar way to Butler's claim in Chapter 2 that the sufferers' address, involuntary and unexpected as it may be, acts as a moralizing force on the spectators, Spivak asserts the fact that sufferers who are deprived of their 'voice', of the appelative power to make others aware of their misfortune, remain forever subalterns or an 'Other'.[22] The Bangladeshi homeless who are portrayed as part of a static landscape become 'Others' with a capital 'o' in so far as their existence remains purely inactive.

In a similar manner, language may 'Other' sufferers when it subsumes them under the general rule of numerical attributes, collective references or statistics.[23] Such semiotic choices *annihilate* the sufferers, in Silverstone's words – that is, they deprive the sufferers of their corporeal and psychological qualities and remove them from the existential order to which the spectators belong.

The first group of questions concerning agency, then, have to do with the sufferers' voice and humanness.

- Are the sufferers given a voice, in language or image?
- What kind of interiority is available for the sufferers? Is there a public–private boundary that gives them a certain 'depth' of consciousness?
- Do the sufferers coexist or communicate with others or other agents of suffering? What kind of ethical responsibility obliges these other agents to act?
- How do the sufferers connect with or communicate with the spectators? What kind of responsibility obliges the spectators to involve themselves in which type of action?

The humanization of sufferers occurs either via the verbal mode or the image. Concerning the *verbal mode*, the choice of the narrative type by means of which the news on suffering is reported plays an important role in the construal of the sufferers' identity as humane. Narration, or storytelling proper, for example, includes dramatic elements that may animate the figures of the sufferers as actors and, thus, humanize them to a greater extent than would a merely factual description of an event. Similarly, the lexicalization of the sufferers and the choice of attributes used to characterize their condition are instrumental in placing them within a hierarchy of active/humane or inactive/inhumane values.

Concerning the *visual mode*, a key choice is camera position and angle. It makes a difference if sufferers are filmed from afar and above in a group or near and from the front, gazing at the camera. The gaze, in this context, is appelative action and choosing to capture the sufferers' gaze with the camera is also one of giving them a voice and humanizing them, whereas choosing to film them using long shots may alienate and dehumanize them. Images of African people struggling en masse for survival in the stormy sea, shadowy figures gazing over their water-swept land or emaciated children's body parts zoomed in on are examples of how visual 'Othering' contributes to sustaining powerful hierarchies of human life.

Another significant choice that regulates the humanization of sufferers is visual juxtaposition. Montages may link the scene of suffering to the zone of safety in various forms of connectivity. One of these may be the cause and effect relationship, which evokes the thought that what happened there may affect us here. Another form of connectivity may set up a request and response relationship between safety and danger, conjuring up the thought that, if this is what is needed, then this is how we should act. Depending on the conceptual relationship established via visual juxtaposition, the sufferers may be placed beyond a zone of contact with the spectators, both spatially (too far out there to reach) and temporally (a figure of eternal misfortune without past or future) or, alternatively, they may be placed in an active relationship with the spectators. The broadcast on the death by stoning verdict against the Nigerian woman Amina Lawal, for example, cuts from violent mobbing scenes in Africa to the streets of Athens and the Amnesty International protest against the verdict that took place there. In establishing a request–response relationship with this instance of suffering, the television text not only brings this sufferer closer to the existential order of the spectators, but, further, it also urges the latter to do something in order to protect and rescue the sufferer, Amina Lawal.

The figures of suffering and the theatre   If in contemplation, the agora model of action at a distance, the what to do vis-à-vis the sufferer depends on the representation of the sufferer as properly humane, in the theatrical model of action at a distance, where the witnessing of suffering occurs mostly via emotions, the what to do has a different twist. The witnessing of suffering is now mediated by the dynamic of social relationships that are already at play in the scene of suffering – of being the benefactor or the persecutor. Agency in the theatre, then, depends on the orchestration of these two primary figures of action who connect the reality of distant suffering to the spectators' private feelings vis-à-vis the spectacle that they are watching.

We should not think of the benefactor and the persecutor only as 'real people' on the television screen, although this is often the case. Rather, we should think of them as symbolic figures organizing and focalizing the affective potential of the spectators towards a particular emotion. It is only when this private potential for feeling leads the spectators to identify with some form of public cause – such as philanthropic care in the case of tender-heartedness or denunciation in the case of indignation – that the spectacle of distant suffering is able to evoke the sentiment of pity.

It is evident in the above that the symbolic figures of the benefactor and the persecutor are taken to be metonymic signs. They are carriers of meaning that use the private feelings evoked by the actors on suffering so as to articulate a 'universal' value of how to act towards the suffering. Whereas the tender-hearted impulse to protect or comfort the sufferers articulates the moral value of care for the 'other', the indignant impulse to denounce or even to attack the evil-doer articulates the moral demand for civil justice. The task of the analytics of mediation, therefore, is to study these metonymic relationships in the suffering we see in the news. Specifically, the task of analytics is to study how the figures of agency – the benefactor and persecutor – literally incorporate the 'universal' moral value associated with suffering in each particular piece of news and how they make it part of a persuasive theatre of action.

The second group of questions, then, has to do with the *presence of* agents in suffering.

- Is the scene of suffering populated by agents?
- If yes, who participates in the suffering and in what capacity?
- Does the text evoke or explicitly represent a benefactor, individual or collective acting to alleviate suffering? Does it evoke a persecutor, individual or collective inflicting the suffering?
- What overall dramaturgical compositional presence do these figures have? Which potential for emotion and/or practical action does this composition induce?

Sublimation The distinction between the two modes of contemplating suffering – agora and theatre – is necessary in the study of the agency of spectators of the news. This is because the option for agency on distant suffering, embedded as it is in the process of mediation, is really a proposal for spectators to engage in pity. Pity, let us recall, is not pure emotion, but a public disposition that incorporates two demands. On the one hand, pity incorporates the political demand for television to function as a public sphere and, hence, observe a measure of objectivity in its representations of suffering, while, on the other hand, it incorporates the ethical demand that television should report on the suffering of the 'other' with a measure of sensibility and emotionality.

Although the work that television does in order to establish impartiality and arouse emotion requires a distinct analytical language, the distinction between impartiality and emotion is difficult to sustain in practice. In the course of the news, there is an inevitable interplay between agora and theatre, objective judgement and emotional response, contemplating sufferers and relating to others who surround the suffering. In fact, the humanization of sufferers occurs to a considerable extent precisely because of the action that television organizes around the sufferers' misfortunes and the feelings and values that such action articulates on behalf of spectators.

This point is thrown into relief once we consider instances of news where the contemplation of suffering does not involve human dynamics at all, either in the form of the sufferer's gaze or the presence of other figures of pity – that is, when the scene of suffering is altogether devoid of agency. Simply watching the scene of suffering objectifies the distant misfortune and, as a consequence, may lead to dehumanizing the sufferer. This is the case in news where the suffering is represented primarily as an aesthetic event and where the horror of the image – be this the September 11th planes crashing or catastrophic powers of nature – takes priority over other activity and emotion in relation to the suffering.

In such cases, we talk about the *sublimation* of the suffering. This is a significant variation on the representation of suffering in the aesthetic register that I examine more closely in Chapter 6. Free of the urgent obligation that the figures of benefactor and persecutor evoke, aestheticized suffering seems to rest on the spectators' indulgent contemplation of the spectacularity of the scene of human pain. Crucial for the moralization of the spectators here is the fact that this aesthetic arrangement does not entail redemptive sympathy, empathetic or indignant, but, rather, sympathy that is detached from its object:

> the beauty extracted from the horrific through this process of sublimation of the gaze, which is 'able to transform any object whatever into a work of art', owes nothing to the object.
>
> (Boltanski, 1999: 127)

Despite the fact that this non-obligation to the suffering object often entails a 'radical rejection of pity', in Boltanski's words, we will see in Chapter 6 that the sublime spectacle may also give to spectators the option to have reflexive distance from the suffering and think through the conditions of that suffering in ways that no other topic enables them to do.

How does the analysis of agency connect to the ethics of the mediation debate? In what way does this dimension of the analytics of mediation help us to understand how television might cultivate a cosmopolitan sensibility? The cosmopolitan spectators, I argued in Chapter 3, become objects of the moral regulation of mediation by being addressed primarily as free subjects – that is, as people who connect to television's suffering by means of their own resources of emotion and capacities for action. Neither too much emotion – the stuff of theatricality – nor too much impartial rationality – the stuff of the agora – are adequate and sufficient conditions for cosmopolitanism.

It is the task of the analytics of mediation to track down, in their concrete singularities, the distinct and specific ways in which the news negotiates the tensions between objectivity and tender-heartedness, between generality of facts and particularity of emotions and the subsequent effects that such negotiations have on the construal of the cosmopolitan disposition in each piece of news.

In this book, the task of the analytics of mediation is to ask if each singular piece of news that I discuss particularizes the suffering too much, indulging in unnecessary emotion, or if it overgeneralizes suffering beyond pity in the pursuit of a heartless impartiality. As we shall see, the cosmopolitan disposition may be emerging out of these multiple representations of the distant 'other' not as a full and positive presence but, rather, as a fleeting glimpse, as a temporary possibility.

Conclusion: towards a hierarchy of news on suffering

In this chapter, I proposed taking an analytical approach to the study of the politics of pity – that is, the study of the various representations of distant suffering in television news. This framework – an analytics of mediation – capitalizes on the poststructuralist views of meaning and power that I introduced in the previous chapter. The analytics of mediation conceptualizes the process of mediation in semiotic terms, as textual difference, and takes the television text as its object of study. The study of mediation as hypermediacy looks into the media technologies that produce the meanings of suffering on screen – what I term 'difference within the semiotic' – whereas the study of mediation as immediacy looks into the social relationships of suffering that these meanings represent – what I term 'difference outside the semiotic'. It is these recurrent double forms of mediation – of hypermediacy and immediacy or difference outside and within the semiotic – that render possible the study of the television text as technology and meaning, as semiotic and social, as aesthetic and political.

By means of multimodal and critical discourse analysis, the analytics of mediation enables us to ask questions about the ways in which the news text is put together in language and image and about how the visual and linguistic articulations of news construe the space–times and forms of agency that connect spectators and sufferers in relation to specific pieces of news on suffering. In so doing, the analytics of mediation also enables us to identify the ethical norms of public action that are already inherent in the genre of television news.

The next three chapters, I put the analytics of mediation into use and study closely a range of news broadcasts from the global channel BBC World and two national European channels, the Greek and the Danish State broadcasting corporations – NET and DR, respectively. Three categories of news emerge from this study. Each of them reports on various instances of suffering around the world by combining the language and images of television in different ways. Consequently, each category proposes its own ways in which the spectators should engage with the scenes of suffering and its own options for possible action on the sufferers' misfortunes. Specifically, the next three chapters are organized to cover each of these categories in turn:

- *adventure news* – a class of news that blocks the production of pity, discussed in Chapter 5
- *emergency news* – a class of news that produces a demand for action on the suffering, covered in Chapter 6
- *ecstatic news* – an extraordinary class of reports on suffering that manages to bring the globe together in acts of simultaneous watching, explored in Chapter 7.

The analytics of mediation contributes to making explicit the ethical values that are embedded in all reports on suffering, from adventure to ecstatic news. Each and every piece of news on suffering is organized using a set of values that appears to be evident and natural, but, when placed in comparison with anothers, reveals its complicity in sustaining the hierarchy of the places and human lives that media critics denounce.

Chapters 5, 6 and 7, then, assess how these values affect the relationships between Western spectators and distant sufferers. In so doing, they also draw attention to the centrality of the mise en scène of the news in providing the conditions for the possibility of the cosmopolitan spectator – the spectator as a public actor with a sense of responsibility towards the 'other'. It is important that news spectators – but also, importantly, news practitioners – have a language with which to describe the production of these hierarchies. Given the urgent ethical and political dilemmas of our world today, such a language would enable us to reflect on the ways in which the news presents the world to the world and, perhaps, to challenge the unequal distribution of pity among the world populations that the news today makes possible.

Notes

1   For a criticism of this position, accusing Derrida of cutting the semiotic system off from social relationships, see Butler (1997: 50–1). See also Said (1978: 703).
2   See also Kress and van Leeuwen (1996, 2001) and Scollon and Scollon (2003).
3   See Howarth (2002: 36–42). Derrida's criticism of Saussure is a philosophical argument that explains the inferiority of writing in terms of the broader historical biases of Western thinking, which takes the form of the opposition between conceptuality/language and materiality/visuality. See also Shapiro (1993: 6–12) for a criticism of the *linguistic reduction* perspective, which suggests that the verbal has a far greater range than the visual, and Jay (1994: 493–542) for a critique of the nineteenth- and twentieth-century suspicion of visual culture – what he calls the 'antiocularcentric discourse' – particularly in French thought. Shapiro and Jay's accounts of the antagonism between linguistic and vision-centred discourses reveal unresolved tensions in the debate.

4 See Howarth (2002: 41).
5 See Kress and van Leeuwen (2001) and Bolter and Grusin (2000).
6 See Grodal (2002: 67–91), Ellis (2000: 193–200) on realism and Nichols (1991: 165–98) for an insightful, but slightly different, discussion on realism in documentary.
7 I here adapt Chatman's (1991) categories of three main text types in communicative practice: *description, argument* and *narrative*. I keep *description* with its original use, as in Chatman, but use *exposition* instead of *argument* because the news genre does not really develop an argument as it usually presents a mixture of descriptions of events with moralizing arguments. Yet, as Chatman also admits, these are semantically familial terms (1991: 9).
8

> Every sign is determined by its object, either first, *by partaking in the characters of the object*, when I call the sign an *Icon*; secondly, *by being really and in its individual existence connected with the individual object*, when I call the sign an Index; thirdly, *by more or less approximate certainty that it will be interpreted as denoting the object*, in consequence of a habit [which term I use as including a natural disposition], when I call the sign *Symbol*.

> (Pierce in Hoopes (ed.), 1991: 251– emphasis added)

In Pierce's categorization, as in Saussure, both sign *and* object are referents already constituted in meaning, rather than assuming that the sign is the meaning element of the relationship with the signified referring to an external reality. For the use of Piercean semiotics in visual analysis and media texts, see Hall (1973/1980), Hodge and Kress (1988: 19–20), Jensen (1995), Messaris (1997: x–xxii), van Leeuwen (2001: 92–118) and Schroeder (2002: 111–16).

9 See Kress and van Leeuwen (1996, 2001) and van Leeuwen and Jewitt (2001) for the grammar of the visual. See also van Leeuwen and Jaworski (2002) and Perlmutter and Wagner (2004: 91–108). The Piercean typology corresponds to other classifications of meaning types, such as Panofsky's. His distinction is between the *representational*, which approximates the index, the *iconographic*, which approximates the icon, and the *iconological*, which appoximates the symbolic or ideological meaning. For a discussion and application of Panofsky's distinctions in visual texts, see van Leeuwen (2001: 100–17).
10 See Chatman (1991: 30).
11 See Grodal (2002: 67–91) for the terminology of perceptual and categorical realism and Nichols (1991: 165–98) for an insightful, but slightly different, discussion on realism in documentary. See also Silverstone (1999: 44–5) on media *poetics* – the textual making of media stories and their 'reality effects' or *vraisemblance*.
12 See Nichols (1991: 171), Messaris (1997: xvi–xvii) and Ellis (2000: 193–4).
13 See Davis and Walton (1983: 45) and Corner (1995: 60).
14 This is one of Foucault's (1970, 1972) basic claims and a major premise for the poststructuralist anchoring of discourse analysis in critical research. For discussions, see Fraser (1997), Torfing (1998), Chouliaraki (2002) and Howarth (2002). There is also a broad literature in linguistics and semiotics on the relationship between meaning and power that draws on the Russian tradition of Volosinov and Bakhtin (Halliday, 1985/1995; Halliday and Hasan, 1989; Hodge and Kress, 1988: 19; Kress, 1985; Fairclough, 1989, 1992, 2003; and van Dijk, 1997a and b).

15 See Boltanski (1999: 3–54) for this conception of the contemporary public sphere.
16 See Fairclough (1992), Laclau and Mouffe (1985), Torfing (1998), Chouliaraki and Fairclough (1999) and Howarth (2002).
17 See Halliday (1985/1995), Halliday and Hasan (1989) and Hasan (2000). For a critical discourse analysis discussion of the multifunctional perspective, see Chouliaraki and Fairclough (1999: 139–55).
18 See Ledema (2001: 191–3) for a typology of the modalities of camera meaning that employs the terminology of *representation* for the ideational metafunction, *orientation* for the interpersonal metafunction and *organization* for the textual metafunction.
19 See Halliday (1985/1995: 23).
20 These questions have been adapted from Morson and Emerson's discussion on Bakhtin's concept of the *chronotope* (1990: 366–75).
21 See Chilton (2004) and Fairclough (2003).
22 See Silverstone (1999a: 34–7; 2002: 761–80) and Butler (2004: 128–51) for a discussion on Levinas's concept of the 'Other' in relation to media representations.
23 See Tester (2001) and Cohen (2001)

5

ADVENTURE NEWS: SUFFERING WITHOUT PITY

Let us look into three pieces of news. These are shootings in Indonesia, a boat accident in India and 'biblical' floods in Bangladesh.[1] The feature that they have in common is that their value was not prioritized in the news broadcast. They were not 'breaking news' or in any way part of their networks' headlines. The status of these pieces of news reflects the fact that television accommodates a selected number of world misfortunes within many less than a minute long news slots.

Which opportunities for releasing pity do these news reports offer? Is there pity without the visualization of the scene of suffering? Is there ethical appeal without the dynamics of action on the sufferer? In addressing these questions, I demonstrate that the properties of such news texts seriously restrict the emotional and ethical appeal of the sufferings that they report. I also make the argument that compassion fatigue – the audience's indifference towards distant suffering – may have less to do with the fact that people are tired of the omnipresence of suffering on their television screens and more to do with the fact that television is selective about which sufferings it dramatizes and which ones it does not.

Suffering as adventure

Adventure is Bakhtin's term for the Greek romance – an early form of novelistic discourse concerning heroes, such as Ulysses, who wander around in strange places and meet strange creatures in a string of unconnected sequences. The adventure, Bakhtin says, takes place 'in the spaces of an alien world [...] filled with isolated curiosities and rarities that bear no connection to each other' (1981: 102).

I use the term adventure to mean the category of news items that, like the Greek romance, consists of random and isolated events and, for this reason, they fail to make an ethical demand on spectators to respond to the suffering they report. Three semiotic features constitute news as an adventure:

- descriptive narratives that only register 'facts'
- singular space–times that restrict the spectator's proximity to suffering
- the lack of agency that dehumanizes sufferers and suppresses the possibility of action in the scene of suffering.

Can we then, though, talk about the representation of suffering without pity as involving a moral mechanism? My answer is yes and it is this positive response that informs the study of news texts as a politics of pity. We can talk about morality without pity, under a certain condition. Morality without pity is possible if we do not use the term morality to mean inherent 'goodness' in the perspective of representation, contrasting it to an inherently 'evil' perspective of representation that is devoid of morality. As I have argued in the Introduction, the analytics of mediation replaces prescriptive views of morality that tell right from wrong with a situated ethics. Situated ethics is a form of critical investigation of the norms of public conduct that, without altogether abandoning the normative perspective, provisionally brackets it in order to assess how the meanings of right and wrong are constituted in particular examples of news on suffering. Behind this form of ethics is the Aristotelian assumption that choices of where, when and with whom the suffering is shown to occur always entail specific ethical disposition, independent of our own evaluative judgement on these dispositions as desirable or undesirable.

By this token, the minimal narration of suffering, the establishment of radical distance from the location of suffering or the refusal to humanize the sufferer may indeed come to interrupt the production of pity, but they should not be regarded as lying outside the enactment of the moral mechanism of mediation itself. The interruption of pity is a variation on this enactment and a moral claim in its own right. Suffering without pity, then, is an ethical option available to the spectator that construes the sufferer in discourses of insurmountable cultural difference as an Other and thereby frees the spectator from the moral obligation to act on the sufferer's misfortune. I shall now discuss the 'Othering' of the sufferer in the adventure news from Indonesia, India and Bangladesh in terms of the key discursive properties that this type of news demonstrates:

- simple multimodality
- singular space–times
- void of agency.

Simple multimodal narratives

Mode of presentation
All of the pieces of news that follow are delivered by anchor presenters and are brief – just four to five clauses each. Their texts are both verbal – drawing on the narrative type of description – and visual – consisting of graphic illustrations and, in one case, video images.

Verbal mode

Descriptive reports
The verbal texts are fact-giving reports. They are mainly descriptions of events rather than either narrations (telling a story with a plot and characters) or expositions (incorporating a point of view or a value judgement). As a consequence, these texts are devoid of emotional elements – apart from occasional token traces of emotionality (*'feared* drowned' and 'the counting of victims *tragic'*). They are also devoid of conceptual complexity – that is, there are no semantic relationships that explain, elaborate on and evaluate the events. Specifically, all three reports are strictly organized in terms of references to *victims* and the *circumstances* that surround their misfortune.

- The victims are referred to in terms of numbers ('More than 40 people missing; 82 people dead and more than 3 million homeless'), nationality, where the Americans are singled out ('Two Americans and an Indonesian') and functional attributes, such as their occupation ('teachers, office workers and schoolchildren').
- The circumstances include specifications of location ('on the road leading to the gold and copper mine in West Papua'; 'in the Eastern Indian state of Orissa ... Jajpur town, a hundred kilometres from the capital Bhubaneswar; across Bangladesh'), manner ('in a convoy of cars'; 'in an ambush'), causality ('separatist rebels were behind the attack'; 'swollen by floods'; 'due to the tropical rains') and time ('in the past four years').

On the whole, these reports narrate events in terms of who, where and how information. Questions of why do not appear. This means that no reasons are given for the occurence of these tragic incidents. The attribution of causality for the Indonesian shootings, for example, is wrapped into the nominal group *separatist rebels,* which hardly explains the context of the attack. The meaning relationships that these news choices establish fall within a *logic of appearances* – that is, they dictate the representation of misfortunes according to particular circumstances – their immediate context and effects – rather than 'historical' circumstances, which are their less obvious contexts and longer-term consequences, or what might be called a 'logic of causality'.[2] Traceable in the semantic features of the text, the 'logic of appearances' is the logic par excellence of the adventure, a logic of things just turning up and disappearing out of nowhere or a logic of 'congealed suddenlys', in Bakhtin's words.

Visual mode

Map graphics
The visual texts that accompany verbal description are maps, screen graphics and, in the case of the Bangladesh floods, satellite video. The red bar at

the lower end of the screen registers the event in Indonesia as 'shootings' and the one in India as a 'boat accident'. Like their verbal narratives, these graphic elements are both only descriptive. They lack a sense of emotionality, let alone urgency. This stands in contrast to the Bangladesh floods' screen graphic of 'biblical catastrophe', which attempts to dramatize the visual effect of the on-location shots. I discuss these visuals in detail below.

Which kind of space–time does this regime contextualize the misfortune in? With which properties of human agency is the scene of suffering endowed?

Singular space–times

The reported events are placed within one space and one temporality only – in a singular space–time. Singular space–time is when a story has been cut off from the chain of events in which it participates and is presented as a random singularity. As a consequence, the reported event does not appear to be connected to other events, nor does it, in itself, contain the potential to predict other events. Singular space–time then restricts the possibility of representing these events in terms of their historicity and their future implications. Furthermore, the space dimensions of the incidents in Indonesia and India are not only singular but also vague. They are construed as being either too remote from or too close to the spectators. In either case, space fails to link the space–time of the event with the space–time of the spectators and so fails to establish some form

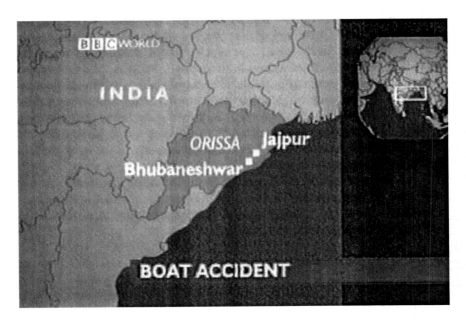

Space–time: singular and decontextualized

of connectivity between the reported suffering and the spectators' own lifeworlds. In the language of Chapter 1, it fails to bring forth the emotional response of either empathy or protest vis-à-vis the reported suffering and, thus, does not motivate the spectator to a form of public action.

Dots on the map

The Indonesian and Indian locations are given on maps presented on a split television screen. At the top right-hand side of the screen, a three-dimensional (spherical) globe locates the countries in focus by framing them in a square. At the left-hand side of the screen, a two-dimensional (flat) national map locates the regions and town in focus as dots. The split screen offers us two map visuals, both of which accurately depict state units on the globe (borders) and regional specifications within states (cities). In which ways do these visuals render the spaces of the reported incidents meaningful?

Maps are representations of abstract space. They are, literally, coloured shapes surrounded by other coloured shapes – unnamed shapes on the spherical map, named shapes on the flat map. Although they offer the advantage of simplicity (why confuse spectators with unnecessary details?), the maps also reinforce a sense of space as a geometrical rather than a geographical entity. In so doing, maps depict locations less as inhabited places and more as decontextualized formations, distant and irrelevant to Western spectators. Split-screen representations of space are less usual in news on Europe or North America, especially when it comes to metropolitan centres rather than Western peripheries. It seems that such Western spatialities are taken for granted as being universally known, but, more importantly perhaps, they are also perceived as deserving more complicated forms of representation than the minimalist split-screen depiction.

Map depictions are not only abstract spaces but they are also devoid of temporality. They say nothing about the living context of the reported events. Has there been a high concentration of 'separatist rebels' in Western Papua, splitting the population into opposing camps? What was the American influence on the island? It is the same with the news about India. Would a map of the Orissa province, with details of the river's route and the direction in which the boat tour was heading, give us a better approximation of the conditions under which the accident took place? Let us compare these simple maps with the elaborate map depictions in the Iraq war footage. In the latter, we have vectors of movement, drawings of vehicles, simulations of bombings and a constant voiceover framing action on the map. As a register of representation, the map can and does combine with other semiotic modes, such as the verbal, the digital or the manual graphic. These semiotic properties inject the lifelessness of the map with dynamic motion and make it possible for spectators to visualize the event not only in terms of an abstract 'where' but also in terms of a concrete 'how', 'who' and perhaps 'why'. This type of map renders the place it represents concrete and active and thus more intelligible, if not more relevant, to spectators.

Although it might be unrealistic (but not necessarily unreasonable) to demand that all news maps follow the example of the imagery used in the Iraq war coverage, the point is to illustrate that, in the minimalist depiction of the map, the representation of specific world locations remains abstract and a-temporal. As a result, the geographical distance between the spectator and the reported suffering is not simply maintained – it becomes the defining feature of their relationship. The Indonesian 'shootings' or the Indian 'boat accident' pieces of news are reduced to dots on the map.

The voiceover provides a different set of spatial specifications for spectators. In the news about Indonesia, we get to know that the ambush took place 'on the road leading to the gold and copper mine in West Papua', whereas in the news about India, we are told that the boat was making its way 'towards Jajpur, a hundred kilometres from the capital Bhubaneswar'. These verbal references shift from the too abstract to the too concrete. Such levels of geographical detail, when not accompanied by illustrative visuals, do little to contextualize the incidents in any meaningful way. On the contrary, the level of unnecessary detail establishes a disjunction between the abstract visual and the all-too-concrete verbal. As a consequence, the narrative fails to construe the proper distance, which would place the suffering in its own location and its own historical circumstances of safety and risk. It fails, that is, to establish the proper distance between spectators and sufferers and, thus, deprives the concrete contexts of suffering, in India and Indonesia, of their particular character. Devoid of internal complexity, either in terms of the groups that fight in the region (Indonesia) or the conditions under which boat accidents may take place (India), the representation of suffering in both pieces of news remains again within the 'logic of appearance'. It occurs outside a meaningful context for interpretation and evaluation and remains too general to motivate engagement on the part of spectators. The temporality of these pieces of news reinforces this effect. The use of the past tense in the verbal text closes the narratives of suffering off, leaving the spectators with one choice only – to acknowledge their factuality: 'the boat capsized', 'have been shot dead/injured', 'the incident happened/occurred'.

Tableau vivant

Could the use of the visual mode, the very imagery of suffering, enhance proximity with suffering and, thereby, activate a politics of pity? Not necessarily, because the visualization of suffering does not always humanize the sufferers. Visualization may cast the suffering in the aesthetic register and, thereby, actually dehumanize them.

Space–time: Generic Space, Eternal Time (Tableau Vivant)

This is the case in the piece of news about Bangladesh. In contrast to the previous two examples, this piece of news consists of a number of images that all depict vast flooded areas. Such images no doubt shift the representation of suffering from the vague – dots on the map – to the concrete – we are eyewitnesses to a catastrophe – yet, we are still 'locked' in a singular representation of space–time. This is due to the fact that all the sequences are filmed using long shots, which portray water, trees and human figures in a static composition. The function of long shots is to universalize, producing spectacles that could be attributed to a number of other world locations at any other time. The meaning, then, that the long shot produces is of the iconic kind – it abstracts from the particularity of the location and the historicity of the event it represents and, instead, foregrounds an abstract condition, which in this case is the water-logged land.

This iconicity of the landscape is, in fact, part of a broader process of aestheticization that occurs in the visual mediation of this piece of news. The dominance of the colour grey, the omnipresence of water, scattered trees on the horizon interrupting the continuity of the water and the outlines of human figures in the foreground attach a distinct aesthetic quality to the representation of this suffering. These compositional features not only abstract from the particularity of the event, but further remove the event from the order of lived experience to the domain of art. They turn the reality of floods into a tableau vivant. The Bangladesh visuals invite not engagement with but gazing at the spectacle of suffering.

What is the consequence of this mode of viewing? The spectators' emotional potential is 'arrested' by the aesthetic register, so a fascination with the landscape is created rather than an emotional connectivity with the fact of suffering. The 'logic of appearances' that traverses the verbal report reaches, in these visuals, its literal as well as metaphorical peak. It is what we see that matters, not how to explain or change it.

The voiceover is more flexible in accommodating subtle shifts in the sense of time that contains the event. It moves from the right now – 'floods *are sweeping* across Bangladesh' – to a causal past tense – 'the rivers *overflowed* and whole regions *were buried* in water' and to a longer-term past temporality – 'the worst *in the past four years*'. Yet, such minimal shifts are not enough to hint at the broader context of a disaster that killed 82 and left more than 3 million people homeless. If floods of this magnitude are repeated as often as every four years, what has been done or can be done about it? What happens to the millions of people who remain homeless, have to be moved, resettled and provided for? Despite the humanitarian issues involved, no future orientation towards possible relief action is given, on the part of governments, organizations or individuals. In a manner similar to the pieces of news about India and Indonesia, the spectators of the Bangladesh floods are denied the option of personal or collective agency. All there is to do is accept the fact of this misfortune.

Void of agency

The lack of a future orientation in the space–time of adventure news is related to the absence of living human beings in the scenes of suffering on this news.

Neither empathy nor denunciation

Benefactor figures are largely absent from all three accounts. There are, instead, minimal linguistic gestures towards a vague sense of empathy with the reported suffering – 'people are missing, *feared* drowned', in the news from India example, and 'the counting of victims *tragic*', as well as the attribute 'biblical catastrophe' in the news of Bangladesh. In this last example, we should notice, too, the epic connotations of 'biblical' that, in a similar way to visual aestheticization, move us away from historical time and into the eternal temporality of the aesthetic register. References to persecutors are explicit only in the case of the Indonesian shootings, but they are vague and speculative, so we have 'unidentified attackers. [Authorities say they suspect] separatist rebels'. No specific body of people, no specific interests or explicit sides of a conflict are mentioned. Persecutors shrink to fit the dot on the map size of this news. Yet, without a minimal reference to the possible cause of the ambush no denunciatory potential can be activated on the part of the spectators. They are not called up to engage with an ethical matter, but as the graphic titling suggests, to simply register the 'shootings'.

With the Indian boat accident and the Bangladesh floods, the search for a persecutor leaves the domain of politics to enter the domain of nature. It is because rivers overflow that boats capsize and floods occur and whole regions are flooded by water. Although human agency, at least in the form of a malevolent persecutor, is usually kept out of natural disaster news, questions about the causes of such events do bring the human factor into the picture because technological intervention always interacts with the physical environment. Could it be that these floods might have been prevented or their consequences minimized had agricultural planning and landscape formation taken into account such risks? Could the lack of preventative technological intervention, as well as a lack of a support mechanism to cope with the aftermath of the floods on the part of local and international agencies be responsible for the humanitarian problem in Bangladesh? Is there an emergency mechanism available to deal with the consequences of the floods for the millions of homeless people? The spatiotemporal economy and the semiotic features of this piece leave such issues untouched. By attributing the catastrophe wholly to the non-human world, this news deletes any possibility of human intervention that might alleviate or prevent further suffering by the Bangladeshi people.

The annihilation of the sufferer
It is not only the figures acting on the suffering – benefactors or possible persecutors – who are absent in adventure news. In all three cases, the sufferers themselves are reduced to an impersonal group of unfortunates.

This form of dehumanization of the sufferer takes place in the process of *aggregation* – that is, when linguistic reference to the sufferer takes the form of a number or functional categorization, such as when sufferers are mentioned in terms of what they do.[3] The unfortunates are aggregated to form a number in references such as '40' victims in India and '88' in Bangladesh. In the news about Indonesia, the reference enumerates casualties, while managing to single out and thematize the Americans by placing them in the beginning of the opening sentence: '*Two Americans* and one Indonesian have been shot dead'.

The classification of sufferers in terms of a salient cultural characteristic, such as national identity, is crucial to establishing a hierarchy of human life in these pieces of news. This is also obvious in the reference to the injured, where foreign versus Indonesian victims are linguistically differentiated: '14 [injured] 9 of them also *foreign nationals*'. When nationality is not an issue, then identity attributes are restricted to a general reference as to what the victims do. These are references to strictly public or official identities rather than personal or kinship ones, so we have: 'office workers and schoolchildren', in the news of the Indian accident. Such references strip the victims of their personal identities as individual mothers, fathers and children and, thereby, minimize the affective impact of their death on the spectator. In the case of Bangladesh, the victims are given no identity attributes at all. Bangladeshi victims are nobodies in particular.

The absence of a person, somebody with a name and a face, deprives the encounter between spectators and sufferers of any sense of humanness. Without the measure of psychological depth necessary for the welling up of emotion, the sufferers from India and Indonesia are annihilated. No matter what the magnitude or the depth of their suffering is, they are unable to produce pity. They remain irrevocably 'Other' – distant, inactive, devoid of feelings and thoughts. This is also the case in the visualization of the news about the floods in Bangladesh. Although visible on screen, the Bangladeshi sufferers appear as figures punctuating a grey landscape. They are portrayed with their backs turned to the camera or in profile, seemingly unaware of the fact that they are being filmed. Without a face, expression or voice, these sufferers lack appellative power – the power to communicate to the spectators the condition of their misfortune. Even the minimal action they are portrayed performing is self-referential, directed towards themselves rather than their environment – they walk away, carry a child, hold an umbrella or row a little boat. They partake in a world of objects, their own human subjectivity erased. In Boltanski's words, the Bangladeshi sufferers – just like the Indian and Indonesian ones – are portrayed as 'radically without will'. The difference between them and the Indian and Indonesian sufferers is that, in shifting from language to image, the dehumanization of the Bangladeshi sufferers transforms itself into an aesthetic spectacle. This is a spectacle of difference between cultures that lie beyond the possibility of contact.

Othering without pity: the moral mechanism

The three aspects of the representation of suffering in adventure news – simple multimodality, singular space–time and the agency void – make up the regime of pity that interrupts the connectivity between spectators and sufferers. The multimodal narrative of adventure news is composed of descriptive verbal text combined with cartographic illustration. This minimal multimodality sets up a very tight frame for the representation of the space–time and the agents of suffering in these pieces of news and, thereby, casts the distant misfortunes in a strictly objective and abstract way, in a representational 'logic of appearances'. The consequence is that pity, which requires that the suffering is construed as an emotional occasion and not only as an objective fact, remains here as an unrealized potential. Adventure news fails to engage the spectators in an emotional and reflexive way with the misfortunes of the Indians, Indonesians and Bangladeshis.

The key feature of adventure news, then, is that its stories of suffering claim objectivity at the expense of emotionality. Objectivity in the news ensures that, whereas the story itself is told from a particular perspective – the space–time of the West – it appears as if it is told from a position of nowhere, a 'universal' perspective. In adventure news, objectivity is established by means of a description of the facts, but also by the use of the map. This is because cartography traditionally bears the scientific disguise of accurate representation, even though the map is itself a discourse of power that reflects how the world is perceived by those who are in a position to define it in the first place.[4] In adventure news, the map 'objectively' portrays the scene of suffering as a formal drawing instead of construing it as a space populated by human beings like 'us'.

How do the discursive features of adventure news participate in the shaping of the broader relationships of viewing? Which social hierarchies does this regime of pity help to reproduce? In my view, the minimalism of adventure news is responsible for (re-)producing two significant hierarchies in the representation of human misfortune. The first of these is related to the restriction that the narrative imposes on space–time. My argument is that singular space–time leads to a specific *hierarchy of place*. The second hierarchy is related to the restriction that the narrative imposes on agency. My argument is that the void of agents leads to a *hierarchy of human lives*. These hierarchies suggest that some sufferers, unlike others, consistently fail to make an ethical appeal to the spectator. Consequently, they get no response to their misfortune. Their suffering leaves no trace.

Hierarchies of place

Maximal distance and a sense of closure around the events are responsible for rendering the Indonesian 'shootings' and the Indian 'boat accident' irrelevant to the experiential world of the spectators. These events are represented as happening too far away, they are just some dot on a map, and random facts that require no further contemplation or action. Despite its visualization, the news on the floods in Bangladesh also lacks a sense of historical dynamism. What happened in Indonesia, India and Bangladesh are brief adventures inserted into the flow of the news as isolated but repeatable narratives in between other extraordinary events that are worthy of our time and emotion.

We can better appreciate the effectiveness of the spatiotemporality of adventure in interrupting the production of pity, when we compare the Indonesian shootings with the Bali night club bombings that happened a couple of months later, on 13 October 2002. The Bali bombings – a major terrorist attack with casualties of up to 218 people – hit world and national channels as 'breaking news' from the first moment. The bombings continued to be headline news for several days. This is understandable as, in the shadow of the September 11th attacks and the rise of a new era of terrorist threat, such an event undoubtedly deserved its prominence. For our purposes, however, the focus is on the way in which the same geographical location – Indonesia – enters the process of mediation in such a different way to the previous story we have been considering. It is this focus that makes me downplay the differences within Indonesia between the West Papua 'shootings' location and the Bali bombings location. What the contrast between the two events tells us is that, when the victims are Western tourists, then the same location, Indonesia, shifts from dot on the map to next-door threat.

In the bombings news, proximity to Bali is established by inserting Indonesia in a broad range of spatiotemporalities. Bali appears now to the

Western spectator as a living scene of suffering. There are on-location reports on the magnitude of the tragedy that include sequences of medical personnel at work, interviews with police investigators and statements by local and international politicians. These modes of presentation place Bali in a chronotopic universe that portrays this place as both a former popular resort and as a presently suspected nest of terrorist activity. The multiple articulations of local space with international networks and the contemporaneity of the bombings with the past reputation of the place and future threats involve a sophisticated politics of pity. The live reporting in streets and hospitals seeks to evoke empathy with the sufferers, while the attribution of responsibility to terrorists aims to move the spectators' emotion towards indignant denunciation.

At the same time, by focusing on the theme 'holiday resorts turn into inferno', the news expands the space–time of danger out beyond Indonesia and towards other destinations that the spectators visit regularly as tourists. We can describe the semiotic mechanism of reorganizing space in this manner as an *anatopism*. Anatopism renders places such as Bali equivalents of other places, such as Kenya, on the basis of a hitherto irrelevant feature shared by the two: their lack of safety.[5] The safe spectators no longer register the facts of a distant world but are faced with the threat of experiencing such suffering themselves. By the same token, the temporal dimension of the news expands from closure – the fact of 'shootings' – to dramatic open-endedness – what is next? The increasing threat of random terrorist attacks accentuates the spectators' sense of insecurity and gives rise to a new cartography of risk. In this cartography, Kenya had preceded Bali by a few weeks, with European capitals such as Madrid and London to follow. There is a lot to say about the political agendas involved in the anatopic moves of the news text. My point now is that the news about Bali shifts the space of mediation from distance (Bali in shootings) to proximity (Bali in bombings) by rendering the event relevant to the Western spectators' lifeworlds. Geographical distance, per se, is irrelevant to rendering a location proximal to or remote from spectators in television news. What is relevant is a logic of mediation that organizes the prominence of places according to a dominant cultural and political hierarchy and deems an event newsworthy on the grounds that it affects the space–time of safety.

In the piece of news about the Bali bombings, the connectivity between spectators and sufferers rests on a rich flow of language and images that confronts the spectators with both the objective fact of terror and the emotions that this fact wells up. The loss of the innocent lives of mainly Western tourists, sudden and unfair as it was, evokes emotions. It provokes empathy for the victims, indignation towards the bombers and solemn reflection as to the consequences of increasing terrorism. At the same time, the new cartography of terror that emerges out of these reports shapes the spectators' connectivity with the scene of suffering in a new sense of proximity: proximity as vulnerability. The public value that the news of the Bali bombings brings forth, then, is concern for the safety of the Western spectators and the political necessity of the war against terror, wherever and however this war is possible – a political agenda that is still unfolding at the time of writing.

Hierarchies of human life

How does the representation of agency in the suffering of adventure news have an impact on the hierarchy of human life? I refer, on the one hand, to the system of agents acting on the scene of suffering and, on the other, to the imagery of the sufferers themselves.

First, the sufferers in India, Indonesia and Bangladesh are placed in a regime of pity where benefactors and persecutors are either minimal or absent. These figures are neither visualized nor described individually in adventure news, although the sporadic references to 'shootings', 'tragic' and 'biblical' catastrophes beg the question as to who acts or who should act on the reported catastrophes. Second, the sufferers themselves have no agency at all. They do not speak, nor are they reported as having spoken. When visible, they do not gaze towards the camera or attempt to engage with it. In India and Indonesia, the sufferers are numerical entities. In Bangladesh, they are passive objects, integral to the landscape.

This separation of the humane condition of the spectators from the condition of the sufferers best defines the quality of this sufferer as an absolute Other: 'Over him [sic] I have no power', Levinas says. 'He escapes my grasp by an essential dimension, even if I have him [sic] at my disposal' (1969: 39). What Levinas' quote eloquently captures here is the insurmountable asymmetry of viewing relationships in news on suffering without pity. There are the safe spectators with the sufferers at their disposal on their screens and there are the sufferers. These are sufferers who escape the Western grasp by an essential dimension – their lack of humanness – and their misfortunes thereby lie beyond the spectators' modal imagination. The spectators are unable to think that these sufferers' misfortunes are real somewhere out there in the world.

In order to appreciate the role of the politics of pity in hierarchizing human life in adventure news, let us compare the Indian 'boat accident' with the news on a train accident in Sydney covered on BBC World again a few months later on 28 January 2003. Not only did the Sydney train accident take on the status of 'breaking news', but it was almost immediately accompanied by live links and extended visuals from the scene of derailment. Map graphics showed the region of greater Sydney with a focus on the train route from the city centre to its destination, the southern town of Wollongong. As in the Bali case, the news about Sydney shifted between multiple spatiotemporalities, from on-location reports to city maps to officials accounts. Far from being dots on the map, these shifts in place rendered Sydney a living space, a space populated with people like 'us'.

Simultaneously, the 'breaking news' status of the event placed the accident within the temporality of an emergency. This was semiotically achieved by means of an open-ended narrative that had an explicit orientation towards the future. There was talk about the short-term future, orientated towards the relief of sufferers, and about the long-term future, orientated towards the travellers' safety conditions. We could ask if it was the sheer number of casualties and, hence, the magnitude of human loss that granted the Sydney accident its news prominence – what in media studies is called the principle of *correspondence*.[6] The answer is no. The prominence of the Sydney accident should not be inferred from the size of human loss. Tragic as it was, the Sydney accident had 9 casualties, mostly commuting office workers, whereas the Indian boat accident had 40, office workers too, but also schoolchildren – let us recall the aura of sacredness that surrounds children's lives in Western culture.[7]

This point clearly suggests that the proximity–distance arrangements in adventure news not only reproduce an implicit order of space relationships, which prioritize places that are already relevant and culturally familiar to spectators, but they further hierarchize the relevance and acuteness of the sufferers' pain for the spectators, distinguishing between human lives that are worth mourning for or saving and others that are not.[8] This hierarchy of human place and human life not only dictates that the loss of two Americans is worthy of distinct reference whereas the many more Bangladeshi or Indonesian ones are not but it also dictates the horizon for possible political or humanitarian interventions in the reported sufferings. Let me take the Bangladesh floods as the last example in this chapter.

Floods also occur in space–times of safety, with Europe experiencing some of the worst floods in the last century in July 2002. Differences between safety and danger in terms of beneficial and preventative action on the effects of floods lies, no doubt, in unequally distributed technological and economic infrastructures. There is more of it in Europe than in Bangladesh, but the difference lies in the manner of their mediation, too. It lies in the activation of a politics of pity in the case of Europe and in its interruption in the case of Bangladesh. In the former case, global news reports emphasized proximity and urgency (the threats to populations, agriculture and economy and to the cultural heritage of central Europe), organized a vast field of actors (expert interventions, governmental action, EU policy decisions, multinational beneficiary agencies) and thoroughly humanized the sufferers (visualization and voicing of farmers' or urban residents' distress). In Bangladesh, the floods are inscribed in a natural disaster discourse, with its consequences constructed as unfortunate but inevitable and beneficiary action as irrelevant to the news itself. The difference is a distinction in the mediation of suffering as a cause of emergency or as an adventure.

The spectator as sufferer

Adventure news fails to produce the disposition of the cosmopolitan spectator. It fails to provide a perspective that presents each incident of suffering as, at once, a unique singularity and a general cause for action. Adventure news fails to set in motion the two elements that may make the spectators care for the sufferers. On the one hand, adventure news fails to represent the particularity of suffering, allowing for some measure of personal pain to come through, and, on the other, fails to convey the generality of suffering, the abstract information that places the suffering in a broader picture. Instead, adventure news hovers between unnecessary detail in the voiceover, and unhelpful generality in the map. A major consequence of this discursive arrangement is that adventure news construes the spectators as potential sufferers themselves and seeks to protect them from the trauma of the multiple witnessing of suffering. This construal of spectators as sufferers introduces to the analysis of adventure news the concern with 'working through' (Ellis, 2000). *Working through* refers to the psychological mechanism of television that manages the spectator's encounter with the 'other' by containing the spectator's uncertainty vis-à-vis what is unfamiliar, alien and incomprehensible. The assumption behind working through is that witnessing distant suffering is regarded as potentially damaging to the spectator's well-being. What the news' examples from Indonesia, India and Bangladesh show is that certain distant misfortunes are subject to the strictest of restrictions that working through imposes on what is reported and how, so as to minimize the disturbing impact of such misfortunes on spectators.

These examples further suggest that the psychological work of television is clearly implicated in the political hierarchies of place and human life. Ellis indicates this connection when he situates the limits of 'working through' in those instances of mediation where the stereotype of the cultural 'other' comes into play:

> the bomber, the Taliban, the burning of Salman Rushdie's book *The Satanic Verses*, the veiled women. More often than not, he continues, [i]t remains a thing, 'Muslim fundamentalism': out there, unified, mysterious and threatening. This is [...] a failure in the process of working through, which serves to highlight how important the process is elsewhere.
>
> (2000: 86)

Ellis' claim that working through places a serious constraint on the political and humanitarian sensibilities of the spectator towards the Muslim is of course valid. Yet, ironically perhaps, we might observe that then the Muslim at least has an identity – even if it is that of the fundamentalist. The Bangladeshi, Indian and Indonesian sufferers have none. My point is that it is for instances of suffering without pity that the limits of working through become most obvious. This is because, unlike the Muslim who usually appears as the persecutor in an active and, therefore, potentially changeable field of social relationships of suffering (Muslims can also be portrayed as victims, of course), adventure news entails a curious pattern of relationships, where the figure of the sufferer is constantly suppressed.

The safe spectator is protected from the emotional demand made by a distant 'other' because the spectator may suffer from watching the 'other's' suffering. No demand is thus placed on the spectator-victim by the sufferer-victim. The distant sufferer ceases to make a moral appeal to the spectator.

The moral dimension of this pattern of relationships comes forth in Silverstone's discussion of the collusion between television's bias in reporting and the spectator of distant suffering. Collusive denial – far from being an intentional indifference to the 'other' – reflects a banal kind of complicity between television and the spectator. It is a complicity that takes on the benign face of our domestic concerns and daily priorities, our 'entirely understandable desire for simplicity, comfort and order in our everyday lives' (2002a: 777). It is this mundane but pressing routine that, ultimately, manages to push the distant 'other' aside as, after all, suffering occurs everywhere all the time and there is nothing we can do about it. This attitude of denial and indifference to the distant 'other' on the part of the spectator is known as compassion fatigue and is often held responsible for corroding the potential for civil action in public life.

The thesis of compassion fatigue

Compassion fatigue is a powerful expression of the pessimistic thesis concerning the ethical role of mediation because it denies the idea that the cosmopolitan spectator may come into being in the work of mediation. Cosmopolitanism requires connectivity that may lead to action, not the indifference that the spectator, tired of news on suffering, exhibits.

Nevertheless, qualitative research on audience responses suggests that compassion fatigue is not about the spectator's individualism and indifference, but may be directly connected to the ways in which news messages portray distant suffering (Tester, 2001: 47). News broadcasts, Tester reports, 'present problems but not their solutions' and this leads to a sense of fatalism among spectators who, willing as they may be to do something for distant sufferers, feel inadequate about acting on a world that lies beyond their reach and their control.[9] Even though this tendency of the news is identified in a large corpus of questionnaires to viewers rather than extrapolated from the textual properties of the broadcasts, there is a telling connection between these audience responses and my analysis of adventure news.

To present suffering as a problem without a solution and, hence, render the spectator a powerless recipient of distant misfortune is the consequence of one semiotic feature of adventure news – its lack of agency. How can spectators feel that things can and should happen about the Bangladesh floods when neither the Bangladeshi sufferers appear humane nor the other figures of pity mark their presence in this news story?

The spectators' feelings of powerlessness to act on the distant suffering become even more acute when we consider the radical distance between safety and danger that the map of adventure news construes on the television screen. How can the audience understand what caused or what can repair these disasters when all access to them is restricted to four sentences and a map?

   This dialectic between audience apathy and television text is further nuanced by Cambell's (2004) pictorial analysis of photographs of suffering. Compassion fatigue, Cambell argues, is produced in the intersection of at least two distinct but symbiotic 'cultural economies'. The first is the economy of 'taste and decency', which has to do with the ways in which television regulates the spectacles of atrocity on screen by censoring shocking images of destruction. The second is the economy of 'display', which cleanses the spectacle of suffering of any disturbing details, so that it is decent and can be shown on the screen. The consequence of these two media economies, Cambell suggests, is that they never confront us with the immediate reality of suffering and, therefore, do not raise the urgent question as to what can be done about it (2004: 55). The cause of compassion fatigue, then, lies not in the omnipresence of suffering on our television screens, but in the significant absence of the distant sufferer from the community of Western spectators. It lies in news of suffering without pity. I do not mean to claim, in a dogmatic manner, that it is the news texts that one-sidedly shape the spectators' attitudes towards distant suffering. It would be fairer, as Silverstone does, to locate the cause of compassion fatigue in the relationship between the spectators' zone of comfort and the minimalism of news texts, as the two feed into each other and reconfirm one another. This relationship makes television producers as well as spectators responsible for the general indifference of the West towards distant suffering.[10] However, trying to define where compassion fatigue begins (with the spectator or the media) is perhaps not as important as we may think. What matters is where, in a practical way, we can begin to reverse the process of fatigue.

   I would suggest that we begin not with the audience side of the argument, with compassion fatigue, but with media fatigue – television's representations and norms of reporting. This, for me, is the political problem, rather than the capacity of the public to engage with and act on distant suffering.[11] Important as the critical alertness of the audience may be (a long-term project of mass pedagogy that, no doubt, needs to be undertaken), the point of departure in reversing compassion fatigue is to actually tap into the texts of mediation and work on their pedagogical potential for evoking and distributing pity in the news.

   This is why Silverstone's hands-on proposal for a change in television's regulative policies in the UK is significant in this context. Singling out the question of the 'other' as being the number one item on the agenda that regulation policies of television should address today, Silverstone recommends that the focus of regulation – currently 'concerned with the protection of our own securities and of those we hold dear' – should now shift to a fairer representation of 'those who are distant in space or culture, the strangers amongst us, our neighbours abroad' (2004b: 446). The pedagogical value of such a shift is absolutely fundamental to any serious attempt (be this media literacy or humanitarian education programmes) to shape the ethical disposition of media publics towards the distant sufferer.

From adventure news to emergency news

I have so far examined the boat accident in India as a piece of adventure news. The truth is, however, that this event was presented in two different ways, at different hourly slots in the BBC World news flow. It was only in later editions that the Indian accident was restricted to a short report – when 'breaking news' from Palestine took the top place on the agenda. In earlier editions, and more in line with the BBC's broadcasting ethos, this piece of news was extended by a 20-second long telephone link with Delhi, in which the local correspondent gave an account of the conditions and the efforts being made to retrieve survivors and bodies.

The conversation was accompanied by a graphic with two on-screen photos – the reporter's, with his name underneath and the specification of place as 'Delhi', and a central square in Delhi. The reporter's verbal account added another layer of complexity to the representation of suffering and brought into the narrative a more nuanced politics of pity. First, it expanded the space–times to encompass a report on the monsoon season and explained that such extreme weather conditions regularly lead to overly swollen rivers and an increased number of boat accidents in the area. Second, it manifested an orientation towards agency in its reference to the efforts of rescue teams to find survivors or retrieve bodies.

Both elements – the expansion of space–time and the orientation towards agency – make a difference to the portrayal of this piece of news as they point to a subtle move towards suffering with rather than without pity. However, this is only a reluctant move. The telephone link brought us closer to the scene of suffering, but, at the same time, still kept us resolutely away from the living context of the suffering. The reporter's verbal references were accompanied by visuals, but these bore no intrinsic reference to the suffering narrative. The graphic illustration was static and uninformative, moving the spectator only vaguely closer to the location of the reported event as Delhi is 1000 km away from where the accident happened. Importantly, there was no image of the scene of the accident. The sufferer was still a number, the appeal to empathy was minimal. In this sense I would argue that, while this version of the Indian boat accident gestures to elements of emergency, the piece of news remains on the adventure category. For a piece of news to work on an emergency level, we need for stories of suffering to become stories of humanitarian intervention. This means that these stories make an explicit appeal to spectators, raising the question as to how they can act on the sufferers. The sufferers are still cultural 'others', but their suffering is not deprived of pity, it is organized around it. In Chapter 6, we shall study three variations on the subject of suffering with pity in emergency news.

Notes

1   The shootings and the boat accident pieces were shown on BBC World on 31 August 2002, whereas the floods in Bangladesh news was shown on national Greek television on 23 July 2002. The first two pieces were inserted into the flow of BBC World's hourly news broadcasts and the third in NET's main evening news broadcast. BBC World shifted, just after the Indian boat accident, to 'breaking news' on the Palestine–Israel conflict. NET slotted the flood story in just before its sports coverage. Due to bad image quality the illustration of the flood on p. 103 comes the Getty Image Bank/Scanpix pictures, which, however, conveys the very same sense of aestheticisation that I develop in the news analysis.

2   For the contrast between a 'logic of causality' and a 'logic of appearances', see Fairclough (2003: 88).

3   On the classification of social actors in pictorial representation, see, among others, van Leeuwen and Jaworski (2002: 255–76), and in language, Fairclough (2003: 145–50 and 222).

4   See Black (1997: 20).

5   On anatopism, see Bakhtin (1986: 10–59).

6   The correspondence model of news selection dictates that:

> news selection provides an accurate and reliable reflection of reality, selecting events only according to their seriousness [...] a political massacre with 200 victims is more likely to be reported than one with 20 victims.
>
> (Cohen, 2001: 170–1)

7   See Tester (2001: 82–6), among others.

8   As Cohen notes, 'each month, the Times Mirror News Interest Index confirms the obvious in fascinating detail: that domestic stories receive more attention than foreign news, unless Americans are there' (2001: 170).

9   This is research conducted by Kinnick et al. (1996: 690), reported in Tester (2001: 47).

10   See Tester (2001: 54–71) for a discussion that casts doubt on the certainty of the compassion fatigue hypothesis:

> The conclusion seems to be clear. It is impossible to predict in advance whether, how or which journalistic production will be or become morally compelling. Social action is actually much too complex to allow for prediction.

11   See Cohen (2001: 192) for the term 'media fatigue' and support for this argument.

Appendix: Adventure News Verbal Texts

'Shootings', BBC World, August 31st, 2002

1. BBC studio. Newscaster: Two Americans and an Indonesian have been shot dead in an ambush by unidentified attackers in an American gold mine in Indonesia. Fourteen other people have been injured, nine of them also foreign nationals.

Cut to map of Indonesia and bordering countries. Dots on map: Jakarta, Jayapura. Left side of screen, globe with Indonesia in square. Red bar: Shootings.

Newscaster voiceover: The incident happened on the road leading to the gold and copper mine in West Papua, the victims were travelling in a convoy of cars. Authorities say they suspect separatist rebels were behind the attack. Most of the victims were teachers at the school set up for foreign families.

Cut to studio.

'Boat accident', BBC World, August 31st, 2002

2. BBC studio. Newscaster Lucy Hockins: More than forty people are missing, feared drowned, after river-boat capsized in the Eastern Indian state of Orissa. The boat overturned in the river Baytarani which was swollen by floods.

Cut to map of India and bordering countries. Dots on map: Jajpur, Bhubaneswar. Left screen side: Globe with India in square. Red bar: Boat accident.

Newscaster voiceover: The accident occurred as the boat was making its way towards Jajpur town, a hundred kilometres from the capital Bhubaneswar. The boat was carrying mainly office workers and school-children.

'Biblical catastrophe', July 23rd, 2002, Greek national television

3. *Long shot of landscape covered in water; in background, small group of houses, in foreground six people, one of them with an umbrella, staring at landscape, two of them walking away, one carrying a child. Shift to long shot of landscape, no human figures. Grey colours. Graphic, top right: the local, Bangladeshian channel logo.*

On top of it the Greek text: Biblical Catastrophe. Voiceover: Floods are sweeping across Bangladesh. The counting of victims tragic, eighty-two people dead and more than three million homeless.

Long shot of flooded landscape with two small boats floating, two people on left side of frame watching; cut to long shot of flooded landscape with a couple of trees at background, no human figures.

Voiceover: Due to the tropical rains that hit the area, the rivers over-flowed and whole regions were buried under water.

Continuous long shots of landscape in water. Return to opening shot with six people, the umbrella holder staring at lansdcape, the child carrier walking away.

We are talking about the worst floods in the past four years.

Cut to studio: sports news.

6

EMERGENCY NEWS: SUFFERING WITH PITY

From news stories that *interrupt* pity, I now shift to news stories that *produce* pity in their representations of suffering. These are prime-time news items on a rescue mission for illegal African immigrants in the Mediterranean, a famine crisis in Argentina and the death by stoning sentence for a Nigerian woman.[1]

I argue that emergency news is a regime of pity that radically rearticulates the multimodality, space–time and agency of mediation and, in so doing, it offers the option for action on distant suffering that adventure news denies to the spectator. Who acts and how on the scene of suffering, however, is an open matter. Each piece of emergency news has a different response to these questions, creating an internal hierarchy of sufferers and actors on the television screen. In this respect, I consider emergency news to be a complicated regime of pity that best throws into relief the possibilities – as well as the limitations – of public action that are available in Western societies today.

Suffering as emergency

The African immigrants, Argentinean children and Nigerian woman share one feature of pity that was absent from adventure news: they call for immediate action. It is this demand for immediate action on distant misfortune that produces the regime of pity I call *emergency news.*[2] The enactment of pity as emergency entails complicated news narratives, with multiple connections between safety and danger and novel possibilities for action for both the participants in the scene of suffering and the spectators. In so far as emergency news participates in shaping the relationship between the sight of suffering and the spectator, we should consider emergency as the exemplary manifestation of television's politics of pity. Pity appears now as a specific structure of address, to recall Butler's term, that certain news narratives put forward: 'Watch this suffering. It is distant, but its distance can be bridged in ways that enable other, experts/ your own nation/yourself, to reach it and make a difference'.

I would describe the distinction between adventure and emergency news in terms of three major shifts in the representation of suffering.

- The move from visually static and verbally minimal descriptions with low affective power, to visually and verbally complicated narratives with increasing degrees of affective power.
- The move from singular and abstract space–times (the map) to concrete, specific, multiple and mobile space–times (chronotopes). Chronotopes place suffering in the order of lived experience and often give suffering historical depth and future perspective. Chronotopes may also connect suffering with the space–time of safety and propose a frame of action to the spectators themselves.
- The move from non-agency (numerical and/or aestheticized sufferers and the absence of other agents) to conditional agency (active and personalized sufferers and the presence of benefactors and persecutors). Conditional agency implies that the sufferer is only able to be active in a limited and ineffective way – hence the need for external intervention. Yet, the very fact of acting endows this sufferer with a quality of humanness that we do not encounter in adventure news.

Complicated multimodal narratives

The obvious difference between adventure and emergency news is that the former manifests a much simpler narrative structure than the latter. Rather than a brief report plus the map of adventure news, there is a variety of narrative types and a multiple visualization of suffering in emergency news. These features give rise to hybrid and multifaceted regimes of pity. For this reason, I now discuss in separate sections how each piece of emergency news reports on its stories of suffering. The discussion on multimodal narratives focuses on:

- the *mode of presentation of the news*
- the *working relationship between visual and verbal semiotic modes* on screen
- the *aesthetic quality* of each piece of news.

The mode of presentation
All three pieces of news mentioned earlier involve moving images – that is, video or archive film, accompanied by voiceovers. This visualization of suffering is a key feature of emergency news because the act of seeing places the spectators in the position of witnesss and confronts them with the facticity of suffering that the image so powerfully carries. At the same time, the voiceover has the power to link images from diverse times and places together in a coherent whole. Thus, the credibility of each piece of news is established via the narrative logic of the voiceover on the image.[3]

Even though all three examples share more or less the same mode of presentation, each piece resolves the tension between verbal narrative, (description, narration or exposition) and images of suffering in distinct ways. In so doing, each piece gives rise to a distinct claim to reality. Evidently, the most conventional claim to reality presupposes a relationship of correspondence between what we hear and what we see on screen. However this claim to reality – a form of *perceptual* or *empirical* realism – is not the only claim to reality that the news can make. It is also evoked by the stirring of strong emotions, empathy or anger or by making references to commonsensical views that are difficult to question – a sense that 'of course things are like this'. Both these are forms of *psychological* realism – a term that I illustrate in the news examples given below. For now, it is enough to repeat that such differences in the mode of presentation of emergency news invite the spectator to attach to each piece of news on suffering different feelings and different moral values.

The working relationship between visual and verbal modalities

There are three types of news realism, each of which brings a distinct type of meaning to work in each news narrative: *indexical*, *iconic* and *symbolic* meaning. The authenticity and aesthetic quality of the news pieces depend on the capacity of each type of meaning to represent suffering via its distinct claim to reality.

The piece of news on a rescue mission for African immigrants in the Mediterranean claims an indexical correspondence between the news story and the reported event, making the spectator a witness of the rescue mission as it unfolds in the rough sea. In this sense, this piece of news is an example of perceptual realism. The other two pieces – the news of the Argentinean famine and Nigerian convict – make use of *iconic* and *symbolic* meaning, respectively, in order to engage language and image at different levels of abstraction and move suffering away from pure description and towards dramatic narration or an evaluative exposition. In this sense, these are examples of psychological realism that represent reality as it appeals to our sense of humanity and justice. Let me emphasize that iconicity and symbolism do not make the realism of these pieces of news any less 'real' than the perceptual realism of the news about the African refugees, but, on the contrary, may render the reality of suffering even more imposing and compelling. These terms, however, make us sensitive to the fact that the reality of suffering is an act of meaning making that bears not one but many faces and brings about many emotions and options for action.

The aesthetic quality

The mode of presentation and the verbal–visual relationship between talk and image produce the distinct aesthetic quality of each piece of news. In adventure news, you will recall, the aesthetic quality was that of a factual minimalism, with brief reports on what had happened being given before moving on to other news. In emergency news, the aesthetic quality is that of a more complicated semiotic product that is specific to each piece of news and entails various combinations of narrative and image. These combinations show that there is complicity between the mise en scène of suffering and the public appeal of the news. This is because of the demand for action towards suffering that emergency news makes on the spectator.

Absent from adventure news, this demand for action in emergency news does not carry the force of an authoritative imperative or a paternalistic adhortation. Instead, it appears as a moral obligation that springs from the spectators' own judgements about the suffering as it is presented to them objectively, without a privileged point of view. Television's ability to exercise power relies not on an explicit 'should', but an indirect authority that seeks to shape the spectators' conduct by playing on their emotions and civil sensibilities. Television's proposition of 'take action' in this respect always articulates political stance by virtue of a certain aesthetic quality. For example, the famine in the news about Argentina draws on an 'icons of starvation' aesthetic, which seeks to touch the spectators' hearts and urges them to act in the role of cosmopolitan philanthropist. The news of the Nigerian woman takes us a step further from philanthropy. It moves from tender-heartedness towards the demand for justice and its aesthetic quality, 'symbols of inhumanity', and calls the spectators to participate in protests against the unfair verdict of the sharia court.

Chronotopes of emergency

Complicated multimodal narratives set the context for a more complicated spatiotemporal regime within which suffering now occurs. Let us, at this point, recall an important distinction. There is the space–time of news presentation, which is the place where the news story is reported from, whether this is the studio or on location, and the space–times of the news event itself, which are the multiple locations and temporalities by means of which the suffering is either verbally narrated or visually portrayed using either the 'involved' camera or long shot or the present or past tense. Although both types of space–time are properties of the multimodality of news text, this distinction draws attention to the possible manipulations of space–time that can occur within the news narrative independently of the location and its presentation.

Chronotopic complexity is effected by montage – that is, by breaking down and reconnecting bits and pieces of spatial and temporal realities. As in film, the main property of television news is visual discontinuity, which is achieved when 'short shots replace one another' so that the news 'point of view changes from shot to shot', as Manovich puts it (2001: 144). Discontinuity characterizes all three of our news items, but particularly those about the Argentinean famine and the Nigerian woman. There is montage in the news of the African refugees too, but whereas this latter piece is mainly temporal montage (that is, cutting film so as to squeeze a 16-hour-long operation into a short sequence), the other two pieces are characterized by spatial montage. Spatial and temporal discontinuities are woven into coherent stories by means of the voiceover, which tells us what happened to whom, where and when.

However, this manipulation of space–times in the montage process does not automatically establish a desirable sense of proximity to the scene of suffering. The key feature of the chronotopicity of emergency is not proximity for proximity's sake, but proper distance – a concept that I discussed in detail in Chapter 2. As the montage effects in the news of the Nigerian woman illustrate, engagement comes about only when a certain combination of proximity with distance manages to pay service to the news story on the screen. Here is Amina Lawal in a Nigerian courtroom [shot of the young mother with baby], the threat of violence she is faced with [mobbing sequence] and here is 'us' protesting against this threat [report on Amnesty International protest in Athens].

The concern with proper distance, then, requires a more nuanced conception of the spatiotemporal mutations of montage than the straightforward categories of proximity or distance would allow. For this reason, the analytics of mediation differentiates four distinct chronotopic properties across the emergency news texts. These are concreteness, multiplicity, specificity and mobility.

Concreteness and multiplicity

All chronotopes of emergency are characterized by concreteness and some form of multiplicity. Both have to do with the presence of the camera in the scene of action. The visualization of suffering introduces spectators to the *concrete* spaces of suffering – where people actually live and act, which in our news items are the boat, hospitals, city streets. For example, in the news of the famine in Argentina, we watch emaciated children in hospital beds – a testimony of suffering that language fails to convey. At the same time, montage also enables spectators to experience the scene of suffering as a multiple space – that is, as a space consisting of many contexts of suffering, including those where efforts to alleviate the suffering take place. In the same piece of news, we follow a sequence of shots from city streets, to hospitals, to a press conference, to a customs' office. These sequences portray famine as a multifaceted and dynamic reality and give a sense of 'depth' to the scene of suffering absent in adventure news.

Concreteness and multiplicity, then, are constitutive properties of the enactment of pity and, as such, are also necessary features of emergency news.

Specificity and mobility

Concreteness and multiplicity are not sufficient on their own to bring about the strongest form of ethical appeal to the spectators – that which creates engagement in action. For this, the news narrative needs to activate two other spatiotemporal features – specificity and mobility.

Only some representations of suffering provide these features. Spatiotemporal specificity introduces verbal and visual information that renders the scene of suffering unique, so that we know it is this one and could be no other. Specificity can be realized linguistically – when the voiceover accompanies images of suffering with details of location and time, for example. This is the case in the news of the famine in Argentina, where the naming of a specific province (Tucuman) and a village (Santa Anna) particularize the alternating visuals of starvation and add both credibility and a new sense of proximity to this distant location.

The most effective form of spatiotemporal specificity, however, is the visual. Visual specificity involves individualized images of the sufferers – human beings with a face and a gaze – on which the plot of the news narrative is focalized. In the news about the famine in Argentina, we have the focalization of the narrative on the eyes of the Argentinean children. Unlike the en masse portrayals of African refugees, the camera zooming in on the children's gaze compels the spectators to 'stay' with these sufferers. Even stronger is the impact of visualizing sufferers as a single figure.[4] This is the case with the Nigerian woman – she is more than a face, she is a person with a name, 'Amina Lawal', an age, 'young', and she is also a 'mother'.[5]

Finally, chronotopic mobility has to do with the capacity of montage to connect the space–time of suffering with that of safety. Mobility is a key quality of the chronotopicity of emergency, because it enables the spectators to inhabit both spaces – the space where dangerous things happen and the safe space where people like 'us' demonstrate in protest. In conjoining the two space–times, mobility suggests that there is, or there should be, a link of action between the spectators, and the sufferers.

Introducing the possibility of action is a key moment in the mediation of suffering, but a difficult one to manage in language. The difficulty lies in the nature of the social control that television enacts. In the news of the Nigerian woman, an imperative of the 'do something' sort would sound too prescriptive, but the shift from the scene of violent mobbing in Africa to the one where the Amnesty International activist speaks out against stoning, humiliation and mutilation articulates a 'universal' value that urges the spectators to do more than just shake their heads in disapproval. It urges us to take public action. It is chronotopic mobility, then, that negotiates this subtle semantics of propositionality and the visual editing of suffering that, before it becomes a verbal call, manages to visualize the moral demand for public action.[6]

Below, I examine the gradual progression of space–times from the news of the African refugees, where the chronotope is only concrete and minimally multiple (the high adrenaline spectacle), to the news of the Argentinean famine, where the chronotope is concrete, intensely multiple and specific (icons of starvation), to the news of the Nigerian woman, where the chronotope, apart from being concrete, multiple and specific, is now also mobile (symbols of inhumanity).

Conditional agency in emergency

There are two main concerns in the analysis of conditional agency. First, there is the concern to establish the attributes by which the sufferer of emergency news is qualified as a human being. Second, there is the concern to establish how the figures of action in the scene of suffering – the benefactor and the persecutor – organize the emotional disposition of the spectators vis-à-vis the sufferers' misfortunes.

The humanization of the sufferer

The human quality of the sufferers in emergency news is semiotized as their capacity to act. The action of the sufferers has different visual manifestations. It may be visualized as *motion*, where the sufferer participates in concrete, purposeful activity; as *gaze*, where the sufferer enters into an active relationship with the camera; or as *condition*, where the sufferer symbolizes a 'universal' human state of existence.

Motion is the humanizing property we see in news of the African refugees. Their action is visualized as the jumping from their boat to another, that of the Maltese coastguard. Minimal as this action may be, it endows these sufferers with a degree of agency absent in the aestheticized figures seen in the piece on the Bangladeshi flood victims. *Gaze* is the humanizing property shown in the news of the Argentinean children. Their eye contact is action that seeks rapport and makes an appeal for help to the audience. Indeed, as the voiceover asserts, 'their gaze does not leave you space for complacency.' The appellative force of the sufferers' gaze carries a universal sense of humanity beyond the specific circumstances of their suffering. A similar operation of humanization takes place when what is visualized is a *condition*. In the case of the Nigerian woman, the gaze is replaced by the image of a woman with a baby in her lap, calling up the most universal quality of (Western) humanity, motherhood.

Yet, active as they may be, the sufferers of emergency news cannot effectively change the condition of their misfortune. Jumping from one boat to another saves the refugees' lives, but does not promise them a better destiny. Looking into the camera invites the spectators' engagement with the children's gaze, but does not improve their life conditions. Film of a mother holding her baby touches on a powerful Western imaginary, but does not remove the death threat from Amina Lawal's life. Endowed with a minimal facility for on-screen action, but, in effect, unable to make a difference to their own fates, the sufferers of emergency are what Bakhtin calls 'merely the physical subject of action' (1981: 105).

They are sufferers caught in one or another form of ambivalent existence that simultaneously asserts and denies their humanity. The term 'conditional agency' points to the inescapable duality of agency, a duality reminiscent of the conditional freedom of the spectator, as discussed in Chapter 3. In both cases, agency is a condition of existence that subjects people to certain restrictions on their conduct, while simultaneously enabling them to act as free individuals in the space that these restrictions provide. This said, conditional agency is by no means a homogeneous category. Sufferers who just move, albeit purposefully, are endowed with less humanity than those who directly confront us with their gaze or the single figure of a mother holding her baby. This heterogeneity in the semiotics of agency introduces a gradation in the representation of the emergency sufferer. From being the 'Other' – the subject of radical existential and cultural difference – the sufferer gradually becomes an 'other' – still an outsider, but now closer to the spectator's own experiential world and within reach.

The scene of emergency action
Whatever the agency of the sufferers, the spectators' own capacity for action cannot be immediate and direct – it is always action at a distance. Suspended between the spectators' potential commitment to action and the sufferers' own minimal capacity to act, the agency of emergency news depends heavily on the presence of other participants in the scene of suffering. This is a form of theatrical agency as it focalizes the spectator's feelings towards the sufferers and, in so doing, also participates crucially in humanizing the sufferers. Let us remember that, in theatrical agency, the spectators' emotions are displaced to either focus on the benefactors, feeling gratitude vis-à-vis their acts of charity, or on the persecutors, feeling indignation at the causes of the sufferers' misfortunes. In emergency news, action is largely focalized on the figure of the benefactor – the coastguard crew rushing to the rescue of African refugees, governments assuming responsibility for starving populations or activists fighting for human rights, for example.

At the same time, beneficiary action cannot be described in a single stroke. It follows a progression from the benefactor as the specialized coastguard crew, then as a State agency and finally as potentially everybody. The progression in the agency of the benefactor is simultaneously a progression towards a more involved spectator. From simply observing the African refugees' rescue mission, the spectators are then presented with a case of international humanitarian aid and, finally, with the concrete petition campaign against Amina Lawal's execution. It is important to follow these variations in agency, because they point to changes in the potential for pity and, hence, the moralization of the spectator as a cosmopolitan actor. I discuss the implications that the agency in emergencies has for the possibility of cosmopolitan sensibility under the heading 'The spectator as actor' later in this chapter.

Let us now analyse the pieces of news we have been looking at in more detail in relation to the conclusions drawn so far about the features of emergency news.

The rescuing of African refugees: high-adrenaline spectacle

Multimodal narrative

- *Mode of presentation*: perceptual realism.
- *Visual–verbal correspondence*: indexical meaning.
- *Aesthetic quality*: spectacularity.

African refugees' spacetime: Concrete and multiple

Perceptual realism

This piece of news is presented by means of video footage with voiceover. The event takes place in the open sea and is filmed mostly with a camera situated on the upper deck of a Maltese coastguard's boat. The coastguard has approached the refugees' wooden boat and lashed their vessel to it so as to enable the transportation of the passengers. The video records the development of this single event, with the voiceover following the action on the visual plane. Consequently, the reality of the suffering that this mode of presentation proposes to us is perceptual realism. What is said is closely anchored to what is seen. Narrative cohesion is established primarily by means of montage – the visual editing of the mission's stages. From the initial shots of the approach of the coastguard towards the refugees' boat, we cut to scenes of the evacuation, followed by the arrival of a rescue helicopter, then the departure of the coastguard for Valetta and, finally, the arrival of the refugees on dry land.

The position of the camera, on board the coastguard's boat with resultant erratic shots and its lens getting wet, provides the spectator with a privileged point of view – that of the uninvolved onlooker. From a perspective of impartial observation, the spectator is an eyewitness to a drama that unfolds in 'real' space and time.

Indexical meaning

The tight image–speech correspondence frames this piece of news in indexical meaning that takes the rescue event as its external referent and uses language to illustrate it. Indexical meaning is responsible for the aura of objectivity that surrounds the rescue mission news, an objectivity based precisely on the combination of an 'uninvolved' visual perspective and descriptive narrative: 'the first illegal refugees begin to get on board [...] throw their poor luggage on the deck [...] are watching the wooden boat being taken away and sinking'. These are all voiceover sentences that assert facts and follow visual action.

However, descriptive narrative is not pure. It is cast within a broader frame of narration that capitalizes on the drama of the visuals by employing classic devices of fictional discourse. These devices are *real-time storytelling*, *focus on danger* and *happy ending*. Real-time storytelling construes the event as unfinished, as if it occurred right now, so we have 'the boat crew has sent an SOS'. Real time is sustained throughout the text via the use of the historical present (the past narrated in the present tense) as well as the position of the camera (we are right here).

Focus on danger accentuates the suspense of the story by expanding on the drama of the visual imagery by means of verbal commentary. The verbal mode not only describes the mission operation as it develops on screen but also provides extra-visual information on the mission's risks. For example, the images of the refugees jumping on board are verbally illustrated with the words 'they rush to get on board the coastguard boat, *running the danger of finding themselves in the sea and getting crushed.*' The danger reaches its peak with the arrival of a rescue helicopter, under worsening weather conditions. This frame – especially the imagery of a rescuer hovering over the grey sea holding on to a rope – adds to the scene of action the visual quality of a Hollywood adventure. Finally, the narration closes off the story with a *happy ending*: 'the mission ends without bad surprises'.

However, neither the description nor narration are devoid of exposition – the narrative type that carries the value judgement in this piece of news. Notice, for example, that all three of the descriptive clauses mentioned above – 'begin to get on board', 'throw ... luggage' and 'are watching' take 'illegal refugees' as their subject, not 'shipwrecked travellers', 'Africans' or 'Somalians'. Something similar happens with the concluding sequence. We now move on to watch the refugees, crew and military forces getting off board. We are told that the 'illegal refugees [may be] obliged to return to their country. Perhaps in order to begin yet again the dangerous journey towards a better life'. The final visual frame brings us back to the initial pictures of the vessel in mid-sea. There is a strong fictional element here, too, casting the news as a never-ending story and the protagonists as people trapped in a time loop. Embedded in it, at the same time, is a strong presupposition as to how the event is to be interpreted and assessed. An event that brings into visibility the issue of mass immigration flows travelling from Africa, either as illegal refugees or as asylum seekers, is here construed as a journey without destination, as a tragic game of fate.

Spectacularity

Visual action is central to the significance of this piece of news. The verbal text essentially follows the stages of the rescue operation in an intertextual mixture of narrative types. These are description, which authenticates what is going on; narration, which dramatizes the intense action; and exposition, which offers a point of view on the spectacle as a game of fate. The aesthetic quality of this news narrative can be summed up as a high-adrenaline spectacle.

What are the consequences of intense spectacularity on the representation of suffering in this news? The first is that the language does not rise beyond the immediate imagery to sufficiently inform us about the event's circumstances, both local (when did this happen?) and general (how often do such events occur, what are the causes, what is being done?). We can talk about a representation of suffering as emergency but it nevertheless does not depart from a 'logic of appearances' – the logic of where, when and who, but not why.

The second and related consequence is that the spectacularity of the rescue mission, without a broader frame for its comprehension, tends to move this piece of news from the domain of the historical world on to the domain of cinematic entertainment. Emergency – the hectic tempo of action on the sufferer – is *internal* to the narrative organization of the event, beginning and ending with the viewing experience, with spectators' consumption of the rescue mission.

Space–time: concrete and multiple

This piece of news mostly unfolds in a singular space – the sea. This is not the singularity of a map that connects space and time in a technical and abstract manner, but the concrete singularity of the two vessels where human action is unfolding moment by moment. There is a further differentiation of this concrete space, which is visualized as the two vessels' decks. The deck of the coastguard's boat signifies safety, while the deck of the refugees' boat means danger. This visual differentiation between safety and danger already introduces a minimal multiplicity of space–times, which is instrumental in organizing human agency in this piece of news. The report is about the refugees' abandonment of the boat, which is the move from danger to safety itself. It is about a rescue mission, as the screen text illustrates. Rather than the dot on the map of adventure news, we now have images of people fighting for survival and a voiceover that talks to us about the risks these people are taking. 'Othering' here cannot take the form it has in the news about India, Indonesia and Bangladesh. It cannot be a reference to humans without humanness. Suffering is now a condition inherently linked to people's lives.

At the same time, however, the sufferer is still an 'other'. This is because the space–time of the rescue operation, concrete as it may be, still remains a-historical. Visually, it is a seascape – an undifferentiated location that could be anywhere – while in the voiceover we are told that it is 'twenty miles away from Malta'. The main temporalities of the news have no historical specificity either. They are internal to the mission itself, its duration (16 hours) and its closure (the safe arrival). No attempt is made to insert the event into a broader chronology in which explanation or other possible courses of action could be contemplated. The only future reference – the closing line, 'perhaps in order to begin yet again the dangerous journey' – attempts to contextualize the suffering in the logic of explanation, hinting at the humanitarian dimension of contemporary immigration flows, but it does not go any further than that. As a closing remark, this chronotopic opening to the future traps the African sufferers in the eternal temporality of the Sisyphus torture, where all attempts to escape are doomed to failure – 'In order to begin yet again.' These sufferers are human beings who exist outside the flow of history, outside the geography of power relationships and its political necessities. Their need might be urgent but cannot be acted on by the spectators. Following the position of the camera, we observe this world in proximity but from the upper deck of the coastguard's boat and outside the scene of action.

Conditional Agency

- *Sufferers*: dangerous 'misérables'.
- *Benefactors*: professional crew.

Dangerous misérables

The African refugees have already demonstrated a great deal of initiative. They have taken the risk to cross the Mediterranean. On screen, we meet them at the point where their audacity turns into despair: 'They have just sent a SOS'. In terms of language, the African refugees, like the Bangladeshis, are cultural aliens: a number '228', a group of anonymous 'misérables' ('poor luggage') without a future ('obliged to return, start anew') and without a voice ('authorities suspect that they come from ...'). Visually, they appear active in the sense of managing to jump from their own vessel to the coastguard's. To be sure, this minimal action is enough to endow them with a conditional agency that the Bangladeshis lack. Nevertheless, their lives are in the hands of their rescuers.

Interestingly, their benefactors appear to be putting themselves at risk, too – fighting the sea. They are also getting physically close to the sufferers. Images of the crew in face masks and uniforms suggest that the benefactors are in need of protection from bodily contact with the sufferers. This visual medicalization of the rescue mission is a key semiotic element in the 'othering' of the African sufferers. Not only are these refugees cultural aliens, they are also polluted. The imagery gets stronger, when the refugees are guided off board. The crew's masks and uniforms are now complemented with guns – a visual militarization of the scene, suggesting that the refugees are also dangerous. There are obviously health and security calculations involved in such operations and it is these calculations that the images denote.

By the same token, however, these images simultaneously introduce a basic ambivalence into the figures of the African sufferers. They are both threatened, as they are in need of rescue, and threatening, as they are in need of confinement. They are passive *and* active. Ambivalence takes us away from indexical meaning and the perceptual realism of a 'this is how it happened' type that dominates the news text. The ambivalence about the sufferers adds a level of symbolic meaning to this representation of suffering. This is the primordial and unreflexive belief of our culture, that the racial 'other' contaminates and threatens our own 'purity'. Such 'symbolics of threat' capture a fundamental anthropological distinction, which is present in the majority of racist public discourse, namely the distinction between the sanitized existence of the West and the danger of disease and disorder in the 'black continent'.[7] I take up the moral implications of this 'symbolics of threat' below in the final section of this chapter, under the heading 'The demand for reflexivity'.

Professional crew

The benefactors are the crew of the coastguard's boat, part of the Maltese navy. They form a specialized body with a strong professional identity. It is only the coastguard's crew and nobody else who could be properly active in the rescue mission. At the same time, as a consequence of the medicalization and militarization of the scene of action that we saw above, whereby the professional crew appears in medical uniforms and wearing masks or holding guns, the benefactor of this story is represented as, at once, protecting and in need of protection. This ambivalence however does not 'other' the benefactor. Rather, it signals the heroic dimension of these professionals who save people's lives by putting their own at risk. In thematizing courage and vulnerability, duty and self-denial, this piece of news celebrates the benefactor as a humanitarian hero and, in so doing, reinforces the news's own cinematic quality as a high-adrenaline spectacle.

The Famine in Argentina: 'icons of starvation'

Multimodal narrative

- *Mode of presentation*: categorical realism.
- *Visual–verbal correspondence*: iconic meaning.
- *Aesthetic quality*: philanthropic campaign.

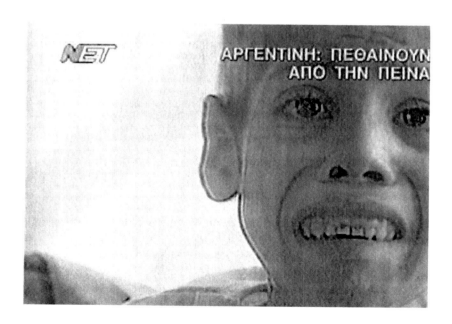

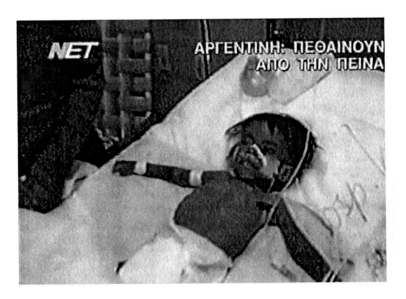

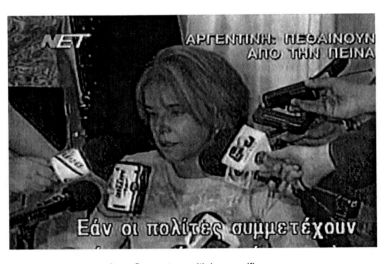

Argentinean famine space–time: Concrete; multiple; specific

Categorical realism
This news item is introduced in the studio by the anchor: 'Argentina suffers the worst economic crisis in its history. In recent days, ten children died of hunger in the province of Tucuman in North Argentina'. Although there is a lack of emotionality in this text, which endows it with the necessary measure of impartiality, the reference to children has a strong sentimental potential that already justifies the status of this news as emergency news. This sentimental potential is capitalized on in the course of the report, which is a combination of archive and satellite pictures.

The satellite pictures, which also constitute the 'news' in this piece, come from a press conference with Hilda Duhalde, who is talking on behalf of the Argentinean government. The press conference sequence is preceded by a briskly edited visual flow of close-ups of children's faces and emaciated children lying in hospital beds. The press conference is then followed by shots of what are reported to be famine-striken city streets, where adults search rubbish bins. The news concludes at a customs office where US medical aid was checked and found to be out of date.

The spectator's point of view is that of omnipresence. We go everywhere the suffering is occurring and where attempts to alleviate it are taking place. The hectic flow of close-ups of children renders this sequence iconic. This is so because the intense proliferation of images lifts them from their particularity and elevates them to a generic status. In their function as icons, images 'surrender' their capacity to refer to specific children from Argentina to their capacity to stand for an abstraction. This abstraction is the category 'starvation', which stands for the life conditions that these Argentinean children are subject to. The realism of this news is categorical because its verbal text abandons the factual reference to the sequence of the visuals – a feature of the rescue mission news, too – and centres on the broad theme of starvation that the visuals come to dramatize and sensationalize. In contrast to the reliance on fact in perceptual realism, categorical realism seeks to strike a cord in the spectators' hearts and makes them feel for the young and defenceless sufferers.

Iconic meaning
Categorical realism relies on iconic meaning – that is, the meaning of resemblance, of family relationships between images or images and words. The montage of icons of starvation weaves a dense regime of meanings around the emergency situation in Argentina. In this regime, images of suffering children portray the reality of starvation in a manner so powerful that words are not needed to describe it. What the verbal text does instead is produce 'transfer effects' of meaning – that is, sustain the loose correspondence that exists between the images of the children and the referent 'starvation'. This transfer is key to this news narrative because, unless the verbal text ensures that the visuals do evoke the raw reality of starvation, then the news story cannot touch the spectators' hearts. This is the reason the dominant narrative type is now exposition – a way of speaking about the pictures that fuses fragments of fact with maximal moral argument and value judgement.

Let us take the opening shot of the news as an illustration of how iconic meaning works. It is a frontal close-up of a healthy-looking boy eating a piece of bread, which is accompanied by a top-screen graphic 'they are dying of hunger' and commented on in the voiceover: 'their gaze does not leave you space for complacence'. Is this boy really suffering from hunger, though? Is this what his gaze tells us? He is not crying, nor in agony. He looks healthy, not starving. He is in fact eating. Speech here has a transfer effect on the visual. The 'dying of hunger' screen text combined with the direct address – 'does not leave *you*' – fills up the image with surplus meaning that is not necessarily derived from the image's own indexical properties but is strategic in providing a desirable meaning horizon for the interpretation of the image – 'empathize, do something'.[8] Such transfer effects carry on throughout the report. Verbal references to 'tragedy', 'despair' and 'death' capitalize on the children's gaze and, later on, more to the point, shots of their emaciated legs, arms and bellies or the sound of their crying sustain and intensify the emotional appeal of the Argentineans' suffering.

Philanthropic campaign
The aesthetic quality of this piece of news draws on philanthropic campaigning – a genre characterized by the priority of feelings over facts. This does not mean, however, that this news item fails to claim that it objectively reports on the reality of the situation in Argentina. Rather, the priority of feelings over facts means that its aura of objectivity is not indexical, as it is in the news about the African refugees, but *a-perspectival* (Boltanski, 1999: 31).

A-perspectival objectivity drops the close correspondence between image and voiceover in favour of offering the broad overview of the circumstances of the suffering. In this piece, it is the quick alternation between places that claims to represent no particular perspective on the suffering because it represents them all. As a-perspectival objectivity does not rely on the detail of any particular referent, the few factual references to the economic problems of Argentina, in this story, are put together with a certain carelessness. It is, for example, reported that the crisis is the 'worst in the history of Argentina' *and* 'the worst in recent years'. In the aesthetic of philanthropy, the spectators do not need to be convinced by way of proof or argument – it is enough that they feel moved and compelled to care for the sufferers. In the formulation 'Argentina is whirling around', the causes of the crisis are displaced on to a natural disaster metaphor – a vortex – whereas in the formulation 'Argentina suffers the worst economic crisis in its history' and 'Argentina is crying for its children', Argentina is personified and its suffering worded by means of references to endurance and pain. Paradoxically, such pure sentimentalism in relation to philanthropy cancels out its own moral appeal to action. Sentimentalism may urge spectators to act as benefactors themselves, but, in effect, it leaves no space for them to do so. In fact, not only are the spectators given no option to act, but they are also left wondering how this disaster came about and who could offer Argentinean people appropriate and effective assistance.

Space–time: specific and intensely multiple

The spatiotemporal order of the Argentina report is concrete, as it was in the news of the rescue mission. However, it also has an intense multiplicity and a specificity that the rescue mission lacked.

It is concrete in that it connects us with people's actions in their context of suffering. It is intensely multiple because visual editing takes us through a variety of contexts of suffering, such as home doorsteps, streets and hospitals. As a consequence of this chronotopic multiplicity, the witnessing of suffering now takes place from alternating positions that give spectators the illusion of 'everywhereness'. It is by diffusing the perspective of observation from one single point to a seeming omnipresence, as I described in relation to the aesthetics of philanthropy, that the news of the Argentinean famine is construed in terms of a-perspectival objectivity.

Finally, the chronotope is specific in that the language of the voiceover progresses towards increasingly precise namings of the location of suffering, from 'that corner of the planet' to 'Argentina' to 'the province of Tucuman' to 'the village of Santa Anna'. Linguistic specification, down to the naming of the village and its province, provides a depth of geographical representation that resembles how Western spectators' view their own national space. This familiarization regarding space was unthinkable in the examples of adventure news discussion in Chapter 5. Equally unthinkable for adventure news is the voiceover reference here to aid packages, which now links the space of danger with that of safety by means of the possibility of humanitarian action. Argentina may be famine-striken, but it is also a nation like 'ours' that 'we' can reach out to and help.

The main temporality of the reportage is the present – the 'right now' urgency of suffering. This is signalled in the top-screen text – 'they *are dying* of hunger' – but also in the verbal references to 'Argentina *is suffering* and *is whirling around*'. References to the past, as a context for understanding the outbreak of famine, are absent. As with the African refugees, the Argentineans are insulated from the historical flow that led the once most prosperous South American country to a serious crisis. However, the prevailing temporality of the present, combined with familiarized proximity, do make a strong case. The famine in Argentina will not wait for a solution – it requires immediate action.

Conditional agency

- *Sufferers*: Children
- *Benefactor*: International aid

Children

Even though the sufferers are still grouped into a collective category – nameless and voiceless – they now have a face and a gaze. 'The sufferer' is the children who look straight into the camera. More than engaging the spectator with the humanity of singular people, the gaze commands an urgent rapport with their suffering. The visual escalates from images of healthy children to ones of emaciated children who are crying, lying in hospital beds. It is not faces we are confronted with now, but body parts – shots of a leg, a back, an arm with a drip. It is clear that these images demonstrate the limits of life when there is famine and, thereby, accentuate the sense of urgency in the report's appeal 'against complacency'.

However, they also raise the question is this sufferer still endowed with humanness? Do the visuals of body parts portray children as children or do they 'fetishize' the children's bodies and cut them off from their humane qualities? In a similar way to that noted in relation to the news of the African refugees, this narrative introduces ambivalence in the representation of the sufferers – an ambivalence that resides at the level of symbolic, rather than iconic, meaning. The camera zooming in on isolated arms and legs subjects these sufferers to a form of dismantling, to *fragmentation*.

Fragmentation, Hall claims, is a technique of representation that, in reducing humans to their parts, turns them into objects, into 'fetishes' (1997: 266). Associating the blatant exposure of body parts on camera with early racist discourses and pornography, Hall reminds us that fetishism is a symbolic condition for marking cultural difference as radical, as 'Otherness'.

The meaning slippage from person to body part places the sufferers in an ambivalent regime of representation where they are protrayed both as human figures and as biological machines. This, simultaneously, appeals to a moral connection with the spectators and distances them from the sufferers.

International aid

The multiple alternations in the space–time in this news, moving us from those who die of hunger to those who govern the famine crisis, produce a topography of suffering where the sufferer and the benefactor belong to the same chronotopic universe. This endows Argentina with an unprecedented form of agency: the Argentinean government can help Argentineans survive. Agency is visualized in Hilda Duhalde's press conference – an appeal to ordinary people to participate in national health projects, 'to organize themselves, get informed'. This form of conditional agency dignifies the sufferers and, moreover, renders the call for external support persuasive.

At the same time, the status and identity of the international benefactor is a complicated matter that I discuss below in the section entitled 'The spectator as actor'. An insight into this curious complexity is offered in the critical reference to the USA's aid action. The reference to the 'rage' of the Argentinean customs officials, which was provoked by the expired medicine in the aid package sent by the USA, performs an interesting inversion in the figures of pity. It turns the benefactor – the USA – into a persecutor and makes explicit a rule of engagement that regulates the philanthropic provision of nations to one another. Emergency aid, the reference suggests, may be premised on an unequal world order, whereby the poor depend on the rich, but this order should, in turn, respect and uphold the dignity of the sufferers.

Death by stoning in Nigeria: 'symbols of inhumanity'

Multimodal narrative

- *Mode of presentation*: ideological realism.
- *Visual–verbal correspondence*: symbolic meaning.
- *Aesthetic quality*: pamphleteering.

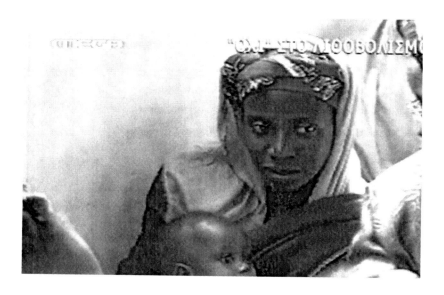

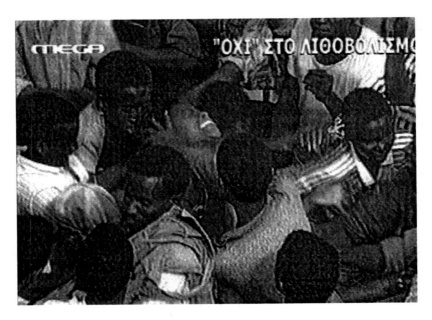

Nigerian convict space–time: Concrete; multiple; specific; mobile

Ideological realism

This news narrative consists of visuals with a voiceover. In the course of it, we are transported from the Nigerian courtroom scene, where the woman sentenced to death by stoning holds her baby in her lap, to Nigerian city streets, where we witness a violent mobbing scene. We then watch an Amnesty International protest happening in Athens, which carries the news value of the story, before we return to the dangerous streets of Nigeria and the repetition of the mobbing scene. The narrative hangs together by means of a series of visual juxtapositions. The first of these is between the scene of the mother with her baby in the courtroom and the mobbing scene in the street. Each of the two images, separately, works iconically. The mother and baby image evokes the Western humanity of the Madonna, whereas the mobbing scene signals the 'savage mind', an alien cultural disposition beyond (Western) rationality and civility.

Terming this piece of news 'ideological realism' captures the function of the news narrative to juxtapose these two iconic meanings in a powerful symbolic representation – the ideological contrast between Western values and Islamic inhumanity. The reality of this narrative, then, is primarily the reality of what we believe is right and humane rather than what we believe to be true (as in the case of the African refugees) or emotionally powerful (as in the news of the Argentinean famine).

Symbolic meaning

As in the case of the Argentinean famine, the narrative here is one of exposition. It takes the perspective that the Nigerian verdict is ethically unacceptable – 'No to death by stoning', the screen graphic asserts. However, the ethical content of this news is produced by means of a different relationship between the verbal and the visual semiotic than the iconicity of the Argentinean news.

The relationship here is primarily symbolic. Symbolic meaning comes about when the verbal narrative, together with the image, evoke some idea or belief that manages to hide its specificity in culture and time and works as if it were a 'universal' truth that the spectator does not need to question. As a consequence of symbolic meaning, the moralizing function of this piece of news is now different from that evident in the previous pieces. There is no explicit urging of spectators to respond to the children's gaze, no sentimental references to 'tragedy', 'death' or 'despair'. What the spectators encounter in this piece is an argument that is articulated on a presupposed nationality, which is all the more powerful for that. How can the young mother of a baby be condemned to death by stoning simply because she gave birth to this baby?

Let us see how symbolic meaning works in the opening sequence of this piece of news. The visual introduces us to the Nigerian court interior, where the woman, with her baby, comes to take a seat. As the voiceover begins with 'The verdict of death by stoning [...] has shocked international public opinion', the camera cuts to a medium-distance frame of the woman and then zooms in on her baby. The visual here clearly focuses on the mother–child bond and, in so doing, strongly evokes the doxa of human innocence and vulnerability. At the same time, the verbal text works to establish a gap between 'us', 'the international public opinion', and the alien culture in which the mother–child bond appears as a crime, the Islamic courtroom. Visual imagery is not explicitly addressed in the voiceover, as it is in the piece on the African refugees, yet the symbolism of motherhood as a sacred condition beyond the punitive scope of law is fully presupposed in the contrast between the West and Islam. It is precisely this contrast between 'our' humanity and 'their' inhumanity that 'shocked' the international community. One way in which symbolism works in this piece of news, then, is that the verbal text is allowed to introduce moral judgement by hinting at, rather than commenting on, the image.

Moral judgement is also introduced in the visual editing. From the mother with baby sequence, we move straight into a powerful mobbing scene, where a crowd is pushing around and beating up a woman trying to escape. The visual juxtaposition of the two sequences – the innocence of the Madonna and the mob violence – works as a symbolic statement in itself, in so far as it now visualizes, rather than verbalizes, the ideological contrast between humanity and inhumanity. This sequencing not only reports on the shock of public opinion, it provokes the shock. In so doing, it effortlessly creates the demand in the spectators to see justice restored. Indeed, the symbolic effect of this contrast is moralizing precisely to the extent that it raises, without hinting at it, the question of action against the injustice of the Islamic sharia court while taking for granted the Western position of critique.

Pamphleteering
The aesthetic quality of the news of the Nigerian woman can be summed up by the political practice of pamphleteering – the public denunciation of the sharia verdict in the name of Amina Lawal's right to life. This appeal to a public cause needs to occur under conditions of impartial reporting. In this news, just like in the Argentinean piece, objectivity adopts the viewing position of omnipresence and, in this manner, diffuses what the voiceover establishes as a privileged moral position ('no to death by stoning') into a position of a-perspectival objectivity ('spectator, see for yourself whatever there is to see').

At the same time, for pamphleteering to effect the spectators' 'swing to commitment', the orchestration of a full cast of pity characters needs to be set in motion. The figure of a humane sufferer whose presence brings the demand for action to the fore is now framed by both evil-doers – the mob and the courtroom that threaten the sufferer's life – and a benefactor – the activist who protests against this threat.

In providing spectators with a concrete option for action, the aesthetics of pamphleteering is no doubt valuable and necessary, but it has its blind spots. It exhausts the exercising of protest to the act of signing a petition. It also leaves unexamined the issue of how best to deal with these 'others', with their conceptions of humanity and justice that we cannot and might not want to comprehend but, by virtue of sharing the same world, we must make an effort to comprehend. I return to these issues in my concluding discussion on the 'cosmopolitan public'.

Space–time: mobile

The Nigerian report involves the most complicated visual editing so far. Its chronotopicity is concrete in that it shows people in their own contexts of action, so we have Amina Lawal in court, a mobbing crowd in city streets and protesters outside the Nigerian Embassy. It is multiple in that it differentiates between locations internal to the space–time of suffering: the Nigerian courtroom, which represents the juridical authority, and the city streets, which represent the 'savage' cultural disposition. It is also specific in that it defines sharia within certain geographical–administrative boundaries – '12 provinces' and 'among Muslims' – whereas it keeps the State authority in a relationship of conflict with the sharia – '*despite* the assertions of the Minister of Justice [...] the *final decision* will be taken by the sharia court.' This set of specifications establishes an antagonism that is internal to the Nigerian space between secular and religious government and construes the land as heterogeneous and dynamic, traversed by cultural and political tensions. Neither a dot on the map nor an undifferentiated landscape, Nigeria may be a space–time of danger, but it is Islam that occupies the extreme end of 'Othering', of difference beyond contact. This internal differentiation of the space–time of danger is instrumental in introducing the novel spatiotemporal feature of this news – mobility, which is both spatial and temporal.

Spatial mobility connects the space–time of danger with that of safety and so creates a zone of contact between the spectators and the sufferer where practical and personal action vis-à-vis the suffering becomes possible. This zone of contact is again achieved via visual editing when it cuts from the mobbing streets of Nigeria to the protest streets of Athens. We move from being witnesses of irrational violence to witnesses of a protest ritual: 'This afternoon, outside the Nigerian Embassy, members of Amnesty International built a pyramid of dignity.' However, for the spectators to perform this shift from witnessing to action, the idea of the cause needs to be construed as having a 'universal' value. What is at stake in this piece of news? What can be done? Has anything been achieved in the past?

Temporal mobility enables precisely this necessary reference to the cause to be made. The news begins with a zooming in on Amina Lawal, the young mother, taken during the initial courtroom procedure. This travels us to time past, reminding us of Amina Lawal's case and establishing the cause against the death by stoning verdict. Subsequently, linguistic references connect the spectators to a variety of options for action. Whereas the temporality of the present points to the necessity of the protest action being taken right now (the Amnesty event), the future tense language used points to intend action that can still be taken. Indeed, the reference to the intermediate status of the verdict – a 'final decision [is to be] taken by the sharia' – is absolutely crucial to sustaining the humanitarian perspective as the case is not yet closed, there is still room to change the verdict. Finally, the reference to a past example – 'Last March', when a similar death verdict was cancelled 'in the last minute *after international denunciations*' – provides both a case that justifies international action and a strong motivation to fight this battle. There is hope for Amina Lawal, if we act in public now, if we all treat her case as a humanitarian emergency.

Conditional agency

- *Sufferer*: Amina Lawal
- *Persecutors*: the 'Other'
- *Benefactors*: Amnesty International and 'us'

Amina Lawal

The sufferer is now a person – Amina Lawal or Amina. Although I have so far referred to the role of *images* in humanizing this sufferer, it is primarily the use of *language* here that endows Amina Lawal with an unprecedented sense of humanity: 'That the young Nigerian woman had her baby outside marriage gave to sharia the right to apply the inhumane laws.' The voiceover avoids the use of legalistic vocabulary. This not only keeps Amina disassociated from the logic of Nigerian juridical discourse, it also appropriates her condition into a Western discourse on the grounds that childbearing is not a criminal act, but the natural right of a woman: she 'had her baby'. The sufferer is thus construed in complete harmony with Western imaginary. Amina is a Nigerian who acted as a Westerner would.

While this process of agentification takes place in language, the visuals propose a different subjectivity for this sufferer. Amina is traditionally dressed, seeks no eye contact with the camera and remains silent, listening to a man next to her. The Madonna icon is passive and voiceless. The language–visual tension projects ambivalence. This sufferer is both an agent and a powerless and silent human being. However, Amina's ambivalence differs considerably from the passivity of the drowning immigrants or starving children we encountered earlier. Hers is a passivity that is thoroughly familiar in a Western imaginary of femininity – it is the passivity of a woman who is persecuted simply for being a woman. Prior to being a Muslim, Amina is the victim of a patriarchal authority that oppresses her autonomy of choice and her wish to live. It is the liberal–humanist discourse of self-autonomy that resolves Amina's suspension between humanness and inhumanness, collapsing the distance between the Nigerian 'other' and the spectator. Amina's identity as a distant sufferer is ultimately domesticated by a 'universal' discourse of Western humanity.

Amnesty international, the 'Other' and 'us'

The aesthetic of pamphleteering establishes the cause – protesting against the Nigerian death by stoning verdict – by populating the scene of suffering with both a persecutor, voiceless and violent, and benefactors, one of which has a voice in the news report and calls for action.

The figure of the persecutor emerges in the mobbing scenes shown in the report, where we witness compelling images of a woman encircled and pushed around, her clothes torn apart as she tries to slip away. This persecutor already resides in Western imagery as a prototypical representation of the 'savage mind' – an alien disposition, devoid of (Western) humanity or morality. Indeed, the top-down shots of the mobbing scenes position the spectators as masters of the spectacle, observing it from maximal distance. There is no viewing from a position of relative proximity, as in the rescue mission, nor is there a face-to-face encounter, as in the piece on the famine. The spectators are now granted an overview from an authoritative position, but no engagement with the action.

In contrast, the sequence on the Amnesty International event places the spectators face-to face with the benefactor and obliges them to listen to his words. The Amnesty activist, like Amina, also has a name and a voice. In his talk, he calls for the 'denunciation *of everybody* against practices of stoning, humiliation, mutilation.' The reference to 'everybody' as taking-protest action considerably expands the definition of 'the benefactor' in this news item. For the first time, the figure of 'the benefactor' includes not only the specialist or the abstraction of a nation state but also individual spectators, who share the same respect for human life as the already existing 23,000 petitioners. The *signature* is an instrumental signifier in the democratization of beneficiary action – that is, rendering such action accessible to all. The simple act of signing the petition shows that effective speech against injustice can make a difference and this is close at hand. Many spectators have done that, any spectator can do it and all spectators should consider doing it.

With this home ground protest, we are a long way from simply watching the refugee rescue mission and certainly a world apart from the boat accident in India. The politics of pity in the genre of the news broadcast has formed a circle – though not a full one, yet. From adventuristic reports on irrelevant misfortunes, we are now into emergencies – people in danger, children suffering famine, a mother on death row. How, though, do such images qualify as requiring emergency action? Which 'universal' values do they manage to articulate in order to give rise to the public disposition of cosmopolitanism for the spectators who watch them?

Suffering with pity: the moral mechanism

Once we are removed from the obvious emergencies, such as the news on September 11th or the Bali bombings that bear clear links to the West, the question of what constitutes an emergency is an open matter. As Cohen reminds us, 'looking at the potential newsworthiness of atrocities and suffering alone, no matrix can accommodate the sheer mass of events, political contingency and the vagaries of fashion' (2001: 171).

Outrageous as it is, people dying on their way to safety hardly constitutes emergency news – 1000 illegal immigrants lost their lives on their way from Africa to Italy alone in 2002. Neither does famine always hit the headlines – in North Korea, an average of one million famine deaths are estimated to have occurred in the past three years. Equally, the loss of innocent life in the name of religion or political belief is routine in totalitarian regimes.[9] Long-term and complicated situations where suffering occurs can only make it to emergency news under certain conditions. They should either reassert their closeness to or relevance to a Western centre, and/or they should make a media-friendly and sensational story.[10] Sufferings, then, become emergencies on the condition that they fulfil the criteria of relevance and newsworthiness. These are precisely the criteria that the category of adventure news fails to fulfil. Although relevance and proximity to the West are not geographical 'givens' but semiotically construed dimensions of suffering, all three pieces of emergency news demonstrate an orientation towards the West, either by virtue of the event itself or active publicity, as in the work of Amnesty International. The refugees' boat was on its way to southern Europe, Hilda Duhalde's press conference was a global appeal for aid in Argentina and the Amnesty campaign was aimed at internationalizing the case of Amina's imminent death by stoning sentence.

The criterion of relevance, however, is a necessary, but not always sufficient, condition for an event to acquire emergency status. The sufficient condition for an emergency is the dramatic visualization of suffering.[11] Is there spectacular imagery relating to the scene of suffering? Can the visuals be framed in dramatic narration? Let us think of the news of the African refugees. Is it not legitimate to claim that their story reached the threshold of newsworthiness simply because images of the mission were made available? How else could we witness anything happening in such an unlikely location unless a camera was there? These African refugees were 'fortunate', unlike many others, in that their struggle for survival was captured on film. Emergency news participates in the production of a power topography of viewing relationships between those who watch in safety and those who are being watched in danger. However, unlike adventure news, which participates in this topography by producing a hierarchy of places and human lives, emergency news produces instead a hierarchy of action. Instrumental in this hierarchy is the possibility of visualizing action on the scene of suffering. Emergency news is, in this respect, less about the objective attributes of an event and more about the spectacular story that construes the event as worthy of spectators' immediate attention and engagement.

The spectator as actor

Action on television is always action at a distance. Nevertheless, emergency news does differentiate between proposals for discursive action (as in the cases of the rescue mission and the starvation victims) and proposals for practical action (as in the case of signing the petition). In all cases, it is the spectator as an *actor* that occupies the ideal viewing position for emergency news.

Below, I identify three hierarchically distinct positions for the spectator as actor in emergency news: the spectator as *voyeur*, as *philanthropist* and as *protester*.

The spectator as voyeur

In the rescue mission, we are confronted with the reality of intense action taking place right now in front of our eyes. We are witnesses of human misfortune as it peaks. Yet, the spectacular aesthetic of this piece of news qualifies the witness's position as one of a *voyeur*. This is the position of a witness who has been freed from the moral obligation to act and so can sit back and enjoy the high-adrenaline spectacle unfolding on the screen.

How can the voyeur act? The voyeur can contemplate in awe. The news footage captured a single moment of danger that could have led to great loss of life. It captures the irreducible singularity of any (potential) death. Indeed, it is one thing to imagine what it is like for hundreds of refugees to cross the rough sea in a small vessel and quite another to witness their struggle in close proximity. In magnifying this moment, the news inserted the representation of the rescue mission into an 'ecstatic' temporality – one that freezes ongoing action, magnifies the detail of suffering and compels the spectators to hold their breath and share the intensity of the experience. This is perhaps good enough. It already fulfils a certain moralizing function – the rare encounter of the safe spectators with the concrete reality of misfortune, even if this misfortune cannot become an object of their own action.

There is a moral deficit in the voyeur position however that we cannot ignore. Its cinematic emphasis on immediacy and adrenaline offers no horizon of historicity within which the massive displacement of refugees today can be understood as a pressing political and humanitarian issue. A brief comparison to national Danish television's (DR) news report on a similar incident less than a year later, on 20 June 2003, illustrates this point. The news was about a wooden vessel carrying illegal immigrants that capsized close to the shore of Tunisia on its way to southern Italy. The news presentation lacked vivid imagery but combined instead map graphics with on-location reporting and voiceover information on victims and survivors. More to the point, the report emphasized the humanitarian aspect of the issue by providing the figures for illegal immigrants entering Europe per year (1.5 million). The report also politicized the issue by connecting it to the EU Summit on the pending European immigration legislation, which, ironically, was taking place that same weekend in Greece.

The point of the comparison is to draw attention to a news story that, brief as it is, provided a useful interpretative context for the accident. In this story, the accident did not 'just happen' – it was connected to a current political reality, with its own policies and human costs. The news piece was still an emergency, in so far as it addressed the demand for immediate action. Tunisian fishermen figured as immediate benefactors on the scene of the suffering, whereas the European Union was referred to as the main long-term political actor. This is an emergency that departs from the 'logic of appearances' and denies the spectator the role of the voyeur. It becomes part of a 'logic of explanation', bringing to the fore the problem of the refugees' security and the controversy surrounding the European policies about receiving them. The 'logic of explanation' may not offer an alternative to practical action, but it decidedly transforms the spectators' disposition to this suffering by linking the event to the historical world and articulating it with the 'universal' of political responsibility. In so doing, this piece of news proposes a reflexive disposition that goes beyond observation and encourages spectators to consider the connectivity between their world of safety and the world of danger.

The spectator as philanthropist

In the piece on the famine in Argentina, we were interpellated by an explicit politics of gaze – the children's eye contact with the camera, then their bodies fading away in starvation. The moral position we are offered here is that of the philanthropist who cares for and, potentially, acts to relieve distant misfortune. Yet, there is no direct link between the individual spectator and the victims of the famine.

How, then, can the spectator as philanthropist act? The philanthropist can feel. We can feel tender-heartedness for the Argentinean sufferers and for the nation's own efforts to comfort the sufferers. We can also feel rage towards the USA for sending medical aid that was beyond its expiry date. The spectators' inability to act practically on the suffering is thus displaced, in the form of feeling potential, on to an agent that *does* have the power to act promptly from afar – the State. What we have here is a suggested relationship of philanthropy between states. States are humanized and treated as collective 'persons', having and provoking emotions. Argentina cries for and seeks solutions, whereas the USA's aid action provokes 'anger' – it is a state, it is implied, that should feel shame.

How far can the philanthropic aesthetic take us when moral action applies in interstate relationships rather than those between individuals?

Philanthropy is about feelings, not facts. It is about icons that move us, not arguments that persuade us. Philanthropy may succeed in striking a chord, but it says nothing about the causes of or solutions to the starvation crisis. Such causes are both internal to Argentina (political, administrative and economic)[12] and external to it (regulations imposed on Argentina's economy by the International Monetary Fund and its dominant partner, the USA).[13] Argentina's fight for survival in 2002 was, in fact, less of a fight about Hilda Duhalde's self-help government programmes and more about life-saving loans from the IMF. Philanthropy's preference for empathy, then, is achieved at a cost. The Argentinean crisis – chronic, complicated and global – is represented as sudden, simple and local.

As a consequence, what this piece of news leaves untouched is the role of international politics in the management of poverty. The spectator, then, rightly feels anger towards the USA – the benefactor failed to deliver its promise and assist a nation in need. However, the political content of this relationship does not become explicit in this piece of news and the general inadequacy of global agencies of governance to confront such crises today is not addressed in this piece of news either. In the symbolics of philanthropy, the political content of this piece of news is transformed into emotion – rage towards the USA's charity.[14]

As a result of this failure, the philanthropic aesthetic restricts the spectators' option to exercise a cosmopolitan sensibility. Effectively powerless to act at a distance, the spectators might at least have been able to turn their indignation into a political voice of protest. Speaking is action – it is symbolic action against the unjust management of world resources. By depriving spectators of the option to go beyond their immediate emotions, emergency news ultimately subordinates its duty to inform public opinion to easy sensationalism.

The spectator as protester

In the Nigerian emergency, it is precisely the public function of the news that takes over. The aesthetic quality of this news story is that of pamphleteering – a quality that sets up polemical antagonisms between political forces. The antagonism here is built around a series of symbolic contrasts between Islam and the West. The moral position that this aesthetic offers is that of the cosmopolitan citizen, who empathizes with Amina and publicly denounces her death sentence.

How can the citizen protester act? Empathy with the sufferer takes, in this news item, a form that neither the spectacular aesthetic of the rescue mission nor the philanthropic sentiment aroused by starving children have been able to achieve. This is the swing from observing and feeling to doing, in which the presence of Amnesty International plays a key role. The Nigerian news item, then, represents an important moment in the mediation of suffering as it demonstrates that emergency news can both articulate the demand for public action and invite the spectators as citizens to participate in it.

Useful and effective as it may be, however, the signing of a petition is minimal public action. In fact, we should regard the petition campaign as only one step in a broader hierarchy of action that scales up spectators' engagement in more demanding and more money- and time-consuming ways. This climaxing of the hierarchy of action – from simply watching and feeling to acting – makes the difference between *emergency* and *crisis* news. Whereas in emergency news there is an urgent but primarily discursive demand for action, in crisis news, urgency leads to more complicated and concrete resolutions. The clearest example of this is the tsunami emergency of December 2004.

Constant on-location footage was accompanied by details of bank account and phone numbers to be used by spectators to give financial support to the victims of the catastrophe. Telethons, music concerts and Red Cross initiatives were also promoted by the news, for the same purpose. Similarly, global channels such as CNN and BBC World promoted aid calls for the victims of the Iraq war in March 2003.

We may be tempted to question the adequacy of the spectator-as-actor to bring forth a cosmopolitan disposition – the disposition that connects the spectators with the distant 'others'. We may also be tempted to sneer at the efficiency of such forms of minimal action, perhaps rightly so. What can all this possibly offer to the massive and tragic sufferings of our world?

Let me postpone these grand questions for a while and turn now to a discussion of how emergency news uses a 'symbolics of threat' in order to work through the spectators' encounter with the 'otherness' of the sufferers. It is via this 'symbolics of threat' that a certain hierarchy of action is reproduced in this type of news.

The demand for reflexivity

There is a property which the sufferer in emergency news has that is crucial to the constitution of the cosmopolitan sensibility in all of them. This is the sufferers' ambivalence. The African refugees were both in danger and dangerous themselves; the Argentinean children were both vulnerable human beings and 'fetishized' body parts; the Nigerian woman was both a woman like 'us' and a voiceless 'other'. Caught in this ambivalent existence, the sufferers of emergencies are and are not endowed with humanness. They are and are not full and proper human beings. This inescapable 'otherness' of sufferers is, as I argued in Chapter 1, an inevitable effect of mediation, partly because it lacks the trust of face-to-face and the physical certainty of copresence.

The inescapable 'otherness' of sufferers is also a consequence of the semiotic choices of television. It is connected with the lack of historicity that characterizes the narratives of emergency news and removes each sufferer's misfortune from the flow of political, social and cultural life. The sufferers of emergencies have no past. As a result, their futures are something that we can only dimly grasp, if at all. Shipwreck, starvation, death by stoning belong to an order of misfortune that can only threaten the world 'out there'. The spectators only encounter them on their screens. Despite the claim that emergency news informs us about the realities of suffering, this is ultimately represented as mythic[15]. It is a realm of evil, fantasy and fear that appeals to the spectators' deep and subconscious cultural patterns and that practices of mediation both produce and address by virtue of the management of a 'symbolics of threat'.

No other example best illustrates the process of managing the threat of the 'other' than the news of the African refugees. The African people were met in mid-sea, confined to the deck of the coastguard's boat and shipped on to Malta under strict supervision, probably soon to be sent back to the countries they came from. Such compulsory, physical proximity with sufferers is not a desirable option because, as Boltanski says, it presents spectators with a threat and brings the mediation of suffering into a crisis. This means that no option for beneficiary action on the sufferers is possible, unless the necessary measures that protect the benefactor from the threat of the 'other' are portrayed in the scene of suffering.

How is the physical encounter between 'us' and the refugees symbolically managed on the television screen? The spectators, let us recall, are onlookers who remain on the edge of the scene of action, whereas the members of the rescue crew, inevitably in direct contact with the refugees, are shown to be wearing uniforms and masks and, on shore, carrying guns. It is this combination of signs of self-protection and latent aggression together with beneficiary action that make up the 'symbolics of threat' in emergency news.

Oscillating between the moral quest for action and the spectators' doxas and imaginary threats, emergency news keeps opening up the option of action, only to lock itself back in the zone of safe viewing. Paraphrasing Nichols, emergency news is less about engaging directly with the world and more about engaging with more news about the world (1991: 80). But if we hastily reject the emergency news' proposal for action as fake, we may end up with no other alternative than adventure news and its complete suppression of the option to act.

What I propose that we do instead is capitalize on the potential for emergency action already inherent in news broadcasts and imagine a different regime of pity where the sufferers, far from being the physical subjects of action, are themselves actors within the historical world – even if their agency is not capable of changing their lives. The best example of this is the news about the Nigerian woman. Amina Lawal is as close to a fully fleshed human being as it gets. She is both placed in a proper distance relationship to the spectators, by means of the multiple and mobile chronotopicity of the news, and endowed with a proper degree of humanity, due to her attributes of age and motherhood and the full choreography of figures of pity who surround her. Similarly, Nigeria is a living nation torn by religious rivalry and cultural tension. It is not accidental that it is this news story, and not the others, that confronts the spectators with the option for practical action.

The key to this representation of the sufferer is historicity. Historicity, in this context, does not mean a deep and comprehensive overview of the causal factors that are at play in the development of a particular event, but a minimal horizon of reference in which singular events can be understood as part of an interconnected environment, emerging out of rival forces in tension with each other – the global and the local, Islamic and Christian, rich and poor, powerful and powerless. In the narrative economy of the news, a sense of humble historicity evokes minor references to what may have caused a certain suffering or might change the condition of that suffering.

Conclusion

The appeal to action in emergency news is better than the indifference of adventure news. Yet, this appeal to action may well work as a symbolic vehicle that gestures towards a token engagement only with distant sufferers and, ultimately, feeds on the spectators' denial and fatigue. Instrumental in a regime of pity that humanizes sufferers and encourages reflexive spectators is the quest *to historicize the scene of suffering*.

In the next chapter, I examine the semiotic properties of a regime of pity that presents us with a very different sense of historicity than we have so far encountered. As a result, it also confronts us with sufferers we feel for and think of as 'our own'. This is history at its rarest, where time stands still and a minute seems to lasts a lifetime. This is ecstatic news.

Notes

1   These pieces come from Greek national television (23 July 2002 for the news of the African rescue and 8 November 2002 for the economic crisis in Argentina and the death by stoning sentence in Nigeria). I selected them because each piece gradually propels my main argument that there is an internal hierarchy

of emergency news on television and helps me illustrate this argument with clear examples. Although emergency news may seem to be particularly relevant to national contexts, which readily provide the concrete audiences for civil action, I would argue that the basic semiotic features of these examples are by no means idiosyncratic to national television. They are part of the broad repertoire for the public staging of suffering available in contemporary Western media, which includes both Danish television and the BBC World service. All emergency news plays out a politics of pity that incorporates the question of what to do, in various formulations, and makes humanitarian concern a key theme of the representation of suffering. I argue this on the basis of news on the Israeli–Palestinian conflict in July 2002 and the Liberian civil war in July 2003 shown on in BBC World (Chouliaraki, forthcoming).

2 See Calhoun (2005) for the term *emergency* and an insightful analysis of what he calls 'the emergency imaginary', defined as the dominant, media-induced perception of Western societies about what distant suffering is.

3 See Corner (1995: 61–3) and Nichols (1991: 21) for their thoughts, which are specifically on documentary but also applicable to news in so far as the effect of speech on image is an effect of authenticity and persuasion.

4 See Tester (2001: 90–2).

5 See Tester (2001: 80–1) for a discussion of 'particularization' as a rhetorical element that motivates 'compassion' in the news.

6 See Corner (1995: 61–2) for the concept of *propositionality* and its relationship to visual editing.

7 The distinction originates in Douglas's seminal work *Purity and Danger* (1966), but see also Bhabha (1983), Mercer (1994: 173–85) and Hall (1997: 225–79).

8 See Corner (1995: 63) for the *transfer effect* concept.

9 Calhoun (2005) offers a persuasive argument on the immense size of natural and human conflict disasters – the latter claiming a toll of more than 2.3 million lives within the past decade. Drawing on statistical data from the International Movement of the Red Cross and the Red Crescent in 'World Disaster Report' (2001), Calhoun also places the figures in a geography of power: 83 per cent of 'natural' disaster victims come from Asia, whereas human conflict disaster victims come from Africa, the Balkans and Central and Southern Asia.

10 See Golding and Murdoch (1991) for news selection. See also Cohen (2001: 173–7) and Morley (1998: 136–58, especially 136–43).

11 'Clear, dramatic pictures are the key to both "good television" and to the impact a given story will have on viewers' (Perlmutter, 1999: 2). Ellis (2000) goes as far as to say that the 'newness' of the image overrides all other criteria of worthiness: 'News is concerned with the images of its events that are as new as possible. All other criteria are secondary. So, the quality of the footage is hardly relevant: news will accept poor-quality images and poor-quality speakers of the immediacy and the importance of the events will justify them' (2000: 98).

12 For the internal chronic government trouble in Argentina, and the incapacity of the State to manage the crisis, see *The Economist*, 1 February, 2003 and BBC News's website (http: news.bbc.co.uk), search for 'Country profile: Argentina'. For an overview of Argentina's international debt, see *The Economist*, 25 January, 2003, and the *Global Exchange* website, five case studies on the IMF and World Democracy (www.globalexchange.org/campaigns/wbimf/imfwbReport 2001. html) and World Bank/IMF Factsheet (www.globalexchange.org/campaigns/wbim/facts.html).

13 Caught between the demand to assist a nation in starvation and the defence of its own economic interests, the IMF did push Argentina's dignity to the limit and, crucially, the nation's life standard, before agreeing 'in the last instance' to yet another life-saving loan. In fact, the national press described the IMF's delay on Argentina's request for new loans as 'outside all norms of respect and protocol' (*La Nacion*, Buenos Aires's daily newspaper, quoted on Third World Network's website, 27 August 2001).

14 This displacement – from politics to emotion – reveals an inherent undecidability in the philanthropic aesthetic as a whole. Its wish to single out a persecutor is often overriden by its desire to stir feelings of tender-heartedness. Relevant, here, is Boltanski's commentary on the topic of sentiment – which motivates philanthropy – as an inherently unstable topic:

> which, in order to provoke pity, must pick out the figure of persecutor and, then, abandoning the chase, shift attention towards the gentle emotions which move the unfortunate and touch the spectator.
>
> (1999: 94)

15 See Silverstone (1984: 388) for the *mythic* dimension of television narratives.

Appendix: Emergency News Verbal Texts

Rescue of African refugees at Malta

Top right graphic: **Rescue mission**

Long relatively erratic shot of small boat, wooden vessel with white flag, over-loaded with refugees in rough sea, floating on the side of police coastguard.

Voiceover: The wooden vessel crew has sent a SOS. A commercial boat nearby approaches the wooden vessel and protects it from the rough sea. The drama is taking place outside Malta, 44 miles off its coastline.

Longer shot from commercial boat, with size of police coastguard more in focus.

Voiceover: The rescue mission begins.

Shot from high deck of police coastguard filming down on lower deck. Sailors in action and the refugee boat floating aside.

Voiceover: The boat crew tie the wooden vessel with ropes and the first illegal refugees from Somalia and countries of Northern Africa begin to get on board the police coastguard.

Zoom on the coastguard deck. Refugees jumping in, leaving their boat; coastline police officers in protective white uniforms, hoods and face masks offering their hands in assistance.

Voiceover: As the wooden vessel starts to sink, they rush to get on to the big vessel, running the peril of finding themselves in the sea or crushed between the two vessels.

Zoom onto faces in the wooden vessel, onto those who have already jumped in the big boat; distinct voices speaking loudly. Momentary zoom on uniformed officers.

Voiceover: The coastguard men are trying to impose some order and the illegal refugees throw their poor luggage on the deck.

Medium (high deck) shot of refugees throwing their clothes and bags onto coastguard vessel.

Visual editing: Cut to shot of helicopter flying over the boats, with rescue staff tied with rope holding a refugee up in the air and being dragged up into the helicopter.

Voiceover: The helicopter's staff are forced to take action and some are dragged up by the rescue team with ropes. The mission lasted no less than sixteen hours because of bad weather and ended without any suprises.

Visual editing: Cut to long shot/zoom of empty vessel abandoned in rough sea. High deck shot of lower deck full of refugees lying or sitting down. Long shot of wooden vessel sinking – camera lens wet.

Voiceover: The 228 illegal refugees and the coastguard's crew, safe by now, are watching the wooden vessel being taken away and sinking, only a few minutes after their rescue.

Visual editing: Cut to coastguard shot from the ground as it is anchored in Malta port, at night.

Voiceover: As it is getting dark, the coastguard arrives at the port of the capital Valetta.

Zoom onto uniformed staff walking on deck, port police officers and military forces, with white masks and guns, escorting refugees off ship.

Voiceover: The Malta authorities believe that the small vessel had set off from Lybia, with Sicily as its destination. Insofar as the illegal refugees are concerned, unless they apply for asylum, they will be obliged to return to their country. Perhaps in order to begin yet again the dangerous journey towards a better life.

Visual editing: Cut to earlier shot of small boat full of refugees in rough sea. Studio.

Famine in Argentina

Studio: Argentina suffers the worst economic crisis in its history. In recent days, ten children died of hunger in the province of Tucuman in North Argentina.

Graphic: *They are dying of hunger*
*Visual editing: Cut to medium shot of **child facing camera**, by door step of brick house. Alternating frames, in medium shots or close-ups, of **children's faces in eye contact with camera**, some eating bread; fifth close-up, a severely under-nourished child crying; fourth frame, an emaciated child in hospital bed, with drips; fifth, sixth, seventh, eighth shots emaciated children, zooms on a leg and on a body, in medical environments; background sounds of child crying.*

Voiceover: Their gaze does not leave you space for complacence. In this corner of the planet, the children do not have the right to happiness and play, because they are struggling to survive. Images of terror. Argentina is crying for its children who fade away in hospitals because they have nothing to eat. Ten children died of hunger in the province of Tucuman. The numbers reveal the size of the tragedy. In Santa Anna sixty percent of the children suffer from malnutrition. Argentina is whirling around the worst economic vortex of recent years. A way out is desperately sought after. The President of the country, Eduardo Duhalde, has spoken of a rescue mission and of the strengthening of the social welfare state.

Visual editing: Cut to middle shot of Hilda Duhalde, at press conference: Si la gente participa, si la gente se organisa ... [*Greek translation in subtitles: If* citizens participate, if they organise themselves, if they get informed about this programme, for example, if a family is malnourished and is close to a health centre, then we'll be able to help].

Visual editing: Cut to two adults looking into rubbish bags at street corner, at night. But it will be very difficult for the Argentineans to stand on their feet. Miserable people who look for food in restaurant rubbish bags are a familiar image in the big cities.

Visual editing: Cut to customs office interior. Officers open up boxes with medicine bottles in them; they looked expired: In the meantime, the rage of the Customs Director was provoked by the humanitarian help sent by the USA, which contained medicine beyond its expiry date.

Nigerian case of death by stoning

Shot of Nigerian court interior: turquoise wall colours, cement floor, wooden bench, where Amina Lawal in traditional African clothing with head covered and holding her baby comes to sit, facing higher platform with three judges behind desks.

Light blue bar: Reportage, journalist's name.

Top right graphic on screen: No to death by stoning. Voiceover: The verdict of death by stoning against the Nigerian woman, Amina Lawal, two months ago, has shocked international public opinion. *During voiceover: Cut to medium shot of the Nigerian woman with baby on her lap and a male figure on her right talking to her. Zoom to baby. Graphic persists.*

Despite the assertions of the Minister of Justice that the young mother won't be stoned, the final decision will be taken by the sharia court, which applies the Islamic law.

Cut to street shot of group of people mobbing, hitting and tearing the clothes of a woman trying to get away from them. Graphic persists.

Voiceover: That the young Nigerian woman had her baby outside marriage gave to sharia the right to apply the inhumane laws.

Cut to street shot of Nigerian embassy entrance in Greece where activists have set up a construction out of paper boxes containing a petition of 23,000 signatures against the woman's stoning. Activists hand boxes with signatures to Embassy official, at the building's entrance.

Voiceover: This afternoon, outside the Nigerian Embassy, members of Amnesty International built a pyramid of dignity with the 23,000 signature petition for the abdication/saving of Amina.

Male Greek activist makes a statement, with background of paper box pyramid: 23,000 Nos to Stoning. Light blue bar: Member of 'Amnesty International', name: … but also as a reaction and condemnation of everybody against practices of stoning, humiliation, mutilation.

Cut to another Nigerian woman, probably in court headquarters, making her way through group of Nigerians with female lawyer on her side.

Voiceover: Last March, another Nigerian woman, the thirty-five year old Safila Huseini, accused of unfaithfulness in marriage, had been condemned to death by stoning. In the last minute, after international denunciations, the woman escaped death.

Back to street shot of Nigerian woman amongst group of people mobbing and hitting her, trying to get away.

Voiceover: The inhumane law was applied in the past two years in twelve provinces of Northern Nigeria and only among the Muslim population.

Return to studio. Let us now move to the Athens Courts, where…

7

ECSTATIC NEWS: SUFFERING AND IDENTIFICATION

Some events are so extraordinary that they cannot be contained in an ordinary news broadcast. Their footage belongs to a special category of news that I call 'ecstatic'. My example of ecstatic news is the September 11th terrorist attacks. I focus on three extracts from the footage, all of which took place during the first two and a half hours in which the news broke.[1] The first extract is from a telephone link between the news studio and the Danish Consulate in New York, accompanied by random street shots from Manhattan just after the Twin Towers collapsed. The second extract is an update on the events of the morning, with shots from the second plane collision and President Bush's first public statement. The third extract is a long shot of the Manhattan skyline burning, with verbal commentary from the DR studio's expert panel.

Each extract enacts a specific mode of representing suffering, a specific topic of suffering. The first evokes empathy with the sufferers, the second is a denunciation of the persecutors and the third an aesthetic contemplation of the spectacle of suffering. I argue that these alternating topics and their genres are characteristic of live footage, the master genre of instantaneous and global transmission. As a result, the live footage establishes a regime of pity and a manner of moralizing the spectator that we have not encountered so far. The moral disposition of the live footage is grounded in a sense of space–time as *ecstatic*, in a conception of the sufferers as *sovereign agents* on their own suffering and in a relationship of *reflexive identification* between these sufferers and the spectators.

Suffering as ecstatic

The question as to what type of news the September 11th coverage is does not meet with a straightforward response. It is not 'news', in the sense of being neatly contained in television's usual daily schedule. It overflows the genre. Nor is it a media event for, although it interrupted our viewing routines to confront us with the extraordinary, it is not a coronation, a conquest or a contest (Dayan and Katz, 1992). It overflows these genres, too, while sharing with them a transformative quality.[2]

What makes the September 11th coverage interesting as a media phenomenon is its undecidability. At the centre of this undecidability lies a dialectic of openness and closure, a dialectic with space and time dimensions. In terms of space, the event is mediated simultaneously as a local tragedy and as a global political fact. In terms of time, the event is mediated simultaneously as contingent, as news, and as making history.[3] I use the term *ecstatic* to refer precisely to this undecidability that brings the event and space–time together in a unique and rare relationship to one another. Ecstatic time breaks with the ordinary conception of time as a succession of 'now' moments and presents us with *truly historic* time: 'moments when a minute lasts a lifetime, or when a week seems to fly by in next to no time. This is what Heiddegger calls "ecstatic temporality", or time taking place in its authentic moment of ek-sistence' (Barker, 2002: 75).

This last formulation of the ecstatic perceptively captures the spectator's shock and disbelief at the moment when the second plane crashed into the World Trade Centre – a moment 'when a minute seems to last a lifetime'. In fact, it is the whole September 11th event that can be described as ecstatic because it did confront us with this different sense of time, the fleeting disquietude that makes us wonder 'how a particular event can be properly accounted for' (Barker, 2002: 75). Ecstatic news, in this sense, is that which seeks to resolve the radical undecidability of the event it reports during the act of reporting itself.[4]

My analysis of the September 11th news takes the liminal quality of the event as its point of departure. Although ecstatic news shares the demand for action with emergency news, the two categories differ drastically in their overall representation of suffering and, therefore, in the ways in which each organizes the ethical relationship between the spectators and the sufferers. I describe the distinction between emergency and ecstatic news in terms of three major shifts in the representation of suffering.

- The generic move from news broadcast to live footage. This is the move from a conventional news narrative – punctuated by single, finite and unrelated pieces of news – to a constant flow of images and verbal narratives with various degrees of affective power. This flow enables the spectators to engage in multiple topics of suffering and so empathize, denounce and reflect on the suffering.
- The move from the emergency chronotope – that is, from concrete, specific, multiple and mobile space–times – to an ecstatic chronotope. This entails a temporality that places suffering both in the order of 'lived' experience and that of historical rupture and a spatiality that connects this specific suffering to the globe as a whole, making 'humanity' the simultaneous witness of that suffering.
- The move from conditional agency to sovereign agency. Sovereign agency construes each actor in the scene of suffering as a thoroughly humanized and historical being – somebody who feels, reflects and

acts on his or her fate. Specifically, sovereign agency entails three typical features:

- the sufferers and benefactors coincide – Americans rescue American victims
- the sufferers are in a position to both mourn for their suffering and analyse it – ordinary people and journalists
- the sufferers have the capacity to respond to the persecutors' infliction of suffering on themselves – politicians and military experts.

- This construal of the sufferer as a sovereign being is instrumental in further construing the relationship between Western spectator and sufferer as a relationship of *reflexive identification*, whereby the spectator engages with the misfortune of the sufferer continuously, intensely and on multiple occasions.[5] It is this relationship of identification that subsequently enables the emergence of a *universal* moral stance vis-à-vis the September 11th event and, at least partly, legitimizes the political project of the 'war against terror' that followed it.

I begin with live footage as a genre of mediation that is related to the function of *witnessing* – each extract from the footage making its own distinct claim as a witnessing of the event. It is the successive articulation of these three claims to witnessing in the flow of the footage that constitute the event as an ecstatic chronotope with sovereign agency.

The live footage

Live footage is the genre of the witness, par excellence. Witnessing relies on the instantaneous presence of the camera at the scene of the action – a presence that is instrumental in live news's claim to factuality, to showing things as they really are.[6] The camera claims to be there when the event actually happens and brings back home the rawness and contingency of the event as it unfolds. This 'mechanical witness', however, needs to be combined with verbal narratives that harness the rawness of the event and domesticate its 'otherness'. This is the work of the various subgenres of the live footage – subjective testimonies, objective summaries and reflective commentaries. Such genres seek to explain the event for the spectators and protect them from the act of witnessing. The three September 11th extracts illustrate how each subgenre of the live footage makes use of images and talk in order to present the scene of suffering as a cognitively intelligible and emotionally manageable television spectacle.

Dayan and Katz refer to media events that act as catalysts for change on our certainties and commonsensical truths as *transformative events*.[7] Although the authors emphasize the ritual aspects of these events – such as the assassination of John F. Kennedy and his funeral – I would argue that September 11th is also a transformative event. It shares with ceremonies 'the moment of interruption of routinized social time', which, as Dayan and Katz claim, 'stops history in its tracks' (1992: 60–1).

At the same time, the September 11th footage differs from ceremonies. Far from a predictable ritual, the footage worked in the opposite way. It provisionally cancelled the 'breaking news' routines that usually manage the contingency of live transmission and made the audience witness the breaking of television conventions themselves.[8]

The ecstatic quality of the September 11th news is contained, I believe, in this dual act of witnessing – that is, the spectators witness the breaking down of journalistic conventions as a result of the breaking down of the reality norms themselves. It was the reversal of space–times that tore the tissue of normality and forced us to come to terms with a new thinkable. The attacks in New York and Washington DC reversed the dominant space–time of the 'centre', which was the space–time of safe viewing, and the 'periphery', which was the space–time of dangerous living. It is now the West witnessing the West suffer.

To be sure, Western television varied considerably in the ways in which it reported the event. For European television, for example, this was evidently an across-the-Atlantic piece of news.[9] Yet, the live footage established a degree of proximity to this across-the-Atlantic space and a degree of identification with the American sufferers that we have not encountered so far. The West, as a cultural and political imagined community, rendered the United States a sufferer like 'us' and Europe a potential sufferer just like 'them'.

Such extreme instances of identification are typically associated with the aggregate function of the live footage. As we recalled in Chapter 1, this is the function of television that enables people to vibrate together, to create a non-present communion. Whereas, for Mafessoli among others, tele-sociality has no explicit political function, my analysis of September 11th coverage as ecstatic news shows that a more complicated spectatorship is produced in the course of the live footage – a hybrid subjectivity that does not neatly fit into the categories of either pure information or pure pleasure. Let us examine the 'direct link with New York', the 'update' of events and the 'Manhattan skyline long shot', taking a close look at their multimodal affordances and the space–time and agency options they make available to spectators.

The 'direct link with New York': empathy

Multimodal narrative

- *Mode of presentation:* psychological realism.
- *Visual–verbal correspondence:* iconic meaning.
- *Aesthetic quality:* testimonial documentary.[10]

Psychological realism
In a six-minute long sequence, the coverage is of a telephone link between
the news studio in Copenhagen and the Danish Embassy in New York.
The anchorman interviews the Embassy Consul, who describes the situation as a witness, expresses his personal feelings and evaluates the event's
longer-term consequences. The visual frame is the studio's interior with
the anchorman and a two-person expert panel.

Space–time: Instantaneous proximity

Almost halfway through, this frame is briefly interrupted, twice, to move to street shots from Manhattan. The main features of the Manhattan visuals are random shots, erratic camera movements, imperfect focus and framing, the camera lens covered with white dust. The reality of suffering that this mode of presentation proposes is psychological realism. This is because we obtain access to the reported event via the witness's verbal account. His experience, his feelings and his thoughts shape our contact with the event. His reality becomes our reality and his emotions touch on and provoke our own sensibilities.

Narrative cohesion is established primarily by means of the anchorman's questions and the witness's responses. The visuals do not interact with the verbal text and, therefore, do not interrupt the flow of talk. Running parallel to the talk, the visuals complement and frame the Consul's dramatic narration. Indeed, the position of the camera, in the thick of the action, is itself 'involved'. It provides the spectator with the participants' point of view. Via these random shots the spectators become the eyewitnesses of a drama that unfolds in real space and time.

Iconicity

The main semiotic mode of this telephone link is the verbal. The Consul's talk consists of description and exposition. Description is present in the Consul's vivid accounts of vehicle alarms howling, hospitals on emergency and bridges closing down, as well as those of the authorities doing their best to assist victims and inform the wider public.

Exposition is present in the Consul's emotions and fears about the consequences of the event in expressions such as 'dramatic', 'impossible to overview', 'very touched by the situation', 'very concerned', and it is, partly at least, triggered by the anchorman's question: 'You are the General Consul updating us on the terrible events in the USA, but you are also a human being. How does it feel to witness such a terrible catastrophe?' The Consul's response is emotional: 'worry', 'deep anxiety', 'for the political consequences of all of us'. At the same time, the random shots appearing on the screen project an unstaged reality. Through them, we enter the concrete, almost tangible, reality of Manhattan. The omnipresence of dust and ashes; scattered bits and pieces of brick, stone, concrete; people, covered in dust, walking or running away; professionals with helmets on, suggesting that relief work is already under way. Indeed, other shots show ambulances, fire brigades and municipality workers setting up street barriers. There is no correspondence between these visuals and the verbal text to anchor the Consul's narration on to specific images.

The verbal–visual link is not indexical. Rather, the two hang together in a loose relationship of iconicity, with the image illustrating the aura of danger and disorder that the verbal narrative evokes. In this sense, the Consul's dramatic talk is, at once, condensed within and expanded on in the images of chaos in the Manhattan streets.

Testimonial documentary

The Consul's voice enters the studio as a credible witness, if not of the actual event itself then at least of the aura that surrounds it. His verbal testimony is valid by virtue of his relative proximity to the scene of the suffering. The camera gains its testimonial status as an eyewitness by virtue of being 'mechanical' and, therefore, capable of objective recording. The two testimonies, verbal and visual, are used in combination to provide an accurate record of the event and document facts as well as emotions. Indeed, I chose to use the term 'testimonial' documentary for this footage sequence precisely because it brings together both subjective and objective witness perspectives in one narrative.

The aesthetic quality of this witness genre stems from, what Peters calls, 'the two faces' of witnessing: the passive one of seeing and the active one of saying. The spectator is both called to consume images of raw reality, recorded by technology, and invited to engage with the deep feelings and thoughts of the person who witnesses – the Consul.[11] As Boltanski puts it, it is not enough for the spectator to witness the suffering as an objective fact: 'at the same time he [sic] must also return to himself, go inwards and allow himself to hear what his heart tells him' (1999: 81). This release of emotion that the coupling of the two faces of the witness allows the spectator to experience is instrumental in the evocation of empathy. Unlike the topic of denunciation, which mobilizes indignation towards the unfairness of the event, empathy rests precisely on such an explication of emotion, on the 'universal' value of human life. The Danish Consul functions, in this context, as that agent of pity who exteriorizes his inner feelings and shares his sorrow and agony for the misfortunes of the American people with the European spectators back home.

Space–time: Instantaneous proximity

Which space–time are we entering here? The involved camera moves us right there, into the scene of suffering, right now as events are unfolding. This is a space–time of *instantaneous proximity* – the space–time par excellence of witnessing and the 'direct link' genre. Simultaneously, this same projection of unstaged reality in real time gives us a sense of distance from the scene. This is evident, for example, in the ways in which the very technology of the mediation makes itself visible – the camera is covered in dust, the satellite transmission fails for a brief moment, there are no sound-effects – which cleanses the sense of presence in the scene of action, and finally, the visual environment of the screen frames the spectacle with other signs, such as the broadcasting channel's logo and the screen bar. All these visible traces of technology foreground the hypermediated properties of the spectacle. In thematizing the textual quality of the footage, these traces also accentuate the spectators' awareness of watching television rather than 'being there'.[12] Indeed, we are called to witness suffering, yet we are made acutely aware of our own situatedness. We are watching it from home, with plenty of time to comment on and analyse it as we inhabit the space–time of safety, of the 'centre'. Given the distance that separates the spectators from the 'there', how is the problem of their action on the sufferer resolved? Who is represented as acting on the screen? Which is the topic of suffering that organizes the options for action in the 'direct link'?

Agency: the presence of a benefactor and the 'universal' value of humanity

There are two elements in the direct link that suggest the September 11th event is constituted via the topic of empathy. First, there is the figure of the benefactor and, second, there is the move towards the 'universal' value of common humanity.

The figure of the benefactor emerges in the course of the act of double witnessing – the witnessing of the camera, with its random images, and the oral witnessing of the Danish Consul in New York. The ambulances, the fire engines, the closing of the bridges and the hospital emergencies constitute a collective agent who is present in all 'first aid' operations. The benefactor, then, is not an individual person but a generic category, visualized and linguistified as the resource for alleviating the suffering in a context of frantic activity and at a time when instant action needs to be taken. Unlike emergency news, where the sufferer and the benefactor belonged to different worlds, here the benefactors are part of the same space–time as the sufferers. They act on the spot and under dangerous and still unstable conditions.

The second characteristic of the topic of empathy is the 'universal' value of common humanity. This is openly expressed by the Consul when he is called on to evaluate the consequences of the event. In his response, he shifts from a descriptive 'they', for the sufferers, to an all-inclusive 'we', which refers to humanity as a whole. Spectators and sufferers appear here connected in a common fate, sharing the same destiny. The future of the globe is uncertain: 'we don't know how it will escalate [...] worry, deep anxiety, deep political consequences for all of us'.

This attention to 'what we all share' is another crucial trait of the topic of empathy because, for this sentiment to properly appeal to the emotions of the spectators, it has to make the leap from the particular to the 'universal', from the instance of suffering to a contemplation of common values that this suffering brings to the fore. The moralizing function of this move lies in inviting the spectator to engage with the sufferer not as a cultural 'other' but a 'universal' being endowed with a humanity like 'ours' and reflect on their suffering as, ultimately, part of our common fate as human beings. The topic of empathy is, in Boltanski's words, a 'strong "gesture of humanity"' that recognizes and formulates 'the common interest which links the one it touches to others' (1999: 92).

The update: denunciation

Multimodal narrative

- *Mode of presentation:* perceptual realism.
- *Visual–verbal correspondence:* indexical meaning.
- *Aesthetic quality:* historical documentary.

Space–time: Omnipresence in immediate past

Perceptual realism

This is a two-minute text put together to provide Danish spectators with a chronology of events up to the time of this broadcast and it was inserted into the flow of the live footage at regular intervals.

It is primarily a visual text that capitalizes on the enormous news value of some of the September 11th shots. It begins with shots from the first burning tower, then shows the second plane crashing, cuts to Bush's first public statement in Georgia before showing the two towers collapsing, it then moves to Washington and shows the Pentagon burning. The verbal text includes no commentary, no evaluation. It consists only of time and space details of the events, information on the flight number and route of those planes involved as well as the passenger numbers on board. President Bush's statement is not quoted or reproduced but directly shown.

The reality of the suffering that this mode of presentation proposes to us is framed by perceptual realism. What we see on screen is verbally located in space and time as it is named and sequenced in a stream of intelligible events. Narrative cohesion is, thus, woven through the bulletin by means of a voiceover that connects the disparate pieces of video footage to form a single news story.

Indexical meaning

The bond between image and talk is now indexical. Language follows the image, contextualizing and illustrating what we see. As we saw in Chapter 6, indexicality plays a key role in authenticating the image of suffering. However in the case of September 11th, the indexical reference acquires further significance because of the initial disbelief everyone experienced as they watched this particular spectacle of terror unfold. Watching the plane crash into the tower is not enough. We need to be told, repeatedly, that indeed a plane crashed into the second World Trade Centre tower and be given details of the when, how and who. For this liminal experience to acquire meaning, it has to be referred on to the historical world, to be connected to the everyday world of unfolding events around us. Similarly, the authenticity of the images is derived less from the force of the images themselves (this might have been a Hollywood movie sequence, as many observed) and more from the strictly informative journalistic discourse that frames it, which turns these unreal pictures into evidence of a real event.

Historical documentary
I use the term 'historical' in order to capture the ambivalent status of the update of events. I propose that we see the update not only as a recurrent part of the live footage but also as television's first attempt to constitute the event as 'history'. The update is, in this sense, an attempt to contain the excess of the event in a neat narrative and render it part of a past that we urgently need to articulate in order to act on it.[13] Witnessing is central to this process, just as it was in the direct link but there is a different twist.

Witnessing now does not entail the subjective perspective, the 'involved' point of view, but is distantiated and uninvolved. The video footage moves from context to context and the camera's gaze consists mostly of isolated long shots that register events as they happen – the plane crashing or the Pentagon burning, for example. Although other shots, such as the towers collapsing, are filmed by a camera on the street below, showing a reporter in shock or people in panic, they never adopt a subjective perspective. Human reactions add an aura of authenticity to the documentation of these facts, but they do not contaminate with emotion the strict objectivity of the documentation.

This is due to the function of the verbal mode. The voiceover is strictly descriptive. It consists of short, informational sentences, pauses and the verbatim repetition of Bush's statement. There is no overt interpretation, explanation or expression of feeling. Furthermore, the voiceover uses the past tense, which disconnects the events from the present time, and includes meticulous time and location references, which further render it an accurate reconstruction of the past. The aesthetic quality of this historical documentary is that of a 'grand narrative'. It assumes that past events can be mastered, registered faithfully and recounted in their factual details before they begin to be interpreted or evaluated. The spectators of this historical documentary are witnesses of 'History', with a capital 'H', social agents who engage with the past in order to comprehend the present and act on the future.

Space–time: omnipresence in the immediate past

The update situates the spectator in a *space of omnipresence* – everywhere the camera takes us (Manhattan, Georgia, Washington DC and the Pentagon) – at the *time of the immediate past* – that same morning of September 11th.

As we saw, this is a space–time of witnessing, but one that does not occur within a 'real space, real time' perspective, activating empathy with the sufferers. Rather, the witnessing of suffering now takes place from alternating positions that provide the spectators with a standpoint of *a-perspectival objectivity*. This form of objectivity – which, as the terminology intimates, makes possible the act of observation as if it occurs from no particular perspective – is crucial in conferring on television representations the legitimacy of the public sphere because it hides its own specificity.

A-perspectival, however, by no means implies a perspective from nowhere. Rather, a-perspectival means a series of chronotopic shifts that move the spectators through multiple concrete and specific space–times and give them the illusion of 'everywhereness'. This is the achievement of visual editing that juxtaposes disparate images and of a voiceover that brings them together in an story of 'this is what happened'.

It is precisely in its capacity to appear to be objective information that the update is a key genre for the topic of denunciation. In appealing to pure facts, the update echoes a courtroom discourse that judges and condemns the persecutor on the basis not of emotion but hard evidence.

Agency: evocation of the persecutor and the call for justice

The two elements that constitute the September 11th footage in terms of the topic of denunciation are the figure of the persecutor and the claim to justice. The persecutor is faceless and will remain largely invisible, even though eventually the persecutor will be given a face. Nonetheless, the persecutor, as the causal agent of suffering, is already evoked in this text. The semiotic technology is the visual editing. The second plane crash is shot with filmic spectacularity, the camera fixing on the tower for several seconds after the plane exploded, with no verbal text, and then the report cuts directly to Bush's first public statement from Georgia. The presidential address begins by condensing the national sentiment – 'today we've had a *national tragedy*' – and locating the source of evil 'in an apparently *terrorist* attack against our country'. As a consequence of the editing, the visual and the verbal are woven together in an anaphoric link – a link whereby Bush's speech 'looks back' and refers to the plane crash itself. This intertextual link succeeds in evoking the figure of a persecutor in the reference to terrorism and in organizing the spectators' feeling potential around the cruelty and unfairness of the persecutor's act – the 'terrorist attack'.[14]

The evocation of the persecutor is closely related to another one of denunciation's properties – the appeal for justice. This is formulated in the concluding part of the address, in the President's promise 'to hunt down those folks who committed this act'. The President articulates here the collective expectation that justice will be done for these crimes.

This call for justice is not devoid of emotion. On the contrary, it plays on strong feelings of shock, anger and indignation. Yet, the emotional potential of denunciation is carefully formulated to appear devoid of blind passion. Rather, the presidential address connects the call for justice to a rational assessment of the facts – '*two planes crashed on the WTC* in an, apparently, terrorist attack against our country' – and regulates the pursuit of justice by means of coordinated and calculated action: 'I have talked to the *Vice-president*, the *Governor of New York*, the *Director of the FBI*'. In this manner, the aura of strict objectivity that marks the voiceover in the update also surrounds the President's statement.

Both texts manage the shift from *indignation* (the national sentiment) to *denunciation* (the appeal for justice) by carefully backgrounding the personal emotionality of the speakers. In this manner, the discourse of denunciation, Boltanski says, 'appears at the same time indignant and meticulous, emotional and factual' (1999: 68).

Unlike empathy, which rests on the explication of emotion and a 'universal' value of humanity, the moral horizon of denunciation is undercut by a 'universal' appeal for justice. The promise to restore justice by 'hunting down' the persecutor contains a further promise – that of practical action. This disposition to act practically on the inflictor of the suffering, anticipated as it is in the USA's doctrine of retaliation, led to the 'war against terror' in Afghanistan a month later.

The Manhattan skyline: sublime

Multimodal narrative

- *Mode of presentation:* ideological realism.
- *Visual–verbal correspondence:* iconic/symbolic meaning.
- *Aesthetic quality:* reflexive contemplation.

Ideological realism

This text is an eight-minute shot of the Manhattan skyline burning, which is an unusually long piece of film for television, that is taken from a

Space–time: Anatopism and Anachronism

distance. We are given plenty of time to visually study this overview of
the scene of suffering. The image takes us away from the here and now of
the direct link, as well as from the everywhere in the immediate past of the
update. We are now looking at the scene as if it were a painting, depicting
'still action'. As with a panoromic painting, we are in fairly close proximity and can see everything there is to see. The temporality is an *eternal
present* without contingency or evolution. This is the time of reflection
and analysis. The voiceover consists of the Danish expert panel talking,

speculating on possible causes, commenting on international reactions and evaluating political consequences. This is talk that, in a similar way to the visual element, distances us from the specificities of the lived environment and functions as a 'macro' perspective on the history and politics of the event.

I use the term 'ideological' realism not to describe the existence of pro- or anti-American propaganda in the footage but, rather, to draw attention to a form of realism that attempts to render intelligible a hitherto para-doxical spectacle. 'Ideological' here, then, refers to the function of the panel's talk, which is to invest with meaning an event still awaiting inter-pretation, to construe a new thinkable by drawing on existing discourses of history and politics. This type of realism is not interested in the reality of objective truth (the update), nor in the reality of the emotions (the direct link), but in the reality of discursive argument and rationalization. Thus, ideological realism is the only form of realism that poses questions about the historical causes of the event and its longer-term consequences for the established world order.

Iconic/symbolic meaning

Long shots universalize. They abstract from indexical, context-specific meaning and foreground the iconic. The image of this sequence is generic, though obviously there are particularizing elements, such as the recog-nizable Manhattan skyline. In its generic form, the image works as an icon representing one 'prototypical' space: the contemporary metropolis with its high buildings, modern architecture and dense volume. Ideological realism, however, requires that the image operates on yet another level of meaning – namely, symbolic meaning.

Symbolic meaning, you will recall, comes about when images are used to mobilize a culturally specific set of beliefs – this specificity being taken for granted as natural and universal and, therefore, beyond discussion. In the film of the skyline, the visuals of the city in grey smoke are not addressed as such, but, as in Chapter 6, the move from iconic to symbolic meaning occurs as a result of visual *juxtaposition*, which here is the manner in which the screen layout contextualizes the sight of the cityscape as 'New York' or 'the USA in a state of war'. This long shot becomes symbolic, then, at the point when the graphic framing of the cityscape comes to signify a new thinkable – the 'centre' under attack. The paradoxical quality of this representation stems from the tacit – and therefore all the more powerful – rationality that the centre is immune, invincible.

The ideological work of the extract is accomplished via two specific meaning operations that reverse this certainty and push the spectators' imagination towards a novel conception of spatial and temporal relationships. These are what I examine below as the chronotopic effects of 'anatopy' and 'anachronism'.

Reflexive contemplation

The aesthetic quality of this genre is that of the tableau vivant – the depiction of still action that lends itself to aesthetic appreciation. The camera's gaze centres on the fumes covering the city and, simultaneously, couples two image themes – the grey sky and the clear turquoise seawater. In aesthetic terms, the camera couples the horror and awe of the sublime with the domesticity and friendliness of the beautiful. These two elements visually cohere on the basis of a set of equivalential contrasts:

- landscape – land in smoke and peaceful water
- colour – grey and turquoise
- activity – obscure, suggestive in land and explicit, readily available to vision in water.

Indeed, it appears as if the boat activity is oblivious to, rather than interacting with, mayhem in the city. In this manner, the visual medium establishes contemplation in relation to the spectacle of suffering. The feeling potential of such contemplative proximity is displaced neither on to the benefactor nor on to a persecutor – it stays with us as an experience of aesthetic indulgence. This is what Boltanski discusses as the *sublimation* of suffering, whereby the scene of distant misfortune appears as a source of aesthetic pleasure for the spectators. This occurs in a double movement. There is an initial movement of horror, when the spectators are confronted with the shocking immediacy of destruction on their television screens. Yet, precisely because this shock is experienced in the safety of their homes, it is then transformed into a second movement of relief, when the spectators sit back and contemplate the horrific in a manner that they could never have done had they been at the scene of action themselves.[15]

Space–time: anatopism and anachronism

Even though the sublime entails the possibility of a radical rejection of pity, in fact, this aesthetic register does moralize the spectator, but in a different way from the previous two topics. Moralization here occurs through symbolic meaning. If the camera abstracts from the particular to project an aestheticized view of the city as an icon, the television graphics and the voiceover particularize this abstraction: 'New York' today.[16] This semiotic combination, as I have argued, works symbolically in so far as it brings into focus the 'centre'–'periphery' inversion – the invincible centre in mayhem. What I now focus on are two strategic inversions that the visual thematization of the 'centre' as a sufferer allows: an inversion in time – *anachronism* – and an inversion in space – *anatopism*.[17]

On the axis of time, the unfolding actuality of the information bars on the screen combined with the eternal presence of the tableau vivant evoke a new temporal context for the representation of suffering in the 'centre' – that of Pearl Harbour and the sudden attacks against the US fleet by the Japanese airforce, which triggered the USA's involvement in World War II.[18] The effect of anachronism is precisely to produce, on present events, a past reference and thus link the two in the eternal flow of history. Is this a 1941 déjà vu? The 'depth' thus attributed to the present event contextualizes it in a discourse of the national past as a recurrent motive that, yet again, requires a response, though the nature of the response – retaliation, as then, or diplomacy – is an open matter.

On the axis of space, the graphic specification of the scene of suffering as 'New York' combined with the long shot of the smoking skyline evoke a new spatial context for the representation of suffering in the 'centre' – that of *any* Western metropolis. The effect of anatopism is to establish equivalence among disparate locales, thus producing a new configuration of possible connections among them. Here, 'New York' as the sufferer becomes a crucial signifier, connecting the space of dangerous living with the space of safety inhabited by other cities in the 'centre'. If this is possible there, which place will be next? The spectators engage with this space as potential sufferers themselves. Anatopism, then, introduces into this sublimated representation of distant suffering a new dimension of proximity – proximity as vulnerability. The European spectators feel that this experience may now well become their own.[19]

Agency: *the reflexivity of the spectator*

The complicated space–time of the sublime, with its anachronistic and anatopic effects, construes a moral horizon that is radically different from either of those seen in the previous topics. Due to the absence of a benefactor or persecutor – so freeing spectators from the urgent obligation to feel certain emotions that they would arouse in them – the sublime rests on the spectators' reflexive contemplation of the scene of suffering. Reflexive contemplation, in this context, should not be understood as an exclusively sociocognitive capacity, as a pure state of mind. Here it also entails a strong psychological dimension, to the extent that the sheer spectacularity of the terror makes an impact on the spectators' fantasy. *Fantasy* in this context is a particular form of pleasure derived from the viewing relationship as the safe spectators are stimulated to project themselves into scenarios of violence and fear that are highly improbable in their real lives.[20] In a similar way to the horrific phantasmagoria of the sublime, which nonetheless is not deprived of a certain political potential, fantasy, too, is not only about play, escapism and the 'forgetting' of suffering but also a certain form of moral engagement:

'perhaps,' as Silverstone puts it, 'the play can, on occasion, be a rehearsal for the real: a practice' (1999: 65).

Indeed, anatopism and anachronism carve out a 'What if?' mode of engagement with the event, whereby proximity as vulnerability emerges in the interface between fantasy and reflexivity. Reflexive contemplation can thus be understood as the effect of a semiotic arrangement, which turns the scene of suffering into a passive object of the spectators' gaze and the spectators into gazing subjects aware of their own act of seeing and feeling. Crucial, now, for the moralization of the spectators is the fact that this arrangement entails neither empathy nor indignation, but emotion distantiated from the sufferers.[21] The implication of this emotional distance from the sufferers is this: the spectators are given the option to make links between the September 11th and other temporal and spatial contexts and so evoke points of contact with the past and with the rest of the world.

Although both links belong to predictable discourses of Western history and politics, it is crucial to notice that the space for a reflexive and analytical exercise is opened up. It is perhaps not by chance that, in the expert panel's talk, what was subjected to the most critical scrutiny was the concept of sympathy itself. The September 11th attacks were discussed as an opportunity for the USA to gain long-lost sympathy from all over the world as these events show that the superpower, far from being invincible, has its own *vulnerabilities*. This sympathy, however, was conditional on the superpower's mode of response to the event – 'retaliation', it was said, would put such 'sympathy under strain'.

It is in the topic of the sublime, then, that the 'universal' certainties of common humanity (empathy) and a world alliance against terror (denunciation) become explicitly formulated and critically evaluated.

Reflexive identification: the moral mechanism

Ecstatic news is the category of news that attempts to represent the extraordinary, the liminal, the historically unprecedented. The live footage of the events of September 11th covers both the television genre of instantaneous transmission and a liminal event that had the globe holding its breath in front of its TV screens. Obviously, my description of the three extracts does not aspire to capture the full dynamic of the footage as it unfolded in time – the *'eventness'* of this event, in Bakhtin's words. In fact, none of the topics of suffering is able to bear the weight of representing September 11th on its own. All three constantly alternate and fuse with one another in an attempt to resolve the acute undecidabilities of the scene of suffering at the moment of mediating the suffering itself.

Each topic is put together by combining different media, the salience of which varies by topic. Empathy, in the direct link, relies on the telephone and the visual shots from Manhattan. Our sense of reality here is psychological. It is based on emotion. The spectators enter the reality of suffering through the street camera and its snapshots of people acting on the aftermath of the towers' collapse. The *accidental gaze* of this camera signifies the same contingency and vulnerability that the Consul's emotional talk conveys when he is on the phone.[22] The combination of talk and image enhances the drama of the suffering by bringing the spectators as close to the urgency of beneficiary action as was possible at that moment.

Denunciation, in the update piece, combines high-value visuals with a brief voiceover. Our sense of reality here is perceptual – it is based on facts. The spectators enter the reality of the suffering via a witness perspective that allows them to see everything that there is to see – the planes crashing, the towers collapsing , the Pentagon burning. The *helpless gaze* of these multiple cameras – a term that describes how cameras only record suffering, they cannot affect it – does not evoke empathy but strengthens the spectators' engagement with the historical world. This engagement becomes a direct accusation via Bush's speech, which is shown after the planes crash. The combination of the impartial voiceover and the edited together pieces of visual text invites the spectator to shift from empathetic emotion to a denunciation of the perpetrator of evil.

Finally, the sublime prioritizes camera work and establishes a relationship of visual contemplation with the city's skyline – a tableau vivant. Identification is reflexive. It is based on the calculation of causes and consequences. The *professional gaze* of this camera – a term for camerawork that evokes no emotion but reports clinically – organizes the scene of suffering away from the figures of a benefactor and a persecutor. In so doing, it distances itself from the immediacy of strong emotions and opens up a way to analytical discourse and journalistic objectivity.

The moralizing effect of ecstatic news relies on this multiple discursive operation of the live footage. It is an operation that constantly repositions the spectators vis-à-vis the sufferers and, thus, offers a rich repertoire of options for agency both in and on the scene of suffering. This possibility of agency as something fully shared by both the actors in the suffering and the distant spectators differentiates *sovereign* agency from the *conditional* agency of emergency news. As a consequence, the psycho-geography of action in ecstatic news becomes 'universal'. This does not necessarily mean that everyone from everywhere actually acts on the scene of suffering. Rather, 'universal' agency works to invite spectators to concede that action vis-à-vis this suffering is not only possible but also necessary and relevant to all.

The shamanizing of the spectator

If the proposal for 'universal' action is one major effect of the act of witnessing in the September 11th footage, then protecting the spectators from the trauma of the witnesses is another, although the two are closely interrelated. In this section, I explore the procedure by which ecstatic news attempts to work through the spectators' feelings of shock and disbelief. My argument is that the politics of pity in this footage manages the working through by modelling it on the ritual pattern of *shamanizing* – an anthropological term applied to media events by Dayan and Katz (1992: 147–87).

September 11th, as with many transformative events, is traumatic because it confronts spectators with a new definition of the possible: the sudden and dramatic reversal of the safety–danger space–times. The three extracts I examined above serve as attempts to turn the unthinkable into a coherent story. It is this function of the footage, to rationalize the new thinkable, that shamanizing comes to define. The term shamanizing is used to refer to the symbolic work of ritual healings and transformations in establishing unity and nurturing well-being amongst members of a tribe. In ecstatic news, the role of the shaman, the tribal leader in charge of the healing ritual, is played by television.

How exactly does the shamanizing process work in ecstatic news? It works by providing a narrative pattern within which the transformative event begins to make sense. This narrative pattern involves three *moments*:

- a *signalling/modelling* moment, which is visual and prepares the spectators by anticipating the transformative event
- a *framing* moment, which is linguistic and spells out the content of the transformation
- an *evaluating* moment, which involves thoughts and ideas in the aftermath of the event.[23]

The September 11th footage involves all three moments.

The *signalling/modelling* is the moment of visual action, which in this case is captured in the update with the second plane crashing, the towers' collapsing and the Pentagon burning. Here, the new thinkable appears as gesture, as action charged with meaning. On the one hand, the film of the plane approaching the World Trade Center *signals* the imminent transformation in the timespan of seconds, when the eyewitness exclaming 'Oh, my God' captures the breathtaking imminence of the crash. On the other hand, the images of the crash itself and the subsequent collapse of the towers perform the function of *modelling* – they give shape to the transformation in the visual form of explosion, demolition, fire and human terror. In the course of the footage, the regular repetition of these images of violence enacts over and over again the same signalling/modelling gesture and reasserts the new thinkable: the 'centre' is no longer immune to violence. At the same time, this repetition removes the traumatic potential from the sequence and increasingly renders the crash a filmic experience.[24]

The *framing* is the moment of language – the talk about the transformation – which is enacted in the direct link and in the discursive performance of the Consul. The Consul's emotional description, as well as his first attempt to account for the event's conseqences is an effort to interpret the event from within. His words 'impossible to overview, dramatic, shocking, undescribable' come to express both the disbelief and confirmation of what the spectators are themselves experiencing. Framing is, further, the part of the Consul's talk that hesitantly introduces the spectators to the possibility of a new agenda in the world order: 'worry, deep worry about what is behind this [...] and deep worry about the consequences'. It operates by anticipating the spectators' emotions and thoughts and putting words to them. As Dayan and Katz would put it, the Consul appears as a witness to history who explicitly talks about his experience because the spectator 'wishes not to witness it alone' (1992: 177).

Finally, *evaluation* is the moment of public debate that takes place in the third extract above during the showing of the long shot of the Manhattan skyline. Evaluation is an extension of the framing process in the sense that it is part of the continuing attempt to account for the event, but it goes further than framing in managing to construe the event's longer-term significance. This is a process that is like the shaman recounting the tribe's cultural myths. In television, such shaman talk is performed by the expert panel. It is the experts who selectively draw on the available resources of contemporary cultural myths and, in so doing, contextualize and interpret the event in their preferred discourses of history and politics.[25]

Evaluation is, then, clearly a political process of selection and legitimation that requires some distance from the temporality of the event itself. The live footage establishes this distance not by means of a proper chronological leap, but by using the spatiotemporal dimensions of the long shot. In placing the attacks in the framework of causal–historical relationships between the United States and the Islamic world and speculating on the superpower's possible reactions to the attack, the panel's discussion sketches out an emergent trajectory of global politics that is still evolving today.

In shamanizing – connecting us recurrently and ritually with the suffering 'other' – ecstatic news protects the spectators from the spectacle of suffering and simultaneously engages them with the suffering of the September 11th attacks as the new human, political and historical paradox of the West.

The reflexive spectator

Shamanizing offers to the spectators of the events of September 11th a potential for reflexive identification with the sufferers that is unknown in adventure and emergency news. *Reflexive identification* is the capacity of the spectators to, at once, act as if they were within the scene of suffering and as if they were speaking out their views on suffering in public. It combines, in this sense, the two historical proposals for action at a distance available in the public space:

- the theatre, with its potential for emotional engagement and identification
- the agora, with its potential for impartial deliberation and rational judgement.

Theatrical action occurs in the direct link and empathetic identification that the involved camera offers to the spectators as well as in the update on the events and the denunciatory sentiment against the attack that the overview of the scenes of suffering incited in the spectators.

Agoraic action occurs in the long shot with the analytical distance and temporality of reflection that this semiotic arrangement enables during the playing of the footage.

Reflexive identification brings the spectators of the September 11th attacks as close to the cosmopolitan disposition as it gets, in so far as it presupposes precisely this duality of the spectatorial subjectivity, both feeling for the distant sufferers and speaking out about the suffering as a response to an ongoing public dialogue.

Central to reflexive identification is the work of the September 11th footage in engaging the spectators with multiple truths, in multiple ways – getting them to empathize, denounce and reflect on the terror attacks. Let me briefly comment on three dispositions that the footage enacts for the spectator, namely the *involved* spectator, the *omnipresent* spectator and the *distantiated* spectator.

The involved spectator
In this disposition the spectator is overwhelmed by empathy. Inhabiting the space–time of instantaneous proximity, he or she gets close to the American sufferers, feels for their misfortunes and shares their destiny. The Americans are human beings just like 'us'; our feelings and fate are common.

The weakness of this emotional humanism lies, predictably, in over-emphasizing feeling at the expense of rationality. The 'universal' value of common humanity prevents the spectators from posing questions such as what led to the attacks and historicizing the position of these particular sufferers in the broad field of contemporary political relations. The United States had long been in a relationship of tension – ranging from close alliance to open animosity – with Arab countries and the West–Islam distinction was a key cultural and political theme in the superpower's discourse long before the September 11th attacks.[26] In privileging the *human* dimension of suffering, though, empathy fails to address the reasons that might have motivated the attack, the 'Why?' questions behind the selection of this sufferer as a sufferer from the 'cen-tre'. It further throws into relief the fundamental bias of mediation, which selectively singles out the September 11th sufferers as the privileged objects of our compassion and care in the face of so much other suffering around the world.[27]

The omnipresent spectator

This spectator feels indignation towards the persecutor and demands the pursuit of justice. Inhabiting the space–time of a-perspectival objectivity, such spectators orientation towards anger is, at the same time, surrounded by an aura of impartiality and political legitimacy.

Which consequences does this spectatorial position have? First, the denunciation of evil denies the spectators the possibility of thinking about the event outside a specific logic of justice – the 'logic of reiteration'. In tightly binding the image and its 'immediate' truth of terror together with the promise of hunting down the persecutor and, soon after, a counterattack, denunciation suppresses other possibilities for alternative political, diplomatic or military action.[28]

Second, by the same token, denunciation elevates the American sufferers to the position of the retaliator and seeks to legitimize this status in the spectators' minds. It further pushes towards specifying the identity of the evil-doer who acts as the target of reiteration. This target, though, is far from settled. The controversy surrounding the war against Afghanistan and Iraq is precisely a controversy over who the evil-doer is, throwing into relief the political difficulties and moral impasses of the topic of denunciation.

The distantiated spectator

This is the spectator of the long shot who enters into a relationship of contemplation with the spectacle of suffering and plays on the spectators' fantasy and their reflexivity. Inhabiting the space–time of the sublime, the spectacle of September 11th dispenses with the figures of benefactor and persecutor and considers suffering to be neither heart-breaking nor unfair. The moralization of the spectator acquires a different edge, as the tropes of anachronism and anatopism establish discontinuities in time (World War II) and space (any Western metropolis). How close is the past event to the current one? What is the connection between this city and others?

What these dispositions mean

Although none of these dispositions aspires to exhaust or fully explain the event to Western spectators, the sublime entails the seeds of a representation of suffering that foregrounds historicity. The present is not a direct derivative of what went on before, but a profoundly unfinalizable process that contains multiple potentials. What might or might not happen after the attacks is, now more than ever, an open matter. The invitation to contemplate the Manhattan skyline is, in this sense, more than just an aesthetic experience – it is a potentially historizing and politicizing move that offers to spectators a distance and a temporality of reflection on the causes and implications of what happened.

The promise for the figure of the cosmopolitan spectator lies, therefore, not in the naive celebration of the communitarian sentiment but the possibility for reflexive identification that television's politics of pity is able to enact. The cosmopolitan spectator emerges now as a figure who navigates between the singularity of suffering – which is necessary for feeling with the sufferer, but without indulging in unnecessary emotion – and the historicity of the event – which is necessary for evaluating the suffering, but without adopting a heartless impartiality. Can reflexive identification, however, transcend the exceptional category of ecstatic news and inform the moralization of the spectator in other types of news, too? This is the question that I address in the remainder of this volume.

Conclusion

The news of September 11th cannot be anything but ecstatic. It is news accounting for a new distribution of viewing relationships – the West is now both a sufferer and a witness of suffering. Although the capacity for identification is inherent in the logic of mediation itself, this capacity is now maximized. The spectators reflexively share with the sufferers the same humanity, the same threat and, potentially, the same destiny. As a consequence, the politics of pity in ecstatic news reconfigures the sufferer–spectator relationship in terms of a 'universal' psycho-geography of action. The spectators may not be called to act directly on the suffering, but they are called to empathize, denounce and reflect on the suffering and, in so doing, get as close to the sufferers' psychological and ethical universe as possible.

Ecstatic news, in this sense, brings television's potential for tele-sociality, so eagerly celebrated by certain media theories, to an unprecedented peak, while throwing into relief its political function. It reserves the spectators' capacity to connect for those who are like 'us' while blocking this same capacity for the largest majority of world sufferings – those experienced by distant 'others'.

Notes

1 The extracts come from the national Danish television channel DR.
2 See Dayan and Katz (1992: 25–53) and below.
3 Undecidability also informs Silverstone's description of the September 11th footage. Silverstone (2002b: 3) describes it as a rare instance of tension between television's attempt to maintain its journalistic conventions and the disruptive effects of the event in terms of its *interruption* (in the realm of time), *transcendence* (in the realm of space) and *otherness* (in the realm of ethics).

4 See Ellsworth and Sachs (2003) for this catching-up process in the global news about September 11th.

5 See Nichols (1991: 156–8) on 'identification'.

6 See Peters (2001: 215–17) on the 'mechanical witnessing' of the camera and McQuire (1999: 109–11) on the 'scandalous cohabitation' of camera images with the real.

7 See Dayan and Katz (1992: 147–8 and 160–1).

8 See Ellsworth and Sachs (2003: 6) for a study of this.

9 See Volkmer (2002) and Clausen (2003) for processes of 'domestication' with the first commemoration event of September 11th.

10 My use of the word 'documentary' departs from the narrow definition of the term, as in 'historical' or 'natural life documentaries', and moves towards a broader definition that includes all audio-visual genres that claim to 'document' reality by providing various 'proofs' of its truth claims – ethical, emotional and demonstrative proofs (Nichols, 1991: 141). See Ellis (2000: 11–13) on factual representation and the ethics of 'realism'.

11 See Peters (2001: 709) for a discussion on the active–passive functions of witnessing.

12 See Ellis (2000: 98) and Peters (2001: 719–20).

13 The concept of 'excess' refers to semiotic properties of the spectacle that cannot be accounted for by the narrative that frames the spectacle: 'excess is the random and the inexplicable, that which remains ungoverned within a textual regime presided over by narrative' (Nichols, 1991: 141).

14 The 'Othering' of the Muslim terrorist is not discussed in this context because this process was not fully visible (though certainly underway) in these first hours of the footage. For comments on this aspect of the mediation of September 11th, see Silverstone (2002a: 9), Lazar and Lazar (2004: 223–42) and Chouliaraki (2005).

15 See Boltanski (1999: 121) for this definition of the sublime. See also Stavrakakis (1999: 131–4) for an interesting discussion of the ethics of sublimation and politics, in a Lacanian framework.

16 By 'graphics' I mean CNN-type information bars that show various messages at the bottom of the TV screen. In this case, these include 'New York', 'Pentagon in flames', 'One more plane crash reported in Pensylvannia' and so on.

17 See Bakhtin (1986: 10–59).

18 The link between September 11th and Pearl Harbour was also made in the commentary by an American citizen in Denmark who joined the expert panel in the same live footage session 15 minutes after this long shot. More generally, this 'anachronistic' link was part of the broader repertoire of historico-political discourses used to contextualize the September 11th attacks in public debate forums (see, for example, Virilio's interview in *Lettre International*, 54, September 2001). For a critical comment on precisely this link as a misguided product of media coverage, see Jameson's article in the *London Review of Books*, 4 October 2001.

19 For a theoretical perspective on the theme of international security and the West, see Beck's 'The cosmopolitan state', *Der Spiegel*, 15 October, 2001. For the social function of 'sharing feelings' with the distant sufferer as a discursive device for public belonging, see Martin (2004: 321–44).

20 See Corner (1999: 97–8) for this formulation of fantasy.

21 See Boltanski (1999: 127) for this point.

22 See Nichols (1991: 87) on the three types of camera gaze – *accidental*, *helpless* and *professional*.

23 See Dayan and Katz (1992: 167–85) for more on these categories.

24 The swift transfer of the audience's status from witness to spectator lies, for Ellsworth and Sachs, precisely in the passing from improvizational television, which was catching up with the speed and severity of events, to the usual conventions and routines of television footage. Television, they say:

> reinstates familiar rhythmic forms, as the footage of the jet smashing into the second tower is repeated up to 30 times per hour [...] and the audience's gaze is restructured, from that of witness to that of spectator. The images on the screen cease to be events in themselves, and begin to border on spectacle.
>
> (2003: 8)

25 See Dayan and Katz (1992: 84) for more on this point.

26 See Gresh in *Le Monde Diplomatique*, Greek edition 7 September 2003.

27 In order to thematize this point, the *New Internationalist* publicized a number of statistics that relativize the terrorist attack death toll of 3,000 people as 'the' privileged suffering of September 11th:

> Number of people who died of hunger on September 11th, 2001: 2400.
> Number of children killed by diarrhoea on September 11th, 2001: 6020.
> Number of children killed by measles on September 11th, 2001: 2700.
>
> (2001: 19 in Karim, 2002: 103)

28 See Ali's 'Yes, there is an effective alternative to the bombing of Afghanistan', *The Independent*, 15 October 2001.

Appendix: Ecstatic News

Text 1. Extracts of telephone interview with Danish Consul in New York

Anchorman: We now have a telephone link to New York, the Danish General Consul in New York. General Consul, you are relatively close to the events. How is the situation in New York just now?

Consul: Dramatic, impossible to overview, we are of course very touched by the situation, very concerned and we are doing our best to keep the information levels on the events going through contacts with the branch in which you are in. We are in a state of war emergency and we are trying to have good contact with our Nordic colleagues and we have also had contact with the American authorities [Provides information on Nordic and Danish visitors in New York].

Anchorman: [...] There are 30000 people working in the World Trade Center, both towers have collapsed. What do the American media say about the situation?

Consul: They are giving different numbers but no specific number has been confirmed as yet [...] What is dramatic about the situation is that New York is a city under siege. Manhattan is closed down. There is a terror alert all over Manhattan. All bridges and towers are closed, vehicles are howling, all hospitals are on hundred per cent emergency, shops have closed down [...] there is a certain feeling of panic around that there might be other planes in the air that might hit another target in the American continent [...]

Anchorman: You are the General Consul updating us on the events in USA, but you are also a human being. How does it feel to witness such a terrible catastrophe; what goes through your mind in these minutes?

Consul: Worry, deep worry about what is behind this [...] and deep, deep worry about the consequences this will have on the political front. It is apparently a terrorist attack and it is clear that this is not something that the USA and other countries will just stay quiet about and let it pass, so there will be consequences coming very soon and dramatic both nationally and internationally, we don't know how it will escalate [...] so worry, deep anxiety, for the political consequences for all of us.

Anchorman: General Consul from New York, thank you very much.

Text 2. Summary of events

Voiceover: Just before 9 o'clock local time one of the World Trade Center Towers was hit by a passenger plane.

And only eighteen minutes later the second World Trade Tower was also hit by another passenger plane.

One plane belongs to American Airlines and was hijacked in Boston said the representative of the airline. They were not sure as to how many were on board but the plane had a capacity for 158 passengers.

President Bush: Today we've had a national tragedy. Two airplanes have crashed into the World Trade Center in an apparent terrorist attack on our country. I have spoken to the Vice President, to the Governor of New York, to the Director of the FBI, and have ordered that the full resources of the federal government go to help the victims and their families, and to conduct a full-scale investigation to hunt down and to find those folks who committed this act. Terrorism against our nation will not stand.

Voiceover: Almost one hour after the first collusion the first Tower collapsed following an explosion. And only half an hour later the second Tower also collapsed. (*Eye witness account*: I am coming down 6th Avenue and all the people and traffic were running up … and I look up and the tower just starts crumbling down …).

Voiceover: Approximately 40000 people work in the World Trade Center every day and more that 150000 visit the Towers every day. At the moment, it is not certain as to how many people are dead or injured.

And as if this was not enough, another passenger plane crashed in to the American Defense Ministry, the Pentagon in Washington. At the same time the Ministry of the Interior was hit by a car bomb. And we just got to know that a Boeing 747 has crashed in Northern Pensylvania. So far nobody has taken responsibility for the attacks.

Text 3. Extracts of panel talk

Panel speaker: … There is of course no doubt that this will establish strong consensus within the nation, within the USA and a great sympathy towards the USA by the international community. But the USA's philosophy is that any terror attack against the USA should be retaliated by attacks of the same strength. The question therefore is if this sympathy will be sustained after the USA's future moves.

Anchorman: These pictures we are seeing now from southern Manhattan nobody could have imagined … What is the character of these attacks that we witnessed this morning?

Panel speaker: They demonstrate great knowledge, professionalism and co-ordination of a kind that we have not known so far […]

Anchorman: We have recently witnessed some heightened activity around protective measures against terrorist attacks. In any case there have been worries about possible terror attacks recently, for example in American embassies around the world [...] though not of this magnitude.

Panel speaker: This issue of heightened emergency ... these are also very diffuse attacks. We don't know where they come from. Who are we going to attack back? Nobody knows where the next attack may come from. Nobody knows is there is a ship in the New York harbour with a bomb or if terror will come from pollution in the sewage system of New York or chemical weapons and gas anywhere in the city. This is what makes the terrorist threat so difficult to confront, that it has a very diffuse character. And this makes it really difficult to do something about it. So far there was no proof that such a co-ordinated attack as this would be possible.

8

MEDIATION AND ACTION

News on distant suffering is hierarchical. At the low end of the hierarchy, adventure news offers spectators a position of maximal distance from the sufferers and no options for action towards the misfortune that they watch. At the high end of the hierarchy, ecstatic news offers spectators a position of reflexive identification, by means of which spectators recognize the sufferers as sovereign agents and engage with their misfortune continuously, intensely and in multiple ways.

These positions represent a key aspect of the information divide in the space of mediation. Although the landscape of global news flows is more complicated than this implies, this typology captures a significant bias in the intersection between global and national news flows. Technological changes, let us recall, go together with symbolic changes in mediation and it is the latter that come to reshape our sense of proximity and connectivity with distant 'others'. This means that, despite the expansion in news delivery technologies, all pieces of news are eventually subject to a process of selection and symbolic particularization that defines whose suffering matters to Western spectators.[1] If cosmopolitanism – the ethical disposition that connects the spectator with the distant sufferer – depends on the capacity of television's symbolic practices to produce proximity with sufferers and propose action to alleviate their misfortunes, then the question is which proximity and whose action?

To answer this, let me now briefly go back to the pessimistic and optimistic narratives on the ethics of mediation. The pessimistic narrative – which deplores the failure of television to connect spectator and sufferer in a moral sense – finds justification in the empirical reality of adventure news. The optimistic narrative – which celebrates the creation of global communities by the act of television viewing – finds justification in the empirical reality of ecstatic news. Can these two types of news provide us with the sense of proximity and options for action that are necessary for a cosmopolitan disposition? Do adventure and ecstatic news provide us with a view of public space where the spectator connects to the sufferer by means of a relationship of emotional and practical engagement?

The answer is no. Neither one is able to construe the public space of television as a space of cosmopolitan agency because each type of news model of the public is its very own community – that of Western social life.

The communitarian public of adventure and ecstatic news

Adventure news is paradigmatically associated with the thesis of compassion fatigue. The thesis of compassion fatigue blames television for bombarding spectators with images of human misfortune and, consequently, holds television accountable for trivializing suffering and weakening the spectator's charitable sensibility towards distant suffering. Yet, rather than finding the cause of compassion fatigue in the omnipresence of images of suffering, adventure news demonstrates that it is related to the systematic absence of certain sufferers from the viewing community of Western spectators. This inadequacy of television to represent certain sufferings as deserving of the spectators' emotion and action results in excluding certain places and some human lives from the public space the spectator belongs to and feels able to act within. The main implication of this exclusion is that, in the name of the spectators' benign desire for comfort, television blocks the possibility of public action beyond their familiar community of belonging.

Ecstatic news is paradigmatically associated with the thesis of tele-sociality, which takes as its point of departure in television's capacity to connect dispersed locales to form a community of spectators. In this respect, ecstatic news clearly demonstrates the effectiveness of television in creating a global audience, but, simultaneously, it also shows that this aggregate function is reserved for those rare pieces of news that have historical significance for the West. In the live footage of the September 11th attacks, television offered the Western spectators multiple engagements with the terror attacks. Yet, this therapeutic connectivity worked to rationalize the move from thinking about terrorism as a story about 'others' to thinking about it as a real possibility for somebody like the Western spectators themselves. The community of ecstatic news, global as it may be in its scope, in fact addresses the fears of Europeans who may now imagine that similar attacks are imminent in Madrid or London. History would sadly prove them right. As a consequence, the space of identification and action in ecstatic news is the space the spectators already belong to. In what Butler calls 'a narcissistic preoccupation with melancholia', the shared vulnerability of ecstatic news is the vulnerability of the West, leaving out places and populations experiencing suffering from terror that precedes and follows the Western experience by many and by far (2004: 30–1).

Adventure and ecstatic news, in their different ways, appeal to a spectatorial community that is already constituted as a public space. This public space is either the familiar and safe space of collusive denial, where no call to the cause of distant 'others' disturbs the spectators, or it is the space of common vulnerability, where the spectators' commitment to the suffering 'others' is natural because the sufferers are people like them. It is precisely by virtue of this shared feature – namely that they address the West as an already constituted community – that neither adventure nor ecstatic news are able to contribute to the ethical question of how a space of public action towards distant suffering may be constituted in the process of mediation itself.

The problem with evoking the West as an already constituted community of spectators is that these types of news simultaneously evoke a set of pre-existing assumptions implicit in any communitarian bond as to whose misfortune matters and what there is to do about the misfortune. The communitarian bond, in other words, organizes the content of mediation according to the concerns and interests of specific viewing publics, which may transcend the national but do not encompass the global – they are resolutely Western. The West, from this perspective, is not a 'universal' context of viewing and action but a particular public – a *microsphere* – that coexists with other such microspheres in the global information landscape.[2] The Western claims to care and responsibility vis-à-vis the distant sufferers compete with the similar claims of alternative news flows that, equally, appeal to their sense of commitment and care for their own distant sufferers. Today, more than ever, it is important to compare these competing claims to humanity and pity across public microspheres because such comparisons may shed valuable light on the overlaps and incompatibilities of whose suffering matters most to whom around the globe.[3]

This comparison would further throw into relief the fact that the communitarian bond of the West is not based on 'natural' affinities but textual devices that confer an aura of objectivity in Western representations of suffering. The map, for example, or certain techniques of visual editing and verbal reporting make a strong claim of showing 'the' truth about suffering and portraying reality as it is. Indeed, as we have seen, the communitarian bond in Western television appears to work by means of the impartial representation of 'facts', while, simultaneously, distributing different potentials for pity among different 'facts' of suffering in different types of news. This combination of impartiality with selective pity is the moral mechanism that reproduces the communitarian consciousness and construes the hierarchy of place and human life reflected in the typology set out in this book.

The public space of pity in emergency news

Between adventure and ecstatic news, the category of emergency news covers a middle space that does not completely efface the sufferer nor does it render the sufferer thoroughly sovereign. It is not that emergency news does not evoke the West as the imagined community the spectator belongs to. Of course it does. It is, rather, that emergency news presents the Western spectator with a demand for engagement that does not exclusively follow from the precommitment to implicit obligations from the communitarian bond. Neither the apathetic spectators of adventure news, nor the overengaged spectators of ecstatic news, the spectators of emergency news move through a number of plausible positions of agency vis-à-vis distant sufferers. They watch the rescuing of African sufferers, shed a tear for the misfortunes of Argentinean children or protest against the death sentence meted out to the Nigerian woman.

Free from the 'contractual' relationship to suffering, these pieces of news pose the question of commitment as a problem to be solved and render distant suffering as a case to be judged worthy of action by impartial spectators. In opening up a range of positions from which the judgement of suffering is now possible, emergency news simultaneously opens up a space of engagement that may lie beyond the spectators' local horizon for feeling and acting. This means that, rather than restricting public space to the West as a given community, television now addresses the public as an undefined entity.

The 'undefinedness' of the public points to the fact that mediation does not always assume a given public but may also call a public into being at the moment when it presents the spectators with a cause for engagement. In appealing to the spectators as philanthropists towards Argentinean children or activists protesting against Amina Lawal's verdict, emergency news throws into relief this pedagogical dimension of mediation as shaping the spectators' conduct towards a cosmopolitan disposition. The spectators are now members of a world bigger than just the West, who develop their self-identity and disposition to act on this world in response to visions of the public that television itself proposes.

As opposed to communitarian spectators, who respond one-sidedly to Western suffering alone, the public person of emergency news connects, in principle, everybody with everybody else. In Chartier's words, this public person is not defined by 'participation, as agent and subject, in the exercise of any particular authority but by identification with humanity as a whole' (1999: 25). The way in which the move from the 'undefinedness' of a public to identifying with the concept of humanity is put here is telling. It suggests that a group of spectators may turn into a cosmopolitan public only if the spectators break with any particular identification – partaking, that is, of 'any particular authority' – in order to reach beyond, ideally to all peoples of the globe.[4] This is why the more we insist on examining the nature of mediation – which emergency news enacts vis-à-vis an undefined and always 'in the making' public – the closer we will get to the conditions of possibility for cosmopolitanism, for public action on humanity.

The discourse of cosmopolitan citizenship: 'universal' morality

Emergency news evidently confirms the point that global visibility alone cannot guarantee public action on humanity, but it does more than this.

It further demonstrates that the move from a communitarian to a cosmopolitan sensibility requires a specific kind of public discourse. This is a discourse that assumes no prior ties between spectator and sufferer and, therefore, evokes the idea of public agency precisely at the moment of addressing it. What, then, is the quality of mediation that characterizes emergency news?

Emergency suffering is an ambivalent condition that construes the question of commitment to the cause of suffering in an indeterminate and fragile manner. Emergency news, let us recall, offers no specific distance from which the spectator contemplates the suffering, nor does it propose a specific humanness that characterizes the sufferer on television. The humanness of the Nigerian woman, for example, remains suspended between a condition thoroughly 'universal' – her motherhood – and thoroughly 'alien' to Western experience – her life under the sharia rule. Similarly, the spectator's judgement vis-à-vis African refugees or Argentinean children constantly hovers between these sufferers' desire for life, which is compatible with the spectator's own, and their fate, which is radically different from anything the Western spectator is likely to experience. Emergency news, then, presents the humanness of the sufferer as an inherently unstable condition and it is this very instability that sums up the paradox of cosmopolitan action. The possibility of cosmopolitanism lies in the impossibility of representing the condition of distant suffering as a fully universal cause.[5]

This impossibility, however, is at odds with the dominant discourse of ethical conduct today, which is eloquently condensed in Ellis's words: 'you cannot say you didn't know.' What does this dominant discourse – with all the suppressed guilt and powerlessness that it uncomfortably stirs up for spectators of the news – tell us? Rather than acknowledging the indeterminacy of mediated suffering this dominant discourse dictates that, once confronted with distant suffering, the spectator is under the obligation to respond to it. In the theories I examined in Chapters 1 and 3, it is obvious that spectators of the news, in general, are automatically under the moral obligation of the sufferers on screen – their sensibilities blocked only by technology's unaesthecisizing effects.

We now need to challenge this myth and recognise that it is strictly the spectator of emergency news who may be endowed with such ethical capacity. This is because spectators of emergency news are the only ones to be confronted with a concrete appeal to public action. That is, they are the only ones to be construed by the news as ethical beings, able to go beyond their own interests and take an interest in 'humanity as a whole'. It is precisely this articulation of suffering with a discourse of 'universal' morality – morality beyond the narrow concerns of the communitarian bond – that renders the spectators of emergency news – and no other class of news – potential citizens of the world, regarding all humanity as their fellow citizens.[6]

The public person of emergency news, then, is primarily an ethical figure constituted by means of those values of engagement with suffering that claim to have a 'universal' status, in our culture.[7] In philanthropy, the moral horizon of the spectator is based on the value of common human- ity, which moves the spectator's heart in empathy at the sight of children in need. In denunciation, the moral horizon of the spectator is based on the value of justice, which turns the spectator against the violation of human rights by the sharia law. In the aesthetic register, the moral hori- zon of the spectator is based on fantasy and fear as 'universal' faculties of the spectator's engagement with human destiny and the powers that rule human life. These 'universal' values, articulated as they are in a dispersed and discontinuous manner, make up the conditions of possibility for a public ethics in Western television.

At the same time, these 'universal' values of suffering do not stand on their own. Each piece of news struggles to accommodate its own specific realities of suffering – the threatening misery of refugees, emaciated bodies of Argentinean children or savage cruelty in the streets of Nigeria. There is always a struggle between the 'universal' truths of humanity, which seek to cast suffering in an enabling proximity, and the detail of singular sufferings, which inevitably evoke a certain distance from the scene of misfortune. It is this struggle that ultimately renders emergency news the ambivalent and fragile regime of pity that I discussed above. As a consequence, every single representation of emergency suffering balances between alienating 'otherness' and a remote sense of human- ness, making the portrayal of each suffering 'other' paradoxical or, in Bhabha's words, 'curiously mixed and split, polymorphous and perverse, an articulation of multiple rather than singular belief' (1994: 82).

Confronted with these 'twilight' presences on their screens, the spectators also become ambivalent figures themselves. Neither true philanthropists, who compassionately care for stranded refugees or emaciated children, nor proper activists, who engage in practical politics of justice, the spec- tators are captured in a fragile, if not impossible, representation, too. Contradictory as this may sound, the spectators' fragility is not a bad thing. On the contrary, I wish to argue, it is precisely this paradoxical and fragile condition that we need to preserve if we wish to sustain the idea of cosmopolitanism not only as a programmatic utopia of mediation, but also a political reality of contemporary public life.

The key is to draw attention to the internal hierarchy of emergency news that affects the quality of each particular and, consequently, also affects the combination of the particular with a 'universal' discourse of action. Whereas all emergency sufferings appear to be concrete and specific for the spectators, only some pieces manage to represent suffer- ing in terms of multiple and dynamic contexts of activity or mobile and practically accessible terrains of action. Similarly, the human presence of sufferers in emergency news ranges from an undifferentiated mass of 'misèrables' to an individual with a personal biography and a cultural history.

Such differences correspond to differences in the forms of realism of the news. Empirical realism magnifies the spectacular value of the African refugees' story, but keeps the story firmly outside a discourse of explanation and public action. Categorical realism casts the Argentinean crisis in the ideal of common humanity, but tells us nothing of what the crisis is about or how it might be overcome. It is, finally, the ideological realism of the piece about the Nigerian woman that manages to articulate suffering as a cause of practical action for the spectators by connecting the concrete reality of a death by stoning sentence with the discourse on human rights and the imperative of social solidarity.

This suggests that, for spectators to be confronted with the call for effective action – action that can make a difference to the sufferer's fate – only a certain articulation of the particular and the 'universal' is appropriate and only a certain type of fragility of the sufferer is powerful enough to present her to spectators as a cause for concern. The capacity of the news about the Nigerian woman to place pity for her, the sufferer, in a historical context and articulate pity with a demand for justice renders its representation of suffering a clear instance of cosmopolitan politics in the typology of news.

The cosmopolitan disposition: historicity and reflexivity

What differentiates the Nigerian case from the other two pieces of emergency news is that it goes beyond bringing a story into the public realm and begs the question 'Why?' It is this question as to why – a question that does not enter the frame in the piece on the suffering of the African refugees and that of the Argentineans caught in an economic crisis – that makes Amina's suffering appear as a dynamic and open event worthy of public commitment.

This is not a 'grand' why, one referring to the structures of society or the traditions of religion. It is, rather, a 'modest' why, embedded in the narrative economy of the news as dispersed historicity, which means that this news incorporates relevant fragments of the trajectory of events around the Nigerian court case, such as the hint at a potential conflict between the secular government of the country and the Islamic law or the reference to another similar Amnesty campaign in Nigeria, thanks to which the person concerned had eventually been acquitted. By pointing to the tensions and potentialities that are inherent in the development of the story, references like these simultaneously establish the multiple, specific and mobile connectivities between the space–times and actors of suffering and the spectators. The factors of who has acted or should act at which place and point in time so as to make a difference to Amina's life organize a regime of pity that does not explicitly moralize spectators into a politically correct activism, but subtly confronts them with the consequentiality of their own actions.

To be sure, the piece of news about the Nigerian woman is precisely this: a single piece of news inserted in to the flow of a longer broadcast. It can only provide glimpses of the event it reports on and not – under any circumstances – determine the nature, causality or outcome of Amina Lawal's suffering. Nevertheless, by begging the question 'Why?', this piece of news does offer to spectators the space in which to reflect on the causes of the action that it proposes. This is what Boltanski calls a 'politics of justice'.[8] As opposed to the politics of pity, where the urgency of wanting to bring an end to the suffering always prevails over considerations of justice, in the politics of justice, the sufferers never simply 'happen to' suffer, but are always subjected to a test of fairness and the question is asked as to whether or not their misery is justified. Why should a woman who had her baby outside marriage be put to death? Why should inhumane practices against women take place without us speaking out in favour of human rights? It is these questions about the justifications for suffering that spectators are called to contemplate.

A crucial feature of 'Why?' questions is that they are not simply propositional. That is, they do not simply formulate issues but are also performative – they enact a certain disposition towards the ethical and political issues that the news articulates. 'Why?' questions, in other words, at once express and construe the reflexivity of spectators – the capacity of spectators to consider themselves as speakers who respond to the suffering that they watch in front of an undefined public. The reflexive response of the spectators – you will recall, I discussed this earlier in its humblest form as a 'whisper'– is linguistically formulated in the voiceover and screen graphic – 'no to death by stoning', for example – but it is also visually embodied in the presence of the Amnesty International activist. Both the verbal and visual semiotics take part in the staging of this news in terms of ideological realism – a realism that shifts Amina's suffering from television story to a fact of life that demands an urgent response. This crucial shift from the fictional to the factual occurs because ideological realism fulfils, what Boltanski calls, the two minimal conditions of an appropriate relationship to reality:

- the demand for public speech – 'no to death by stoning'
- the anticipation of an active attitude – showing and narrating the Amnesty International protest event.[9]

By fulfilling these conditions, the news of the Nigerian woman's situation is unique among the pieces of news I have analyzed in this book in seeking to shape the spectators as reflexive citizens and stands out as a case of cosmopolitan politics in the typology of pity.

Cosmopolitan politics: social solidarity

This form of cosmopolitan citizenship speaks in the name of an international public opinion that uses agencies such as Amnesty International in order to monitor the will of governments to act on world suffering and injustice.[10] Foucault, a theorist of power widely known as denying the possibility of resistance, in fact forcefully advocated such a form of militant international citizenship, reclaiming the right of the governed to act within the sphere of those who are governing:[11] 'Amnesty International, Tèrre des Hommes and Médecins du Monde are initiatives that have created this new right – that of the private individual to effectively intervene in the sphere of international policy and strategy' (*Liberation*, June 1984/2000).

Isn't the call for action in the name of Amina's life made possible precisely by the presence of Amnesty International? This is because, in its capacity as a non-governmental human rights organization, Amnesty International is both a carrier of global civil society values and a powerful political agent that monitors the democratization process around the world. Summarizing Kaldor, Amnesty International enacts cosmopolitanism in a dual sense: as a moral sentiment but also as a political project (2000).[12] This felicitous ambiguity in the agency of Amnesty International enables the representation of Amina Lawal's news to combine a politics of pity with the claim to justice. By representing Amina as a woman treated with injustice and the spectators' agency in the concrete form of the petition, Amnesty International introduces to the news broadcast the practice of social solidarity.[13]

Social solidarity is a bond of mutual commitments that, as Calhoun explains, is based on 'more than similarities of pre-established interests or identities' and includes 'the citizens' engagement in shared projects of constituting a better future' (2001: 170–4). Social solidarity, Calhoun argues, is a necessary dimension of any viable cosmopolitan project because cosmopolitanism is not only about technological or economic development but also the voice of global institutions, which, in addressing the social issues of suffering and poverty, have the power to constitute various publics around the world as non-communitarian publics. The value of social solidarity is important here because, necessary as these institutions may be, unless they make an explicit commitment to the world that is not like 'us', they may well end up reproducing the communitarian concerns of the West. Their views may amount to nothing more than 'a view of Brussels, where the post-national is identified with the strength of the European Union rather than the weakness of, say, African states' (Calhoun, 2001: 91).

Social solidarity enacts the most effective form of cosmopolitanism in television because it incorporates the voice of global authority and, thereby, expands the horizon of Western spectators to include sufferers who live beyond their own communities. This kind of cosmopolitan politics crucially depends on the voices of Amnesty International, United Nations, Nelson Mandela or the Live Aid artists, because all of these bear the expertise, authority and, not least, the celebrity aura necessary to push the ethical cause of suffering through to vast television publics. Unless this form of solidarity politics is in place, transborder broadcasting may still operate within a logic of border-setting, rendering the deterritorialization of news flows and their reterritorialization in local contexts of viewing and action the two sides of the unequal relationship between 'us' and the 'other'.[14]

Indeed, pieces of news such as that about the Nigerian woman are admittedly rare, both in national and transnational television. National television may increasingly draw on transnational broadcasting in its news reports, but it does so in a manner that addresses the spectators as national citizens within the communitarian logic of their own body politic.[15] In a similar manner, transnational broadcasting may have emerged as a strong player in the arena of international politics, setting agendas and giving voice to the disempowered, but it is questionable if it does so in ways that cultivate a politics of social solidarity that includes parts of the world beyond the borders of the West.[16]

If the cosmopolitan politics of emergency news tells us anything, it is that social solidarity in the public realm of television may be an exception, but it is definitely a possibility. It is, in my view, a key question on the agenda of media research today to investigate further, rather than celebrate, whether transnational news flows reproduce the spectators' communitarian concerns in the zone of safety or cultivate new connectivities between spectators and distant sufferers.

Conclusion

Communitarianism and cosmopolitanism are the two ethical norms that define how each class of news enables or blocks public action on distant suffering. Communitarianism suggests that spectators act on suffering that is proximal and relevant to the community to which they belong. Adventure and ecstatic news – despite differences in their politics of pity – enact the communitarian logic in their representations of suffering. Adventure news enacts the communitarian logic by blocking the option of pity for the suffering of people who are not like 'us', whereas ecstatic news enacts the communitarian logic by expanding globally a demand for action on suffering that is 'our' own.

Cosmopolitanism suggests that the spectators engage with distant suffering via a demand for action on 'others' who do not readily belong to their own communities. Far from the direct outcome of globalizing technologies of communication, cosmopolitanism appears to reside as a potentiality in one class of news, which is emergency news. Emergency news entails a specific proposal of action at a distance that incorporates the question of 'Why?' in its representation of suffering and uses global voices of authority to turn distant suffering into a cause for action. As a consequence, emergency news has the potential to introduce the option of social solidarity to the public life of spectators – an option that can make a concrete difference to the sufferers' lives.

Although the landscape of global news flows is more complicated than the typology of this volume, the divide between communitarianism and cosmopolitanism captures a symbolic bias in transnational news flows that selectively shapes our connectivity with distant 'others'. How can we imagine an alternative space of mediation? How can we shift from the actual to the potential?

I move to these questions in the next, concluding, chapter, where the ethical demand to act on suffering brings me to Arendt's conception of the public realm. I argue that her theory of the public as a world-making and agonistic realm is today indispensable if we wish to imagine the cosmopolitan possibility under conditions of technological mediation.

Notes

1   See Rantanen (2002), Boyd-Barrett and Rantanen (1998), Clausen (2003), Volkmer (1999) and Ekecranz (1999).
2   See Volkmer (2002) for the term *microsphere* in this context.
3   See Lynch (2003) and Sakr (2001) for the microsphere of Arab media.
4   See Brown (2001: 8) for the theme of 'humanity as a whole' and the 'universal citizen' in cosmopolitan literature. See also Hannertz (1996), Chartier (1999), Boltanski (1999) and Calhoun (2001).
5   This is not a new idea. Silverstone's work on 'proper distance' reflects, at once, an acknowledgement of this impossibility and an attempt to formulate a norm by which an enabling sense of proximity to the 'other' may be construed on television (2004b: 444–5). Similarly, Butler's work on 'de/humanization' reflects both the recognition that it is impossible to fully represent the human and also the need to understand how this failure becomes embedded in norms of media representation that selectively value and care for the lives of the West (2004: 144).
6   'Universal' morality – a discourse informed by ideas of Christian care and civil responsibility – was first articulated in the public realm in Enlightenment Europe and today constitutes a powerful discourse of ethics in the Western world. As Arendt explains, it was the spectacle of human destitution and poverty confronting the French revolutionaries that shifted the demand for action on poverty from compassionate charity by the good Samaritan to care for the 'other' as a practice to be undertaken by the citizen (1963/1990: 73–5). The historical origins of the politics of pity lie, therefore, in the enlightened awareness of early modern Europe that the suffering of others should no more be acted upon through private charity but through public action.

7   It is no coincidence that Smith's work on the moral sentiment of the public man of the Enlightenment is precisely a theory that seeks to reconstruct 'a morally acceptable politics, around the double figure of an unfortunate and an impartial spectator who observes him from a distance' (Boltanski, 1999: 24).

8   See Boltanski (1999: 5) for a discussion.

9   See Boltanski (1999: 23).

10   For an overview of interdisciplinary literature on cosmopolitanism, see Archibugi and Koenig-Archibugi (2003: 273–91), particularly the sections on 'Cosmopolitan citizenship' and 'Cosmopolitansim as cultural aspiration' (282–3) and 'Ethics and norms in international affairs' (287–88).

11   See Foucault on the announcement of an International Committee Against Piracy in 'Confronting governments: human rights' (1984/2000: 474–5).

12   See Held (1995), Archibugi and Held (1995) and Archibugi, Held and Koehler (1998) for a view of cosmopolitan politics that is organized around different layers of participation in discourse and decision making in institutions of global civil society, such as the UN, rather than the international politics exercised by nation states.

13   As Calhoun (2001: 164) says, social solidarity is introduced to the public 'partly through enhancing the significance of particular categorical identities', such as that of the African woman deprived of her rights, 'and partly through facilitating the creation of direct social relations', such as the activism of the petition and its symbolics of collective action concerning a just cause.

14   See Morley (2000, 2003) for discussion on reterritorialization and deterritorialization vocabulary in the context of this discussion.

15   See Anderson (1983), Billig (1989) and Barnett (2003) for the role of mass media in the construction of national identity.

16   See Volkmer (1999; 2002) for discussion on the emergence of transnational news networks – what she calls *self-referential* networks of public life – that act as powerful political agents in the global space of mediation. The question remains, however, as to whether or not such self-reference emanates from a communitarian or cosmopolitan structure of address. See Held (1996) and Archibugi (2003) for discussion on the *democratic deficit* of global governance institutions which causes them to reproduce structures of global power rather than exercise a politics of solidarity.

9

THE COSMOPOLITAN PUBLIC

In conclusion, let me now move from the question of how things are to how things could and should be. My aim is to think through the ideas of mediation and the public realm in ways that maximize rather than restrict the capacity for a cosmopolitan connectivity between spectators and distant sufferers. Two major insights inform this aspiration. The first is that mediation does not simply act on a pre-existing public, but constitutes this public as a body of action in the process of narrating and portraying distant suffering. The second, and related, insight is that mediation engages the spectators with the demand for action by capitalizing on the aesthetic or spectacular dimension of the public realm.

These insights have been present throughout the discussions so far, but I now wish to address each of them in the light of Arendt's account of the public realm:[1]

> The public signifies two closely interrelated but not altogether identical phenomena. It means, first, that everything that appears in public can be seen and heard by everybody and has the widest possible publicity ... Second, the term 'public' signifies the world itself, in so far as it is common to all of us and distinguished from our own privately owned place in it.
>
> (1958: 50, 52)

Arendt's first notion of the public as 'everything' that 'can be seen and heard by everybody' foregrounds the dimension of the public as a spectacle, as a semiotic accomplishment that orchestrates the effects of image and language in order to present the world to the world. This dimension is often referred to as Arendt's *agonistic* model of the public. Her second notion of the public as 'the world itself, in so far as it is common to all of us' entails the idea that the commonality of the world is not simply given to us, but created by acts of imagination, dialogue and mutual commitment and so is often referred to as the *world-making* model of the public.[2]

Despite Arendt's attachment to a dialogic model of the public realm, the polis, it is clear that her world-making and agonistic dimensions also correspond to a model of public life predicated on mediation. Even though mediation in modern times has expanded and intensified the processes by which the world is presented as 'common to all', it does not render

Arendt's view of the public dated or irrelevant. Mediation today simply forces us to rethink Arendt's contribution on public life in light of the dissemination model rather than the dialogic one. It is important that we do this. If we wish to go beyond a communitarian commitment, caring only for those like 'us', then we need to carefully consider just how mediation renders the engagement of the spectator with the distant sufferer 'public' in the Arendtian sense, as 'world-making' and 'agonistic'.

My argument unfolds in two moves. First, I suggest that the world-making dimension of mediation forces us to rethink the public as a potential agency with no empirical presence that may, however, make a difference in the life of the distant sufferer – the public as a latent body politic, always placed in a structural 'elsewhere' (Keenan, 1993: 135). Second, I suggest that the agonistic dimension of mediation forces us to re-examine the ways in which mediation stages its narratives of suffering and, thereby, selectively orientates the Western sensibility towards certain misfortunes while forgetting others, making us critically aware of the relationship between the public–ethical and the aesthetic dimensions of mediation. Let me consider, in turn, each of these suggestions.

The world-making force of mediation

Emergency news is world-making, in Arendt's sense, in so far as its representations of suffering push the spectators' sense of belonging beyond its existing boundaries and seek to constitute their relationship to distant suffering in terms of a demand for public action. At the same time, the differences that occur between stories within the category of emergency news from active deliberation to passive spectatorship only testify to the fact that the process of world-making, of making the world common to all, is not evenly distributed across these pieces of news. The hierarchy of emergency sufferings is, in this respect, embedded in the same tensions of mediation that organize the broader hierarchy of action in the news, from adventure to ecstatic, that I examined earlier.

The key insight regarding emergency news, however, is that the tensions surrounding action at a distance are not tensions of mediation only. In raising the question of action in multiple ways, emergency news brings forth the idea that action at a distance is a constitutive part of the contemporary political order as a whole. This is the political order of (mainly Western) democracies, where only elected governments have the monopoly on direct action on the political reality of the world, while the governed, as singular individuals, lack the capacity of direct action.[3]

Isn't this the order that Foucault challenges, in Chapter 8, by claiming 'a new right – that of the private individual to effectively intervene in the sphere of international policy and strategy'? Well, yes and no. Even though Foucault relates this new right to organizations such as Amnesty

International or Médècins du Monde, it is clear that such privately mobilized institutions of public action cannot exhaust the agency of the private individual. How many private individuals have the expertise to provide specialized aid to those who need it or, more problematically, how many would wish to join a non-governmental organization in order to live in the zone of suffering? What the cosmopolitan politics of the news about the Nigerian woman's situation illustrates is that public action towards distant sufferers takes the form of *effective speech* – a protest event, yes, but in the zone of safety.[4]

By *effective speech* is meant two specific types of engagement of the spectators with suffering as a moral cause. These are protesting and paying. Each type of engagement inevitably corresponds to the two historical topics for the public representation of suffering that we have encountered earlier:

- denunciation, which leads to political protest
- empathy, which leads to charitable donations.

Protesting and paying, despite their differences, participate in the public realm by performing two similar functions at once. They are both:

- forms of communication, making suffering audible and visible in public
- forms of action, potentially having material effects on distant suffering.

This duality of effective speech expands the concept of public action as world-making action in a new direction.

Effective speech, then, is world-making not only in the sense, mentioned above, that it extends the world in common beyond the community of the 'West' but also because it understands action as that which is beyond the instrumental view of doing something in anticipation of a concrete outcome. Effective speech entails a view of action as establishing connectivities between people and forging relationships of responsibility and commitment with the 'other' without asking for reciprocity or control over the outcome of action.[5] This means that the protesters or charity donors act on distant suffering without being able to fully predict or experience the consequences of their actions. Arendt explains this concept of public action by referring to the identity of the actor as always being already a sufferer:

> Because the actor always moves among and in relation to other acting beings, he [sic] is never merely a 'doer' but always and at the same time a sufferer. To do and to suffer are like opposite sides of the same coin, and the story that an act starts is composed of its consequent deeds and sufferings.

> (1958: 190)

The coupling of the actor and the sufferer in one single identity illustrates the idea that the contingency of effective speech is, at one and the same time, a sign of the actor's own radical vulnerability and dependency on others. Thus, ultimately, it is the awareness of our own vulnerability as human beings that informs – in an existential rather than empirical manner – our commitment to the pain of the other.[6] In this respect, Arendt's account of action acknowledges that the discourse of 'universal' morality lies behind contemporary practices of public action, including those of protesting and paying.[7]

Protesting entails a set of practices for public activism and deliberation, such as demonstrations, petitions, opinion polls or the vote itself. Such practices depend on technological mediation that enables individual citizens to 'bring the testimony of people's suffering to the eyes and ears of governments' (Foucault, 'Liberation', June 1984/2000). Paying – traditionally a private practice of donating to charity – becomes public when it enters the spectacular space of mediation and takes the form of coordinated action on television, such as Live Aid and other such concerts, telethons or other appeals for money in humanitarian crises – a topic studied in detail by Tester (2001) and mentioned in Chapter 6.

In this respect, effective speech in terms of television does not substantially differ from other forms of speech in the public realm. They are all mediated. Indeed, don't the vote or the poll also involve technologies of mediation that give them their public character and don't they both involve the spectator in a minimal and indirect agency on the political process they address?[8] It is telling that these established practices of public action are continuously subject to the same criticism as the mediation of suffering in the news. Just as the television spectacle may distort the reality of suffering, so may the poll or the vote distort public opinion, depending on the methods used and interpretations put on the public voice. Public opinion is just as suspicious a form of public agency as the television spectacle that informs and guides it.[9]

The public as structurally 'elsewhere'

The problem of the cosmopolitan public, then, may be less a question of distance from the suffering and more to do with a 'myth' of authenticity. This is the belief that any form of mediation removes the authenticity of action from a fully present and, therefore, immediately effective public. I examined this argument as the pessimistic thesis of mediation in Chapter 1. At this point, we can see that what I then named the paradox of technology has a strong political equivalent – the paradox of representative democracy (Barnett, 2003: 9–13). Just as technology aspires to eliminate distance only to remind us of its own complicity in mediating a false proximity, so contemporary democracies are supposed to represent the public in its large scale and diversity by virtue of a series of mediations that only manage to deprive the public of a fair representation – ultimately disempowering it. The concern with the ways in which various forms of mediation may distort public opinion or undermine the 'universal' morality of the citizen, is best formulated in Habermas's thesis of the 'refeudalization of the public sphere'.[10]

For our purposes, the same criticism is also formulated with respect to the mediation of suffering and its impact on the moralization of the spectator.[11] The spectacle of human pain, the thesis has it, may be manipulative for spectators. Unless accompanied by practical action or compassionate care, the spectators' pity vis-à-vis distant sufferers may become part of a persuasive machine. 'Pity', Peters says 'is a persuasive technique rather than an ethical value' (2005: 249). This thesis echoes Arendt's own suspicion regarding the 'social question' of suffering as a cause for action in the public realm, on the grounds that it sidelines 'genuine' politics from the public agenda.[12]

What the 'pity is dangerous' thesis fails to take into account is that, today, the world-making dimension of the public realm, the rendering of 'the world itself [...] common to all of us', is performed by means of mediation, via television's own representations of human pain and suffering. Embedded journalists in war zones and, simultaneously, live footage of massive anti-war demonstrations around the world present us with different facets of the same political reality – the frontline of the war and the frontline of protest against it. Both images, despite criticisms on the manner of reporting, constitute a space of mediation where some of the world common to all of us appears in front of the spectators' eyes precisely as common.

Yet, in emphasizing the 'danger' inherent in the physical separation of spectators from sufferers, the thesis of 'pity is dangerous' perpetuates the same utopian belief in the dialogic model of the public realm that we met in Chapter 1. Indeed, isn't there a stark contradiction in Peters' denigration of pity – 'easy to inspire over television' – and his compelling account of contemporary public life organized on the model of dissemination? If today's model of public life is dissemination rather than dialogue, why should public agency remain locked in the idea of acting on the spot? To be sure, each individual spectator is anchored in his or her own lifeworld, in a biographical context from which to experience the world. Nevertheless, by virtue of engaging in mediation, all spectators also engage with specific proposals for agency with what Barnett describes as 'reiterative acts of description that bring into existence the identities that they appear to be merely representing' (2003: 21). Individualized as these acts may appear – casting spectators into the roles of voyeurs, philanthropists or the protesters – let us recall that they belong to a broader structure of address that invites spectators to join an abstraction, an ideal public. The result is that the people addressed by these individualized but ideal acts of identity are, in Barnett's formulation again, 'structurally non-identical with any given event of their manifestation' (2003: 20).

We need, therefore, to go all the way and recognize the elusiveness and fragility of the public as a natural consequence of our recognition that public life today is less about speaking to the one next to us and more about speaking into the air. Recognizing this means that we also cease to regard public action on distant suffering as an expression of the spectators' embodied and emotional compassion. Instead, we should regard public action on distant suffering as always taking place in a 'structural elsewhere' – that is, in a space of agency that may be effective without having a concrete, physical or embodied presence; in fact that is defined precisely by its resistance to being made present' (Keenan, 1993: 135). This is a challenging thought. It appears to suspend, or at least moderate, the powerful discourse of 'universal' morality – the view of the spectator as an ethical being compelled to respond to the call of a sufferer. It appears to suggest, instead, that the question of action on suffering is a radically open question, both in terms of who undertakes it and when and also in terms of the outcomes it has on the suffering. Yet, this is precisely what we need to do[13].

Unless we accept the structural 'elsewhereness' of public agency, we cannot analyse how mediation may bring us in contact with the suffering of distant 'others' and yet leave us untouched and fatigued by it. We can only deplore it as the loss of 'universal' morality. We cannot understand the political dimension of mediation in terms of a historically specific, and therefore reversible, hierarchy of engagements with place and human life, but can only condemn it as an indiscriminate call for 'liberal guilt', in Peters' words.

Public action and the impossibility of 'genuine succur'

The thesis that 'pity is dangerous' in relation to the spectators' 'inner calm' and risky for the expression of 'genuine succour' not only leaves the communitarian logic of mediation unchallenged but also confirms it. This is because the 'pity is dangerous' thesis ends up dismissing the possibilities for public action on suffering that reside in emergency news. In privileging the 'myth' of *authentic* public action over protesting and paying, the thesis writes off these forms of agency as hypocritical or ineffective or both.[14]

On the one hand, mediation undermines the effectiveness of action, because protesting is seen to be too far away from the contexts of 'real' action to be anything other than 'just words'. On the other hand, mediation also fails to register the full presence of the spectators in their acts of engaging with the sufferers. Protesting is dismissed as 'costing nothing' on the part of the spectators, as requiring no sacrifice, and paying is seen as a monetary issue that obliterates the singularity of the particular suffering and enables no bonding between the sufferers and the spectators who help them (Boltanksi, 1999: 18–19).

Once again, let us return to the question: if our encounter with distant suffering is the consequence of a public life that is fully organized around dissemination – the global dispersion of images, information and money – why would our response to suffering either take the form of a sacrifice in the zone of suffering or a testimony of authentic emotion vis-à-vis the sufferers? What the search for manifestations of 'authentic' pity forgets is the world-making force of mediation on public life – the fact that the world today is constituted as common by means of public action that aspires to make a difference but anticipates no immediate outcome as a response.

The political demonstration stands as the prototypical case of world making. This is because the protest makes the moral cause of suffering visible and audible to people and because, in doing so, it also brings people together in a common space of solidarity. Even if demonstrations always sought to render the world common by staging their cause, this possibility is today multiplied and amplified by global media. The instantaneous broadcasting of multiple world demonstrations against the Iraq war in February 2003 testified to a rare moment where public agency becomes embodied and visible to many and, more than this, functions as a point of potential identification with the spectators. This performative function of mediation not only includes the reporting of demonstrations in news broadcasts but also a continuum of broadcasting practices. These encompass, at one end, the 24/7 flow format of global news channels, occasionally operating as pressure points for political agendas (the CNN effect), and, at the other end, infotainment genres, such as debate or interview programmes and documentaries or even drama productions that stage how action on distant suffering is possible.

A particular television genre that provokes public agency in the form of charity donations is the telethon. This is a particular genre because it involves the mediation of philanthropic agency, which, in turn, depends on another form of technological mediation – the transfer of money. This genre has been sharply criticized for subordinating the moral cause of suffering to not only television entertainment but also to the bank cheque.[15] What remains of the authentic emotion in attending to suffering if the call for help takes the form of a celebrity parade on screen or is reduced to a charity phone line?

Such criticism, echoing the 'pity is dangerous' thesis, is haunted by the image of the good Samaritan who alleviates human pain by being there, next to the sufferer. If distance makes practical care impossible, the argument has it, and if effective speech is either ineffective or inauthentic from a distance, then the only alternative is to act as a Samaritan, to offer help to those close to us. As Peters suggests, even if 'the profoundest ethical teachings command love for all people indifferently, ultimately, time allows genuine intimacy and care for only a few of the planet's inhabitants' (1999: 271). It is, precisely, in clinging on to the certainty of proximity and its concrete outcomes that the 'pity is dangerous' thesis subordinates the potential for cosmopolitanism inherent in mediation to communitarian logic and an ethics of proximity.

If, however, we wish to keep the promise of cosmopolitanism open, we need to build on, rather than dismiss, the forms of effective speech that television may promote in its politics of pity. We need to fully acknowledge that, under conditions of dissemination, it is not only the nature of action that becomes disembodied and deterritorialized but also, as Arendt says, the outcomes of action on distant suffering that become inherently uncertain as they are invisible and deferred to the future. Once embedded in multiple technologies of mediation and therefore dislocated from places and bodies, cosmopolitanism itself becomes a radically undecidable regime of action. It is not manifested in a coherent human character but instead expresses itself as a sensibility, an elusive disposition predicated on the willingness to act on the suffering of the 'other' without guarantees.[16]

Genres of mediation, such as the Live Aid concert or a telethon, cultivate this sensibility by embedding the proposal for action in a set of deterritorializing technologies and reterritorializing this proposal in specific practices of popular entertainment. Controversial as such practices may be, they are, in fact, crucial in shaping a cosmopolitan disposition. They do so not *directly*, in the explicit formulation of 'some sort of abstract global civic ethic', as Tomlinson says, but *obliquely* in the performative acts of identification that the spectacles of television engage the spectator with (1999: 202). This point – which places the cosmopolitan public at the centre of the popular practices of television – leads me on to the second and final theme of this chapter, which is the concern with the agonistic dimension of mediation.

The agonistic force of mediation

Agonism is the quality of the public realm as a space of appearance, so that, in Arendt's definition, 'everything that appears in public can be seen and heard by everybody and has the widest possible publicity' (1958: 50). Drawing on a dramaturgical metaphor of action – the public as a 'theatrum mundi' – this view has often been seen as elitist and anti-democratic, privileging the memorable deeds of distinguished individuals over the public action of ordinary social groups.[17] For our purposes, however, this dramaturgical metaphor does not have to take on these connotations. The public as appearance simply draws attention to the fact that mediation appropriates and transforms or, in the vocabulary of Chapter 2, 'remediates' the two historical practices of the polis – the theatre and agora. The idea that mediation does not break with but only disperses these two sites of publicness across space and time is crucial to our understanding of how the cosmopolitan disposition can be cultivated by television. How so? In order to respond to this question, we now need to go full circle and return to the concerns of Chapter 3, with meaning and power.

The concern with meaning brings into focus the need for news broadcasts to reconsider their mise en scène of suffering – that is, the ways in which news narratives stage the spectacle of suffering within a particular politics of pity. I address this concern in the next section. My proposal is that, if we wish to redress the existing hierarchy of pity in the news, then the mise en scène of suffering should stop taking the private emotions of the spectator as the measure against which the reality of the 'other' is portrayed. Instead, the mise en scène of suffering should encompass the value of impersonal action (Arendt, 1968: 3–31). This proposal, which I formulate in the section after the next under the heading 'The narcissism of pity', resonates with Arendt's view of the public as not only the world 'common to all' but also 'distinguished from our own privately owned place in it'.

The other concern, with power, brings into focus the need for television news to combine pity with *justice*. Whereas justice is already an element of the politics of pity, in the topic of denunciation, I propose that we restore justice as an autonomous dimension of the selection and mise en scène of the news, which articulates with, rather than subserves, pity. The sections later in this chapter entitled 'Communitarianism and "global intimacy"' and 'Pity and justice' conclude this book by suggesting that only when news narratives begin to address the concrete questions of why and what to do can television begin to mediate distant suffering in more reflexive and pluralistic ways than it has done so far.

The agonistic properties of mediation: immediacy and hypermediacy

On-the-spot action on suffering suppresses the expression of emotion. In contrast, action at a distance requires the construal of suffering in some form of affective register, so that 'pity becomes eloquent, recognizing and discovering itself as emotion and feeling', Boltanski writes (1999: 6).

The contrast between adventure and emergency news is that between the modes of eloquence pity takes. Whereas the news of the Indian accident blocks the eloquence of pity and places no demand for a response on the spectators, the piece on the Argentinean famine maximizes eloquence and seeks to engage the spectators with emotion and humanitarian action (albeit in an impossible manner). What does this contrast suggest? The multimodality of these news texts – from narrative types to visualization and language–image combination – are simultaneously the dramaturgical features of the news genre. Thus, the politics of pity, as I have argued, is itself an aesthetic process that stages the scene of suffering in a particular place and time and populates this scene with actors and the deeds that they perform on the suffering.

It is this staging of emotions in television that the 'pity is dangerous' thesis regrets as inauthentic. It is against such staging that the thesis counterposes the compassionate ethos of silent but authentic benefaction – the polis to broadcasting. Nevertheless, let us recall that the public of the polis was itself a stage for spectacle, rendering suffering an object of contemplative identification and action for the spectators. Don't the theatre and the agora – the two genres of the Athenian public – also re-present and therefore spectacularize public action at a distance in language or image?

Despite the fact that mediation incorporates these two public genres in order to disperse them in space and time, the nature of dramaturgical performance does not change beyond recognition. There is a shift, to be sure, from the embodied individual, agoraic orator or theatrical performer on the stage of the polis, to the individualized but disembodied actor on the television screen, yet, in both cases, these are public figures who act out parts. In a manner reminiscent of the Athenian orator or actor, the Amnesty International activist or the September 11th terrorist refer less to themselves and more to generic or metonymic figures, as I call them in Chapter 4, who appear on screen in the capacities of benefactor or persecutor of suffering. In this respect, they are part of the symbolic mechanism of pity, always engaging the spectators in reiterative acts of identity.

Even if both the theatre and agora model public action as a space of appearance, as aesthetic performance rather than just political and ethical practice, there is a difference between the two of them. Whereas the agora mobilizes the rational and deliberative sensibilities of the spectators vis-à-vis the suffering, the theatrical model enacts the emotional identification of the spectators with the sufferers. Impartial deliberation and the arousal of emotion are, as we know, the two constitutive properties of the politics of pity, which seeks to construe suffering as a moral cause by presenting the suffering as an objective fact to be contemplated.

These distinctions are difficult to sustain in practice. Agora and theatre, contemplating and feeling are fused together in the course of the news narrative so that it becomes difficult to tell them apart.[18] However, we need to do so because, unless we differentiate watching from feeling on the screen, we won't be able to differentiate among the forms of public agency that pity generates. The pessimism of the 'pity is dangerous' thesis lies precisely in its inability to appreciate the forms of social solidarity and humanitarian care that the news may construe in its reports of human suffering. In dismissing feeling in television as inauthentic, the pessimistic thesis fails to discern the potential for cosmopolitanism that lies in the agonistic dimension of mediation. The value of the opposite thesis – optimism about the power of mediation to democratize care and responsibility – lies in the inability of the optimistic position to evaluate the hierarchies of pity that the news usually construes in reporting suffering. In celebrating the power of mediation as a space of appearance, the optimistic thesis fails to evaluate the dangers that lie in the agonistic dimension of mediation.

The analytics of mediation is an attempt to develop a language of description that makes the tactical distinction between watching and feeling so as to throw into relief how they interplay and their effects. Let us recall the vocabulary:

- *hypermediacy* – the staging of suffering as a technological and semiotic accomplishment – draws attention to the act of watching
- *immediacy* – the presentation of suffering as suffering – draws attention to the feeling that we need to act, and potentially the commitment to act on suffering.

The forms of realism that construe emergency news are, in this respect, aesthetic effects of the ways in which each news narrative puts watching at the service of feeling; hypermediacy is at the service of immediacy. By the same token, the verbal minimalism and map graphics of adventure news foreground hypermediacy at the expense of immediacy and, thereby, manage to evacuate suffering of the urgency to act, disconnecting watching from feeling.

The narcissism of pity

The contrast between adventure and emergency news tells us that, without immediacy, pity cannot become eloquent in television. Without realism – verbal and visual – suffering is about watching the news and not feeling for the 'other'. This theatrical sense of as-if authenticity – of witnessing the scene of suffering and being moved by it – throws into relief the centrality of intimacy in the shaping of the spectator–sufferer relationship. Intimacy, in this context, refers to the mechanism of psychological identification, either empathetic or indignant, that may potentially engage the spectators with the cause of suffering.[19] The evocation of emotion as if the spectator were present in the scene is, of course, constitutive of the theatrical conception of the public. Technological mediation, however, intensifies this mimetic effect via the visual plenitude of the screen and the illusion of presence that this creates. 'The viewer,' as Manovich puts it, 'is expected to concentrate completely on what she sees [...] focusing her attention on the representation and disregarding the physical space outside' (2001: 95–6).

The hope that connectivity with the 'other' is achievable with technological imagery and mimesis may be a cause of disagreement between the two narratives on mediation, but both of them agree on this prior assumption: psychological identification provides the condition of possibility for cosmopolitanism. This is why, in navigating between pessimism and optimism, Tomlinson's own proposal on cosmopolitanism is that 'stories of moral concern need to be told in ways which [...] indeed translate these concerns into the realm of the personal and the intimate' (1999: 179).

This powerful discourse, which links intimacy and cosmopolitanism in a cause and effect relationship, assumes that the sufferers share with the spectators a common humanity. It is this shared humanity that, when not readily accessible, can be theatricalized – staged and translated – into the realm of the spectators' own psychological world. The discourse of 'universal' humanity, then, is as equally constitutive of the politics of pity as the discourse of 'universal' morality. How else would distant sufferers arouse the spectators' emotions, unless their humanness, hidden as it may be, was already there, waiting only to be properly staged in order to reach the spectators' kind hearts?

Nevertheless, there is a danger in theatrically staging suffering. The Argentinean famine as well as the news item on the African refugees show us that the spectators' call for emergency action may be easily reduced to an exercise in private emotion. By relying exclusively on the aesthetics of immediacy, these pieces of news overpsychologize suffering – that is, they choose to thematize the fear, danger or bodily pain of the sufferers and engage the spectators with the intensity of these feelings. As a consequence, these news items reduce the demand for action on suffering to easy sensationalism. They do very little to connect the instances of suffering with the questions of why and what to do.

Such overpsychologizing of suffering cannot be explained away as simply reflecting sociocultural particularities or market demands. Although such explanations are no doubt valid, what I wish to draw attention to is a deeper and, hence, more powerful tendency that informs the mediation of suffering in Western television. It is that the tendency to psychologize the distant 'other' reflects the narcissism of contemporary social life in the West – a quality of social life that shapes individuals' experiences of the world around the emotions of the self. In a diagnosis of late modernity reminiscent of Arendt, Sennet describes narcissism as the key 'pathology' of Western social relationships:[20] 'narcissism is now mobilized in social relations by a culture deprived by belief in the public and ruled by *intimate feelings as a measure of the meaning of reality*' (1976/1992: 326, emphasis added).

Let us think of the African refugees or the Argentinean children in our pieces of emergency news. Don't these representations of sufferers seek to reflect the condition of suffering in a mirror of the spectators' own psychological portraits? Whereas the rescue mission is a theatre that mirrors the spectators' thrill for adventure, the Argentinean famine is a theatre that discovers the spectators' tender hearts in the spectacle of emaciated children. In both cases, the spectators' agency is exhausted in the gasp or the shedding of a tear, bringing the possibility of action at a distance to a stop. In fact, the narcissism of viewing leaves, according to Sennett, no space for the idea of action at a distance.[21] In so far as distance inevitably separates the action accomplished from the actors themselves, the narcissistic spectators fail to see the reflection of their feelings in the action and, therefore, also fail to see their own actions as concrete, effective and authentic. Doesn't the 'pity is dangerous' thesis sustain its reservations regarding action at a distance precisely on the grounds that it lacks the authenticity of full presence?

It is to this narcissism of mediation that Arendt's dramaturgical conception of action comes as a powerful response. For her, the agonistic ethos of the public is about appearing on stage under the condition that we leave behind the needs and drives of the private self. Public action is impersonal because it sustains the distance between the interiority of the self and the role on stage, between 'man and actor'. In the mediation of suffering, the distinction between private self and public role does not reside in the person. Rather, it resides in the structure of the address by means of which television stages the spectacle of suffering. It resides in the relationship between the particular and the 'universal' – showing a single incident of human pain and narrating this specific incident as a moral cause for collective action.

Indeed, you will recall from earlier that no singular story of misfortune is, in itself, capable of evoking emotion. Rather, each story acquires its emotional depth, tender-heartedness or anger by means of the topics of empathy, denunciation or even aesthetic contemplation. The spectacle of suffering, in other words, needs to portray the humane sufferer as one who is endowed with some form of 'conditional' agency and surrounded either by a kind benefactor or a vicious evil-doer. This structure of address – at once public and personalized – demonstrates that the dimension of impersonality still exists in today's culture of intimacy. However, it simultaneously shows that, pace Arendt, contemporary mediation cannot be strictly impersonal – it cannot separate public from private. It is not only that no politics of pity is possible without this distinction but also because the Western experience of modernity as a whole is inescapably bound up with the idea that human particularity, our needs, desires and emotions, constitutes the centre of the self, throwing the 'man' of the polis – the carrier of the 'universal' values of public life – into decline.[22]

Communitarianism and 'global intimacy'

It is impossible to return fully to this lost past. Instead of deploring it, we should accept our condition, which is that the viewing subject of mediation is not theatrical but self-conscious, not heroic but reflexive.[23] This, however, does not mean that the narcissistic spectator cannot become a public figure. It means, rather, that the spectators' capacities to become public figures and connect to the distant 'others' depend on those technologies of the self that tap into their very reflexivity.[24]

This point brings us full circle, returning us to concerns with the nature of power that mediation exercises today on the spectators. Part of what Foucault calls 'technologies of governmentality', the power of mediation works less by imposing ideas about the 'good' and more as a result of construing a hierarchy of 'good' and 'bad' that we spontaneously embrace as 'our own'. This happens less by explicitly restraining our freedom and more by letting us act reflexively, as subjects of 'conditional freedom'. In order to function pedagogically, therefore, mediation should address the reflexive concerns of the spectators with 'How I feel', but it must do so in a manner that avoids self-absorption. Instead, mediation must seek to expand the spectators' emotional concerns beyond the limits of their existing intimate world and cultivate a moral sensibility beyond an ethics of proximity.

This is possible if television news combines the emphasis on emotion – which facilitates the spectators' capacity to 'connect' – with an element of impersonality, which interrupts rather than reproduces their narcissism. In other words, cosmopolitanism depends on the condition that television news keeps the distinction between watching and feeling in a constant, creative tension. Indeed, the collapse between watching and feeling, which I discussed earlier, is simply another way of saying that intimacy lies at the core of dominant conceptions of cosmopolitanism today. How else would the spectator be persuaded to act unless they can forget about the watching and feel for the pain of the 'others' as if it were their own? Innocent as this discourse may sound, there is, nevertheless, growing suspicion against it. 'Intimacy', Silverstone argues, 'does not guarantee recognition or responsibility; it can invite, conceivably, either blank resistance or, alternatively, incorporation' (2002a: 8).

Let me return, for the last time, to the twilight humanness of the emergency sufferer. The symbolics of threat – in the medicalization of the African rescue operation, for example – or the fetishization of the sufferers – in the zooming in on the Argentinean children's body parts, discussed in Chapter 6 – points precisely to the inability of these pieces of news to represent the suffering 'others' outside the emotional horizons of the spectators. They seem to be incorporating the 'otherness' of these sufferers – an irreducible 'being who they are' – into a culture that, instead of making room for irreducibility, reflects on the sufferers, the image of whom the spectators are or should be, in their encounters with these sufferers. This mechanism, which Peters (after Adorno) calls *pathic projection*, is the first to organize a structure of address that mediates suffering via a discourse of intimacy.[25]

By the same token, the dehumanization of the Indian or Indonesian sufferers can be seen as the sign of 'blank resistance'. Isn't television denying these sufferers the status of human beings precisely by resisting to translate their interiority into the spectators' own, reflecting their despair and pain on to 'our' own emotions? This mechanism of *annihilation*, in Silverstone's words, is second to organize the structure for addressing mediation around the discourse of intimacy.

Pathic projection and annihilation are, in this respect, effects of representation that reproduce the narcissistic sensibility of spectators, either by capitalizing on the spectators' emotions regarding the 'others' who approach 'our' humanity or interrupting emotion when the 'others' do not mirror 'our' inner selves. The implication of these effects for distributing pity in a selective manner is obvious. They recreate the communitarian bias. Articulated on the immediate force of emotion, both mechanisms of pity reserve feeling for the 'other', for those like 'us', and spin the rest of the world away from the order of humanness. Instead of cosmopolitanism, these mechanisms of pity establish a form of global intimacy that is, by definition, hierarchical.

Cosmopolitanism and convention

The cosmopolitan portrayal of suffering requires the interruption of emotion by means of a measure of impersonality – a measure of what Sennet calls 'conventional performance': 'convention is about rules for behaviour at a distance from the immediate desires of the self' (1974/1992: 266). Impersonality in mediation is about a structure of address that makes explicit its own conventions of representing suffering and, in so doing, reminds the spectators that their encounters with the sufferers, far from being authentic reality, are a spectacle. Rather than a stiff application of rules, then, convention refers to the use of deliberative genres of television that foreground the distinction between immediacy and hypermediacy and offer the spectators a temporality of detached watching and reflection as if the spectators were part of a public stage – an agora.

The clearest illustration of the capacity of convention to temper emotion with a measure of impersonality is the class of ecstatic news. Central to this representation of suffering is the live footage, a master genre that enables a flow of other genres to engage the spectators with alternating topics of suffering and empathize, denounce and reflect on the scene of suffering. Live footage, by definition, interrupts broadcasting routines and makes the breakdown of convention part of its own staging. It is about following up on reality as it happens via live links or updates and explaining reality by means of constant reference to the machinery of mediation, such as commentary on slow-motion footage, expert interviews on location or panel talks at the television studio.

What does this 'ecstatic' dialectic suggest? Even though, as we saw Tomlinson claim in Chapter 1, the history of mediation is about putting hypermediacy at the service of immediacy, the dialectic suggests that the key to cosmopolitanism may lie in doing the opposite. Cosmopolitanism is about thematizing the tenuous relationship between immediacy and hypermediacy.

Convention, in this respect, is about articulating the two positions of mediation by means of which the spectator encounters distant suffering:

- the as-if they were within the scene of suffering, which is a position of immediacy
- the as-if they were speaking out their views on suffering in public, which is a position of hypermediacy.

This dual position, you will recall, is what I have called a 'position of reflexive identification'. Reflexive identification brings the spectators of the news as close to the cosmopolitan disposition as it gets, in so far as the cosmopolitan disposition presupposes precisely this duality between feeling for the distant sufferer and responding to the suffering as part of an ongoing public dialogue.

Whereas in ecstatic news reflexive identification was accomplished by using live broadcasts and reserving care for somebody like 'us', it is possible to imagine otherwise. It is possible to imagine that reflexive identification occurs outside the genres of liveliness and expands the spectators' reflexivity beyond their communitarian concerns. The emergency news about the Nigerian woman is a case in point. Amina Lawal's story was narrated using more than one of the topics of suffering, which moved the spectators back and forth in the space–times of danger and safety and confronted them with a number of humble stories about the sharia sentence. The intense visual editing that enabled this multiplicity, combined, in turn, a number of other news genres. For example, it combined a reporter's voiceover with archive film and on-location footage with the Amnesty International activist's interview. It is, again, the tactical combination of feeling with watching that throws into relief the power of convention in this piece of news. It is the being there and, simultaneously, showing that the being there is an act of mediation.

The key here is the necessary distance between the spectators and the scene of suffering that the use of multiple genres introduces into the news. This distance is important because the shift between witnessing and deliberative genres breaks with the immediacy of emotion and opens up a space in which to problematize what the spectators usually take for granted: the questions as to why we are being confronted with these specific sufferers and what can be done about their suffering.

The brief interview with the Amnesty International activist establishes this kind of distance between the location of the spectators and that of the suffering, signalling that our feeling for Amina is not enough – she needs our actions, too. In this example, the deliberative genre of the interview not only facilitates a reflexive distance vis-à-vis the spectacle of suffering but it also renders the Nigerian 'other' more visible and intelligible to the Western spectators. Paradoxically, then, conventional distance introduces a quality of connectivity with the distant 'others' that is more equalitarian and fair than the selective connectivities with other news stories. This is, of course, largely due to the fact that the deliberative agent of this piece of news – Amnesty International – works to an agenda of global solidarity.

In summary, the necessary condition for an agonistic ethos in the news' representation of suffering is the balanced shift between witnessing and deliberative genres. In contrast to the suggestion that the news should render the stories of distant 'others' congruent with local horizons and the realm of the intimate, the cosmopolitan disposition seems to depend, instead, on contextualizing the intensely personal in the realm of the public and political. Without the right measure of theatricality and agoraic deliberation, the example of the news of the Nigerian woman shows that there can be no reflexive identification on the part of the spectator; no balance between feeling and watching. There can only be either a 'spontaneous' response of emotion regarding those who are 'naturally' like us or else a 'blank resistance' to those who fail to mirror 'our' quality of humanness.

Pity and justice

Far from being a denial of pity, impersonality is a necessary condition for the cosmopolitan disposition in so far as it prefers the value of detached judgement to the intimate reflex of communitarianism.[26] Is the impersonality of deliberation, however, a sufficient condition for cosmopolitanism? The answer is no.

News broadcasting – both in terms of global and national television – often includes the voice of an expert, the detached commentary of a local reporter or the contribution of an activist. Nevertheless, such proliferation of voices cannot, in itself, cultivate a relationship of care and responsibility regarding the distant sufferes, just as the intense deliberation in the September 11th footage did not put the communitarian bond under pressure – it reinforced it.

The sufficient condition for a cosmopolitan structure of address is that the news extends the reach of reflexive identification towards sufferings that occur outside the community of the West and are of a magnitude and level of impact on local people that deserve our solidarity. Such instances of suffering currently receive either minimal attention or fall completely outside the remit of newsworthiness. Justice, therefore, is a key criterion – not only in the mise en scène but also in the selection of such sufferings. Even though the procedures of news selection – rendering such instances visible to the Western spectator in the first place – fall beyond the scope of this book, the demand for reflexive identification, once these instances reach the screen, is directly connected to our discussion on the importance of the why and what to do questions in the news.

These questions, you will recall, raise the issue of whether or not the suffering of the unfortunate is at all justified. This is an issue that pity, in privileging the urgency of suffering, consistently sidelines. At the sight of emaciated children, as Boltanski claims, 'who [...] would dream of saying that the inhabitants of a country ravaged by famine have what they deserve?' (1999: 5). Yet, as we know, even if the question 'why?' appears scandalous in any particular situation of suffering, it is nevertheless already foreclosed for the majority of world sufferings. The inhabitants of the Sudan or Argentina surely do not deserve to suffer from famine. Yet, if their suffering is not made visible, then the question of who deserves what becomes irrelevant to the Western spectators before it is even articulated. As long as Western television reports on distant suffering exclusively from the perspective of pity, then urgency – with its voyeuristic and sentimental calls for action – will always be more important than inequality.

The result is that the spectators are confronted with a diffused and often confusing collage of sufferings, each seeking to make its own bid for public attention, while it offers them 'no rational way of weighing the claims of one against another'.[27] In making it impossible to judge which distant suffering matters most, the media create an ethical vacuum in the voice of justice and this is what may create compassion fatigue and inhibit action.[28]

It is, therefore, as a response to the bias inherent in a pity-orientated politics of representation that justice comes into the picture. In fusing emotional identification with reflexive judgement, justice brings about a different discourse on the 'others' and their suffering. The voices of the anonymous activist, UN representative, rock star, political personality or demonstrating masses play a key role, in this respect, as they establish the necessary distance from the spectacle of the suffering 'others' in order to tell us why their suffering matters and what we do about it. It is by means of these various forms of effective speech that the spectators are reminded of this simple fact: our action may be more relevant and effective when orientated towards those whose human needs have been neglected precisely because they do not share 'our' own humanity, rather than towards others like 'us'.

It is difficult to imagine how sufferings so far invisible and, hence, irrelevant to us can be singled out as causes of our concern and action. Indeed, as Peters, following Adorno, emphasizes, the key question for communication theory today is 'how ready we are to see "the human as precisely what is different"?' (1999: 230). The responsibility for this difficulty falls, partly, on the lack of a robust and truly effective culture of global institutions that engages Western spectators with the question 'Why?' and can be held accountable for the question of what to do about these distant causes for concern.[29] So far, it is only the Western nation states that are the legitimate receivers of the question 'Why' and mainly national governments that are held accountable for the protection of the civil rights of Western citizens. The politics of justice – to the extent that it is exercised at all – remains a privilege of national public discourse.

At the same time, the responsibility to bring distant suffering as a moral cause on to our television screens also lies with the current structures of mediation – not only as technological and semiotic realities, but also historical and institutional processes. How do current media conglomerates regulate, economically and technologically, the global flows of information? What impact does the rapid development of satellite broadcasting have on the visibility of distant suffering in the West? How can we describe the public microspheres that distribute different potentials for pity in different parts of the globe? Such questions, albeit beyond the scope of this book, do nevertheless delineate an important research agenda that promises to contribute new insights to the problematic of cosmopolitanism and global citizenship.

From global intimacy to worldiness

Changes in the representation of distant suffering on television can and must facilitate a broader shift in the public cultures of Western societies. This shift is necessary because it is now evident that the language of pity – essentially the currently available language of politics and community – is insufficient to properly translate distant suffering for the Western spectator. The key to this shift towards a cosmopolitan public culture is to develop a reflexive distance from the society of intimacy. Even though the Western spectators inevitably interpret the world by means of a preferred set of norms of community and belonging, this is not an irreversible fact of life. Community is not simply given – it is produced and reproduced via public discourse and the acts of identification with the world out there that television makes available to us.[30]

Public discourse that is world-making, in the Arendtian sense described earlier, can educate us to distinguish between acting on the 'others' in a manner that mirrors our own emotions about their suffering and doing so in a manner that makes a difference to them without getting the 'I' into the picture. The difference is between action to 'express ourselves' and that which makes us 'expressive in public'.[31] Isn't the latter the essence of social solidarity that I discussed in Chapter 8?

This cosmopolitan disposition, which distinguishes (without separating) the public–political from the emotional, promises to bring back to the public stage a particular form of civil identity. This is what Arendt calls 'worldliness' (1968).[32] As it is difficult to survive in a culture of intimacy, worldliness proposes an experience of public life that thrives on impersonal action. Although it does not ignore private emotion and desire, Arendt suggestively calls it a 'feeling for the world', worldliness is a mode of relating to the 'others' that takes as its point of departure the affairs of the external world rather than the interiority of the self. The 'how things are' rather than the 'how I feel.'

Public discourse that is agonistic, in the Arendtian sense, can produce narratives of suffering that are historical, in that they are open and dynamic, and portray the distant 'other' neither as somebody like us nor as an 'Other' beyond reach. Just as the concept of proper distance refers less to our intimate proximity to and more to our reflexive detachment from the scene of suffering, so the concept of proper humanity refers less to the sufferers' own emotional interiority and more to their 'conditional' agency vis-à-vis the burden of their own misfortunes.

Equally crucial for the agonistic ethos of mediation is the use of the discursive apparatus of justification and its deliberative genres, because such genres can put forward another way of prioritizing whose suffering matters for the Western spectators. Drawing on the authority and experience of global civil society institutions and popular forms of effective speech, the visibility of multiple actors on distant suffering provides a point of identification for the Western spectators and engages them with 'incessant and continual discourse about the affairs of the world' – a discourse that may humanize the world in more effective ways than pity currently does.[33]

To be sure, the demand for action embedded in the spectacles of mediation is not, in itself, enough to sustain the cosmopolitan vision. It is only when the spectators take up the proposals of television and join a broader public of deliberation and action that the founding act of mediation as an agent of cosmopolitan reflexivity can be accomplished. In this sense, we should regard the act of mediation itself as purely performative. It is a 'promise' about the quality of public culture that we wish to live in, given that certain conditions of possibility – symbolic and material – for enabling the global flow of news and representing the world to the world are ultimately fulfilled.

Whether cosmopolitanism remains a utopian form of identification in the pedagogic repertoire of television or ultimately develops into concrete and effective public action depends on more than the representations of television. It depends on larger political, economic and institutional realities that go beyond this analysis. My aspiration is much more modest. It is to make us aware of certain conditions of this promise, one of which is to carve out the symbolic space in which the cosmopolitan spectator becomes possible in public life.

The idea and ideal behind this aspiration is that public action vis-à-vis the 'other' should not be left exclusively in the hands of humanitarian agencies or global governance. If we still believe in the modernist project of social change and wish to envisage the individual spectator as an ethical being, then we should also be able to envisage how mediation makes public action possible for each one of us. It is in the space of mediation that our ways of being as citizens meet and fuse with our ways of everyday life, multiple and different as these are. It is also in this space of mediation that the present may become a moment that we at once experience and analyse, live in and reflect on, talk about and act on. The promise for the cosmopolitan disposition lies in this worldly engagement with the present that can make each and every one of us 'the friend of many men, but no man's brother'.

Notes

1 See Silverstone (2002a: 766) for an appropriation of Arendt's view of public life under conditions of mediation and Peters (1999: 27–8, 108) on Arendt's concepts of plurality and difference in communication theory.

2 For this distinction, see Villa (1999: 128–54) and Benhabib (1996: 125–6).

3 See Held (1996: 295–360) and Robins (1994: vii–xxvi), among others.

4 See Boltanksi (1999: 170–92) for a discussion on the possibilities and limitations that the media provide for effective action on humanitarian issues and Calhoun (2004: 94 –101) on the problems of engaging with cosmopolitan politics – not least, the illusion of excessive activism and the bias against women's participation.

5 See McGowan (1998: 63–4) and Villa (1999: 193–98) for a discussion on the Arendtian view of action, Silverstone (1999: 135–6) for a similar argument, drawing on the philosophy of Levinas, and Calhoun (2003: 97).

6 See McGowan (1998: 66–70) for the existential element in Arendt's concept of action and Butler (2004: 19–49) for the constitutive role that human vulnerability plays in contemporary ethical practice.

7 See McGowan (1998: 81–95) on Arendt's own critique of the Enlightenment on the grounds that it privileges the moral question of poverty and suffering over public–political issues – the 'social question' over 'politics' (Arendt, 1963/1990: 59–114).

8 See Held (1996: 327–8), Derrida (1992: 87–8), Peters (1997: 5–16) and Barnett (2003: 24–9).

9 See Peters (1997: 6–8), Boltanski (1999: 174) and Barnett (2003: 17–24).

10 See Habermas's *The Structural Transformation of the Public Sphere* (1989). For relevant critical discussions, see, among others, Fraser (1991, 1997) and Calhoun (1992, 2001) and Demertzis (2002).

11 See Arendt (1963/1990: 59–114), for a critical discussion on this position see McGowan (1998: 45–52) and also Boltanski (1999: 3–13).

12 See Calhoun (2003: 100) who, from a political theory perspective, formulates a similar point:

> the ideal of civil society has sometimes been expressed in recent years as though it should refer to a constant mobilization of all of us all the time in various forms of voluntary organizations.

Yet, he suggests, it is unreasonable:

> to base a political order on the expectation that everyone will choose to participate. *A good political order must deal fairly with the fact that most people will not be politically active most of the time.*

(Emphasis added)

13 See Tester (2001: 3–8; 104–114).

14 See Tester (2001: 115–31) for an overview of the criticisms.

15 Fraser, in her *Re-think the public sphere* (1997: 69–98), introduces the term 'weak', as opposed to 'strong', public in order to conceptualize collective activities 'whose deliberative practice consists exclusively in opinion-formation and does not encompass decision-making' and contrasts this to strong publics that also include decision-making (1997: 90). See also Chouliaraki (2000: 311) and Barnett (2003: 70) for discussions of the distinction in relation to the media.

16 See Villa (1999: 116) and Barnett (2003: 26) for a criticism of Arendt's model as reducing the political 'to the pure action of self-creation detached from instrumental concerns'.

17 Silverstone (1999: 29–30) defines the interplay between judgement and emotion as one between *rhetoric* – the power of mediation to persuade – and the *poetic* – the power of mediation to please – as well as the *erotic* – with its power to seduce – and argues that they are instrumental in shaping patterns of spectatorial identification. In a similar manner, for Corner (1999: 100), the interplay between judgement and emotion is one between *scopophilia* – the jouissance of visual experience – and *epistephilia* – the interest in impartial knowledge and distantiated reflection.

18 According to Corner, identification – that is, 'a degree of viewer projection in which alignment is established between a character or kinds of action on the screen and the viewer's own subjectivity' – is the most straightforward notion to account for spectatorial engagement (1999: 100). See also Bondebjerg (2002) for the social effects of spectatorial identification that the hybrids of public discourse with private fascination in various television genres bring about and Bordwell and Thompson (2001) for identification, fantasy and social regulation in film.

19 See Villa (1999: 128–54) for the connection between Arendt and Sennett, on the grounds that Sennett's view of the public as a theatrical stage makes up for what critics call the 'sociological deficit' in Arendt's thinking.

20 See Sennett (1974/1992: 327).

21 See McGowan (1998: 34–95), Villa (1999: 107–27 and 128–14) for critical discussions.

22 See Touraine (2000: 131–5), but also Giddens (1990, 1991) and Thompson (1995, 2000).

23 See Giddens (1990: 2, 3, 20); Foucault (1983: 208–12; 1984a: 46–7, 50) and Flyvbjerg (2001: 103).

24 Peters (1999: 230) quotes Adorno (1974: 105) for the term *pathic projection:*

> The constantly encountered assertion that blacks, savages, Japanese are like 'animals', monkeys for example, is the key to the pogrom [...] The mechanism of 'pathic projection' determines that those in power perceive as humans only their own reflected image, instead of reflecting back the human as precisely what is different.

25 See Villa (1999: 125).

26 See McIntyre (1985: 8).

27 See also Tester (2001: 13).

28 See Held (1996) and Best et al. (2000).

29 See Calhoun (2003: 98).

30 See Sennett (1976/1992: 323–36).

31 See Villa (1999: 131–7, 151–4).

32 See Arendt (1968: 30).

BIBLIOGRAPHY

Adorno, T. (1938/1982) 'On the fetish-character in music and the regression of listening', in A. Arato and E. Gebhart (eds), *The Essential Frankfurt School Reader*. New York: Continuum.

Adorno, T. (1974) *Minima Moralia. Reflections from Damaged Life*. London: Verso.

Alexander, J. (2001) 'From the Depths of Despair: Performance, Counter-Performance, and September 11th'. Working papers. New Haven, Connecticut: Centre for Cultural Sociology, Yale University Press.

Alexander, J., and Jakobs, R. (1998) 'Mass communication, ritual and civil society', in T. Liebes and J. Curran (eds), *Media, Ritual and Identity*. London: Routledge. pp. 23–42.

Ali, T. (2001) 'Yes, there is an effective alternative to the bombing of Afghanistan', *The Independent*, 15 October.

Allan, S., and Zelizer, B. (eds) (2002) *Journalism after September 11th*. London: Routledge.

Anderson, B. (1983) *Imagined Communities: Reflections on the Origin and Spread of Nationalism*. London: Verso.

Appadurai, A. (1996) *Modernity at Large: Cultural Dimensions of Globalisation*. Minneapolis: University of Minnesota Press.

Arato, A., and Gebhart, E. (eds) (1982) *The Essential Frankfurt School Reader*. New York: Continuum.

Archibugi, D. (ed.) (2003) *Debating Cosmopolitics*. London: Verso.

Archibugi, D., and Held, D. (eds) (1995) *Cosmopolitan Democracy: An Agenda for a New World Order*. Cambridge: Polity.

Archibugi, D., and Koenig-Archibugi, M. (2003) 'Globalization, democracy and cosmopolis: a bibliographical essay', in D. Archibugi (ed.), *Debating Cosmopolitics*. London: Verso.

Archibugi, D., Held, D., and Koeler, M. (eds) (1998) *Re-imagining Political Community: Studies in Cosmopolitan Democracy*. Cambridge: Polity Press.

Arendt, H. (1958) *The Human Condition*. Chicago: University of Chicago Press.

Arendt, H. (1963/1990) *On Revolution*. Harmondsworth: Penguin.

Arendt, H. (1968) *Men in Dark Times*. New York: Harcourt Brace Jovanovic.

Aristotle (1976) *The Nichomachean Ethics*. A.K. Thompson (trans.). Penguin: Harmondsworth.

Armitage, J. (ed.) (2000) *From Modernism to Hypermodernism and Beyond: Paul Virilio*. London: Sage.

Bakhtin, M. (1981) 'Forms of time and chronotope in the novel', in M. Holquist (ed.), *The Dialogic Imagination: Four Essays by M.M. Bakhtin*. Austin, Texas: University of Texas Press.

Bakhtin, M. (1986) 'Bildungsroman', in C. Emerson and M. Holquist (eds), *Speech Genres and Other Late Essays*. Austin, Texas: University of Texas Press.

Barker, C. (2002) *Alain Badiou: A Critical Introduction*. London: Pluto Press.

Barnett, C. (2003) *Culture and Democracy: Media, Space and Representation*. Edinburgh: Edinburgh University Press.

Barnett, C., and Law, M. (eds) (2004) *Spaces of Democracy*. London: Sage.

Barry, A. (2001) *Political Machines*. London: Athlone Press.
Baudrillard, J. (1968/1996) *The System of Objects*. London: Verso.
Baudrillard, J. (1983) *Simulations*. New York: Semiotext(e).
Baudrillard, J. (1988) *Selected Writings*. M. Poster (ed.). Cambridge: Polity Press.
Baudrillard, J. (1994) *The Gulf War Did Not Take Place*. Sydney: Powerful Publications.
Baudrillard, J. (2001) 'The mind of terrorism', in *Le Monde*, 2 November.
Bauman, Z. (1990) *Thinking Sociologically*. London: Blackwell.
Bauman, Z. (1993) *Postmodern Ethics*. Cambridge: Polity Press.
Bauman, Z. (1998) *Globalization: The Human Consequences*. Cambridge: Polity Press.
Beck, U. (1986) *Risk Society: Towards a New Modernity*. London: Sage.
Beck, U. (2001) 'The cosmopolitan state', *Der Spiegel*, 15 October.
Beck, U. (2002) 'The cosmopolitan society and its enemies', special issue, *Cosmopolis, Theory, Culture and Society*, 19(1–2): 17–44.
Beck, U., Giddens, A., and Lash, S. (1994) *Reflexive Modernatization*. Cambridge: Polity Press.
Beilharz, P. (2000) *Dialectic of Modernity. Zygmunt Bauman*. London: Sage.
Bell, A. (1991) *The Language of New Media*. London: Blackwell.
Benhabib, S. (1996) *The Reluctant Modernism of Hannah Arendt*. New York and London: Sage.
Bennett, T. (2002) 'Culture and governmentality', in J. Bratich, J. Parker and C. McCarthy (eds), *Foucault, Cultural Studies and Governmentality*. New York: SUNY Press, pp. 47–66.
Bhabha, H. (1983) 'The other question: the stereotype and colonial discourse', in *Screen*, 24(4).
Bhabha, H. (1994) *The Location of Culture*. Cambridge: Cambridge University Press.
Billig, M. (1989) *Banal Nationalism*. London: Sage.
Black, J. (1998) *Maps and Politics*. Chicago: University of Chicago Press.
Boltanski, L. (1999) *Distant Suffering. Politics, Morality and the Media*. Cambridge: Cambridge University Press.
Bolter, D.J., and Grusin, R. (2000) *Remediation: Understanding New Media*. Cambridge, Massachusetts: MIT Press.
Bondebjerg, I. (ed.) (2000) *Moving Images, Culture and the Mind*. Luton: University of Luton Press.
Bondebjerg, I. (2002) 'The mediation of everyday life. genre, discourse and spectacle in reality TV', in A. Jerslev (ed.), *Realism and 'Reality' in Film and Media*. Museum Tusculanum Press, Copenhagen: University of Copenhagen.
Bordwell, D., and Thompson, K. (2001) *Film Art. An Introduction*. New York: McGraw-Hill.
Bourdieu, P. (1990) *In Other Words. Essays Towards a Reflexive Sociology*. Cambridge: Polity Press.
Bourdieu, P., and Wacquant, L. (1992) *An Invitation to Reflexive Sociology*. Cambridge: Polity Press.
Boyd-Barrett, O., and Rantanen, T. (eds) (1998) *The Globalization of News*. London: Sage.
Bratich, J., Parker, J., and McCarthy, C. (eds) (2002) *Foucault, Cultural Studies and Governmentality*. New York: SUNY Press.
Brooks, R., Lewis, J., Mosdell, N., and Threadgold, T. (2003) 'Embeds or in-beds?: the media coverage of the war in Iraq'. Report commissioned for the BBC, Cardiff: Cardiff School of Journalism.

Brown, C. (2001) 'Cosmopolitanism, world citizenship and global civil society', in *Critical Review of International Social and Political Philosophy*, 3. pp. 7–26.

Butler, J. (1997) *Excitable Speech. A Politics of the Performative*. London: Routledge.

Butler, J. (2004) *Precarious Life. The Powers of Violence and Mourning*. London: Verso.

Calhoun, G. (1992) *Habermas and the Public Sphere*. Cambridge, Massachusetts: MIT Press.

Calhoun, G. (1995) *Critical Social Theory*. London: Blackwell.

Calhoun, C. (2001) 'Imagining solidarity: cosmopolitanism, constitutional patriotism and the public sphere', in *Popular Culture*, 14(1): 147–72.

Calhoun (2003) 'Belonging in the cosmopolitan imaginery', *Ethnicities* 3(4): 531–3.

Calhoun (2005) 'A world of emergencies: fear, intervention and the limits of cosmopolitan order', speech at Social Science Research Council Humanitarian Action Seminar, New York (www doc).

Cambell, D. (2004) 'Horrific blindness: images of death in contemporary media' in *Journal for Cultural Research*, 8(1).

Carey, J. (1998) 'Political ritual on television: episodes in the history of shame, degradation and excommunication', in T. Liebes and E. Katz (eds), *Media, Ritual and Identity*. London: Routledge. pp. 42–70.

Chartier, R. (1999) *The Cultural Origins of the French Revolution*. Princeton, New Jersey: Princeton University Press.

Castells, M. (1996) *The Rise of the Network Society*. London: Blackwell.

Castells, M. (1997) *The Power of Identity*. London: Blackwell.

Chatman, S. (1991) *Coming to Terms: The Rhetoric of Narrative in Fiction and Film*. Ithaca, New York: Cornell University Press.

Chilton, P. (2004) *Analysing Political Discourse. Theory and Practice*. London: Routledge.

Chomsky, N. (2001) interview in *Radio92*, Belgrade (downloadable www document).

Chouliaraki, L. (2000) 'Political discourse in the news: democratizing responsibility or aestheticizing politics?', *Discourse and Society*, 11(3): 293–314.

Chouliaraki, L. (2002) 'The contingency of universality: some thoughts on discourse and realism', *Social Semiotics*, 12(1): 83–114.

Chouliaraki, L. (2004) 'Watching 11 September: the politics of pity', *Discourse and Society*, 15(2–3): 185–98.

Chouliaraki, L. (2005a) 'Media and the public sphere', in D. Howarth and J. Torfing (eds), *Discourse Theory in European Policy*. Palgrave, London: pp. 275–95.

Chouliaraki, L. (2005b) 'Spectacular ethics', L. Chouliaraki (ed.), special issue, *The soft power of war, Journal of Language and Politics*, 4(2).

Chouliaraki, L. (forthcoming) 'Distant suffering and the public sphere: A phronetic approach', in *Media and the Public Sphere*, MODINET proceedings Vol. 5, Copenhagen: Samfundslitteratur Press.

Chouliaraki, L., and Fairclough, N. (1999) *Discourse in Late Modernity*. Edinburgh: Edinburgh, University Press.

Chouliaraki, L., and Fairclough, N. (2000) 'Language and power in Bourdieu: on Hasan's "The disempowerment game"', *Linguistics and Education*, 10(4): 399–409.

Clausen, L. (2003) 'Global news communication: 9/11 around the world', *Nordicom Review*, 2: pp. 105–15.

Cohen, S. (2001) *States of Denial. Knowing about Atrocities and Suffering*. Cambridge: Polity Press.

Corner, J. (1995) *Television Form and Public Address*. London: Edward Arnold.

Corner, J. (1999) *Critical Ideas in Television Studies*. Oxford: Oxford University Press.

Darley, A. (2000) *Digital Culture: Surface Play and Spectacle in New Media Genres*. London: Routledge.

Dahlgren, P. (1995) *Television and the Public Sphere*. London: Sage.

Dahlgren, P., and Sparks, C. (eds) (1992) *Journalism and Popular Culture*. London: Sage.

Davis, H., and Walton, P. (eds) (1983) *Language, Image, Media*. Oxford: Blackwell.

Dayan, D. (1998) 'Particularistic media and diasporic communications' in T. Liebes and E. Katz (eds), *Media, Ritual and Identity*. London: Routledge, pp. 103–13.

Dayan, D. (ed.) (2001) 'A chacun son September 11', special issue, *Dossiers de l'Audiovisuel*, Editions CNRS, Paris.

Dayan, D., and Katz, E. (1992) *Media Events. The Live Broadcasting of History*. Cambridge, Massachusetts: Harvard University Press.

Dean, M. (1999) *Governmentality*. London: Sage.

Delanty, G. (2000) *Modernity and Postmodernity*. London: Sage.

Derrida, J. (1982) 'Structure, sign and play in the discourse of the human sciences', in *Writing and Difference*. Chicago: Chicago University Press.

Derrida, J. (1992) *The Other Heading*. Bloomington, Indiana: Indiana University Press.

Derrida, J., and Stiegler, B. (2002) *Echographies of Television*. Cambridge: Polity Press.

Douglas, M. (1966) *Purity and Danger*. London: Routledge and Kegan Paul.

Ekecrantz, J. (1997) 'Journalism's "discursive events" and sociopolitical change in Sweden 1925–87', *Media, Culture & Society*, 19(3).

Ekecrantz, J. (1999) *Modernity, Media and the Global System*, Rapport nr 2, Media Societies Around the Baltic Sea, Södertörns Högskola.

Ekecrantz, J. (2001) *Interpreting popular postcommunism: local and global media imagery*. Paper presented at the 'Inaugural International Media Conference: Global Village or Global Image? Representing Diversity and Difference', London, July 24th–27th.

Ekecrantz, J. (in press) 'Espetaculos midiatizados e comunicacoes democraticas: entre a hegemonia global e acao civil', Belo Horizonte: UFMG.

Ellis, J. (2000) *Seeing Things. Television in the Age of Uncertainty*. London: I.B. Tauris.

Ellsworth, E., and Sachs, R., and J. (2003) 'Media and the un-representable: the brief time of audience-as-witness to 9/11'. Paper presented at 'MIT3: Television in Transition' international conference, Cambridge.

Fabion, J.D. (ed.) (1994) *Essential Works of Foucault 1954–1984: Vol. 3: Power*. Harmondsworth: Penguin.

Fairclough, N. (1989) *Language and Power*. London: Longman.

Fairclough, N. (1992) *Discourse and Social Change*. Cambridge: Polity Press.

Fairclough, N. (1995) *Media Discourse*. London: Arnold.

Fairclough, N. (2003) *Doing Discourse Analysis. Textual Analysis for Social Scientists*. London: Routledge.

Featherstone, M. (ed.) (1990) *Global Culture: Nationalism, Globalisation and Modernity*. London: Sage.

Flyvbjerg, B. (2001) *Making Social Science Matter*. Cambridge: Cambridge University Press.

Foucault, M. (1970) *The Order of Things*. London: Tavistock.

Foucault, M. (1972) *The Archeology of Knowledge*. London: Tavistock.

Foucault, M. (1983) 'The subject and power', in H. Dreyfus and P. Rabinow (eds), *Michel Foucault: Beyond Structuralism and Hermeneutics*. Chicago: The University of Chicago Press.

Foucault, M. (1984a) 'What is Enlightenment?', in P. Rainbow (ed.), *The Foucault Reader*. Harmondsworth: Penguin.

Foucault, M. (1984b) 'Nietzche, genealogy, history' in P. Rabinow (ed.), *The Foucault Reader*, New York: Pantheon, pp. 85–98.

Foucault, M. (1984/2000) 'Confronting governments: human rights' in J.D. Fabion, *Essential works of Foucault 1954–1984: Vol. 3: Power*. Harmondsworth: Penguin.

Foucault, M. (1991) 'Governmentality', in G. Burchell, C. Gordon and P. Miller (eds), *The Foucault Effect. Studies in the Governmentality*. London: Harvester Wheatsheaf, pp. 87–104.

Fowler, R. (1991) *Language in the News. Discourse and Ideology in the Press*. London: Routledge.

Fraser, N. (1989) *Unruly Practices. Power, Discourse and Gender in Contemporary Social Theory*. Minneapolis, Minnesota: University of Minnesota Press.

Fraser, N. (1991) 'Rethinking the public sphere: A contribution to the critique of actually existing democracy', in C. Calhoun (ed.), *Habermas and the Public Sphere*, pp. 109–42. MIT Press.

Fraser, N. (1997) *Justice Interruptus. Critical Reflections on the 'Postsocialist' Condition*. London: Routledge.

Geertz, C. (1973) 'Thick Description', in *The interpretation of Cultures*. New York: Basic Books.

Giddens, A. (1990) *The Consequences of Modernity*. Cambridge: Polity Press.

Giddens, A. (1991) *Modernity and Self-identity*. Cambridge: Polity Press.

Giddens, A. (1992) *The Transformation of Intimacy*. Cambridge: Polity Press.

Gilligan, C. (1993) *In a Different Voice: Psychological Theory and Women's Development*. (2nd edition). Cambridge, Massachusetts: Harvard University Press.

Golding, P., and Murdock, G. (1991) 'Culture, communication and political economy' in J. Curran and M. Gurevitch (eds), *Mass Media and Society*. London: Edward Arnold.

Gowing, N. (2004) *Media, the law and peace-keeping: from Bosnia and Kosovo to Iraq*. The Alistair Berkley Memorial Lecture, London School of Economics.

Gresh, A. (2003) 'Comment on September 11th, 2001', 'Le Monde Diplomatique', Greek edition, 7 September.

Gripsrud, J. (1992) 'The aesthetics and politics of melodrama', in P. Dahlgren and C. Sparks (eds), *Journalism and Popular Culture*. London: Sage.

Gripsrud, J. (ed.) (1999) *Television and Common Knowledge*. London: Routledge.

Grodal, T. (2002) 'The experience of realism in audiovisual representation', in A. Jerslev (ed.), *'Realism' and 'Reality' in Film and Media*. Museum Tusculanum Press, Copenhagen: University of Copenhagen.

Habermas, J. (1989) *The Structural Transformation of the Public Sphere*. Cambridge, Massachusetts: MIT Press.

Habermas, J. (1976/1998) 'What is universal pragmatics', in M. Cooke (ed.), *On the Pragmatics Of Communication*. Cambridge: Polity Press, pp. 21–104.

Hall, S. (1973/1980) 'Encoding-decoding', in S. Hall, D. Hobson and A. Lowe (eds), *Culture, Media, Language*. London: Hutchinson.

Hall, S. (1996) 'Who needs "identity"?', in S. Hall and P. du Gay (eds), *Questions of Cultural Identity*. London: Sage. pp. 1–17.

Hall, S. (1997) *Representation. Cultural Representations and Signifying Practices*. London: Sage.

Hall, S., and Du Gay, P. (eds) (1996) *Questions of Cultural Identity*. London: Sage.

Halliday, M.A.K. (1985/1995) *Introduction to Functional Grammar*. London: Arnold.

Halliday, M.A.K., and Hasan, R. (1989) *Language, Context and Text. Aspects of Language in a Social Semiotic Perspective*. Oxford: Oxford University Press.

Hannertz, U. (1996) *Transnational Connections. Culture, People, Places*. London: Routledge.

Harvey, D. (1989) *The Condition of Postmodernity*. London: Blackwell.

Harvey, D. (1996) *Justice, Nature and the Geography of Difference*. Cambridge: Polity Press.

Hasan, R. (2000) 'The disempowerment game: a critique of Bourdieu's view of language', *Linguistics and Education*, 10(4).

Held, D. (1996) *Models of Democracy*. Cambridge: Polity Press.

Higgins, J. (1999) *Satellite Newsgathering*. Oxford: Focal Press.

Hjarvard, S. (2002) 'The study of international news', in K.B. Jensen (ed.), *A Handbook of Media and Communication Research*. London: Routledge, pp. 91–7.

Hodge, R., and Kress, G. (1988) *Social Semiotics*. Cambridge: Polity Press.

Hoopes, J. (ed.) (1991) *Pierce on Signs. Writing on Semiotic by Charles Sanders Pierce*. University of North Carolina Press, North Carolina: Chapel Hill.

Howarth, D. (2000) *Discourse*. Buckingham: Open University Press.

Iedema, R. (2001) 'Analysing film and television: A social semiotic account of hospital: An unhealthy business', in T. van Leeuwen and C. Jewitt (eds), *Handbook of Visual Analysis*. London: Sage, pp. 183–206.

Jameson, F. (1981) *The Political Unconscious: Narrative as a Socially-Symbolic Art*. London: Methuen.

Jameson, F. (1991) *Postmodernism, or the Cultural Logic of Capitalism*. Duke University Press, North Carolina: Durham.

Jameson, F. (2001) 'Comment on the 9/11 attacks', *The London Review of Books*, 4 October.

Jauss, H.R. (1982) *Towards an Aesthetics of Reception*. Brighton, Sussex: Harvester Press.

Jay, M. (1994) *Downcast Eyes. The Denigration of Vision in Twentieth-century Thought*. Berkeley, California: University of California Press.

Jensen, B.K. (1995) *The Social Semiotics of Mass Communication*. London: Sage.

Jensen, K.B. (ed.) (2001) *News of the World*. London: Routledge.

Jensen, K.B. (2002) 'Media reception: Qualitative traditions', in K.B. Jensen (ed.), *A Handbook of Media and Communication Research*. London: Routledge, pp. 156–70.

Jerslev, A. (ed.) (2002) *Realism and 'Reality' in Film and Media*. Museum Tusculanum Press: University of Copenhagen.

Jewitt, C., and Oyama, R. (2001) 'Visual meaning: A social semiotic approach', in T. van Leeuwen and C. Jewitt (eds), *Handbook of Visual Analysis*. London: Sage. pp. 134–56.

Kaldor, M. (2000) 'Cosmopolitanism and organized violence'. Paper for conference 'Conceiving Cosmopolitanism', 27–29 April, Warwick.

Karim, K. (2002) 'Making sense of the "Islamic peril": journalism as cultural practice', in B. Zelizer and S. Allan (eds), *Journalism after September 11*. London and New York: Routledge.

Keane, J. (1991) *The Media and Democracy*. Cambridge: Polity Press.

Keenan, T. (1993) 'Windows of vulnerability', in B. Robbins (ed.), *The Phantom Public*. Minneapolis, Minnesota: University of Minnesota Press.

Kinnick, K., Krugman, D.M. and Cameron, G.T. (1996) 'Compassion fatigue: Communication and burnout toward social problems', *Journalism and Mass Communication Quarterly*, 73: 687–707.

Kress, G. (1985) *Linguistic Processes in Socio-cultural Practice*. Oxford: Oxford University Press.

Kress, G., and van Leeuwen, T. (1996) *Reading Images. The Grammar of Visual Design*. London: Arnold.

Kress, G., and van Leeuwen, T. (2001) *Multi-modal Discourse*. London: Arnold.

Laclau, E. (1996) *Emancipation(s)*. London: Verso.

Laclau, E., and Mouffe, C. (1985) *Hegemony and Socialist Strategy*. London: Verso.

Lash, S. (1990) *Sociology of Postmodernism*. London: Routledge.

Lash, S. (1994) 'Reflexivity and its doubles: Structures, aesthetics and community', in U. Beck, A. Giddens and S. Lash (eds), *Reflexive Modernization: Politics, Tradition and Aesthetics in the Modern Social Order*. Cambridge: Polity Press.

Lash, S. (2001) *Critique of Information*. London: Sage.

Lazar, A., and Lazar, M. (2004) 'The discourse of the New World Order: "outcasting" the double face of threat', *Discourse and Society* 15(2–3): 223–42.

Levin, D.H. (ed.) (1993) *Modernity and the Hegemony of Vision*, Berkeley, California: University of California Press.

Levinas, E. (1969) *Totality and Infinity: An Essay on Exteriority*. Pittsburgh: Duquesne University Press.

Lewis, J. (2004) 'Television, public opinion and the war in Iraq: the case of Britain', *International Journal of Public Opinion Research*, 16(3): pp. 295–310.

Liebes, T., and Curran, J. (eds) (1998) *Media, Ritual and Identity*. London: Routledge.

Livingstone, S., and Bennett, L. (2003) 'Gatekeeping, indexing and live-event news: Is technology altering the construction of news?', *Political Communication*, 20: 363–380.

Livingstone, S., and Lunt, P. (1994) *Talk on television*. London: Routledge.

Livingstone, S., and van Belle, D. (2005) 'The effects of satellite technology on newsgathering from remote locations', *Political Communication*, 22: 45–62.

Lynch, M. (2003) 'Beyond the Arab street: Iraq and the Arab public sphere', *Politics & Society*, 31(1): 55.

McGowan, J. (1998) *Hannah Arendt: An Introduction*. Minneapolis, Minnesota: University of Minnesota Press.

McIntyre, A. (1985) *After Virtue: a Study in Moral Theory*. Notre Dame, Indiana: Notre Dame Press.

McLuhan, M. (1964) *Understanding Media*. London: Routledge and Kegan Paul.

McQuire, S. (1999) *Visions of Modernity*. London: Sage.

Maffesoli, M. (1993) *The Time of the Tribes: The Decline of Individualism in Mass Society*. London: Sage.

Maffesoli, M. (1996) *The Contemplation of the World: Figures of Community Style*. Minneapolis, Minnesota: University of Minnesota Press.

Manovich, L. (2001) *The Language of New Media*. Cambridge, Massachusetts: MIT Press.

Martin, J. (2004) 'Mourning: how we are aligned', *Discourse and Society*, 15(2–3): 321–44.

Mercer, K. (1994) 'Reading racial fetishism', in K. Mercer (ed.), *Welcome to the Jungle*. London: Routledge. pp. 173–85.

Merton, R.K. (1946) *Mass Persuasion: The Social Psychology of a War Bond Drive*. New York: Harper.

Messaris, J. (1997) *Visual Persuasion*. London: Sage.

Miller, J. (1971) *McLuhan*. London: Fontana.

Minc, A. (2001) 'Terrorism of the mind', *Le Monde*, 6 November.

Misztal, B. (2000) *Informality: Social Theory and Contemporary Practice*. London: Routledge.

Morley, D. (1998) 'Finding out about the world from television news. Some difficulties', in J. Gripsrud (ed.), *Television and Common Knowledge*. London: Routledge. pp. 136–58.

Morley, D. (2000) *Home Territories: Media, Mobility and Identity*. London: Routledge.

Morley, D. (2003) 'What's "Home" Got to Do with it?: Contradictory Dynamics in the Domestication of Technology and the Dislocation of Domesticity', *European Journal of Cultural Studies*, 6(4): 435–58.

Morley, D., and Robins, K. (1995) *Spaces of Identity*. London: Routledge.

Morson, G.S. and Emerson, C. (1990) *Mikhail Bakhtin: Creation of a Prosaics*. Stanford, California: Stanford University Press.

Murdock, G. (2002) 'Media, culture and modern times', in K.B. Jensen (ed.), *A Handbook of Media and Communication Research*. London, Routledge. pp. 40–61.

Nelson, C., and Grossberg, L. (eds) (1988) *Marxism and the Interpretation of Culture*. London: Macmillan.

Nichols, B. (1991) *Representing Reality*. Bloomington, Indiana: Indiana University Press.

Noel, A. and Therien, J.P. (1995) 'From domestic to international justice: the welfare state and foreign aid', *International Organisation*, 49(3): 523–53.

Nohrstedt, S.A., and Ottosen, R. (eds) (2001) *Journalism and the New World Order*. Nordicom Goeteborg.

Nussbaum, M. (2001) *Upheavals of Thought: The Intelligence of Emotions*. Cambridge: Cambridge University Press.

Outhwaite, W. (1994) *Habermas*. Cambridge: Polity Press.

Perlmutter, D. (1999) *Visions of War: Picturing Warfare from the Stone Age to the Cyberage*. New York: St. Martin's.

Perlmutter, D., and Wagner, G. (2004) 'The anatomy of a photojournalistic icon: marginalisation of dissent in the selection and framing of "a death in Genoa"' in *Visual Communication*, 3(1): 91–108.

Peters, J.D (1997) 'Realism in social description and the fate of the public', *Javnost-the public*, 4(2): 5–16.

Peters, J.D. (1999) *Speaking into the Air: A History of the Idea of Communication*. Chicago: University of Chicago Press.

Peters, J.D. (2001) 'Witnessing', *Media, Culture and Society*, 23: 707–23.

Peters, J.D. (2005) *Courting the Abyss: Free Speech and the Liberal Tradition*. Chicago: University of Chicago Press.

Piper, A. (1991) 'Impartiality, compassion and modal imagination', *Ethics*, 101: 726–57.

Plant, S. (1992) *The Most Radical Gesture: The Situationist International in the Postmodern Age*. London: Routledge.

Poster, M. (1990/1996) *The Mode of Information*. Cambridge: Polity Press.

Rabinow, P. (ed.) (1984) *The Foucault Reader*. New York: Pantheon.

Rantanen, T. (2002) *The Global and the National: Media and Communications in Post-communist Russia*. London: Rowman & Littlefield.

Robbins, B. (ed.) (1999) *The Phantom Public*. Minneapolis, Minnesota: University of Minnesota Press.

Robins, K. (1994) 'Forces of consumption: from the symbolic to the psychotic', *Media, Culture and Society*, 16: pp. 449–68.

Rose, N. (1999) *Powers of Freedom: Reframing Political Thought*. London: Routledge.

Ross, D. (1923/1995) *Aristotle*. London: Routledge.

Said, E. (1978) *Orientalism*. New York: Vintage Press.

Sakr, N. (2001) *Satellite Realms: Transnational Television, Globalisation and the Middle East*. London: I.B. Tauris.

Sartre, J.P. (1976) *Critique of Dialectical Reason*. London: Verso.

Scannel, P. (1988) 'Radio-times: The temporal arrangements of broadcasting in the modern world', in P. Drummond and R. Pateson (eds), *Television and its Audience: International Research Perspectives*. London: BFI.

Scannel, P. (1989) 'Public service broadcasting and modern public life', *Media, Culture and Society*, 11: 135–66.

Scannel, P. (ed.) (1991) *Broadcast Talk*. London: Sage.

Scannel, P. (1996) *Radio, Television and Modern Life*. Oxford: Blackwell.

Schlesinger, P. (1991) *Media, State and Nation*. London: Sage.

Schroder, K.C. (2002) 'Discourses of fact', in K.B. Jensen (ed.), *A Handbook of Media and Communication Research*. London: Routledge. pp. 98–116.

Schudson, M. (1982) 'The politics of narrative form: the emergence of news conventions in print and television', *Daedalus*, 3(1): 97–117.

Schudson, M. (1992) 'Was there ever a public sphere? If so, when? Reflections on the American case', in G. Calhoun (ed.), *Habermas and the Public Sphere*. Cambridge, Massachusetts: MIT Press.

Scollon, R. (1998) *Mediated Discourse as Social Interaction: A Study of News Discourse*. London: Longman.

Scollon, R., and Scollon, S. (2003) *Discourses of Place*. London: Sage.

Sennett, R. (1976) *The Fall of Public Man*. New York, London: Norton Books.

Shapiro, G. (1993) 'In the shadows of philosophy. Nietzsche and the question of vision', in D.H. Levin (ed.), *Modernity and the Hegemony of Vision*. Berkeley, California: University of California Press.

Silverstone, R. (1984) 'Narrative strategies in television science – a case study', *Media, Culture and Society*, 6: 377–410.

Silverstone, R. (1994) *Television and Everyday Life*. London: Routledge.

Silverstone, R. (1999) *Why Study the Media?* London: Sage.

Silverstone, R. (2002a) 'Complicity and collusion in the mediation of everyday life', *New Literary History*, 33(4): 761–80.

Silverstone, R. (2002b) 'Mediating catastrophe: September 11 and the crisis of the other', D. Dayan (ed.), special issue, 'A chacun son September 11', *Dossiers de l'Audiovisuel*. Editions CNRS, Paris.

Silverstone, R. (2003) 'Proper distance: towards an ethics of cyberspace', in G. Liestøl, A. Morrison, T. Rasmussen (eds), *Digital Media Revisited: Theoretical and Conceptual Innovations in Digital Domains*. Cambridge, Massachusetts: MIT Press. pp. 469–90.

Silverstone, R. (2004a) 'Mediation and communication', in G. Calhoun et al. (eds), *The Sage Handbook of Sociological Analysis*. London: Sage.

Silverstone, R. (2004b) 'Media literacy and media civics', *Media, Culture and Society*, 23(3): 440–9.

Smith, A. (1759/2000) *The Theory of Moral Sentiments*. New York: Prometheus Books.

Spivak, G.C. (1998) 'Can the subaltern speak?', in C. Nelson and L. Grossberg (eds), *Marxism and the Interpretation of Culture*. London: Macmillan.

Stavrakakis, Y. (1999) *Lacan and the Political*. London: Routledge.

Tester, K. (2001) *Compassion, Morality and the Media*. Milton Keynes: Open University Press.

Thompson, J. (1990) *Ideology and Modern Culture*. Cambridge: Polity Press.

Thompson, J. (1995) *Media and Democracy*. Cambridge: Polity Press.

Thompson, J. (2000) *Political Scandal: Power and Visibility in the Media Age*. London: Polity Press.

Thompson, K. (1997) *Media and Cultural Regulation*. London: Sage.

Thussu, D. (2000) *International Communication: Continuity and Change*. London: Edward Arnold.

Tomlinson, J. (1999) *Globalization and Culture*. London: Sage.

Torfing, J. (1998) *New Theories of Discourse*. London: Blackwell.

Touraine, A. (2000) *Can we Live Together? Equality and Difference*. Stanford: Stanford University Press.

van Dijk, T. (1997a) *Discourse as Social Interaction*. London: Sage.

van Dijk, T. (1997b) *Discourse as Process and Structure*. London: Sage.

van Leeuwen, T. (2001) 'Semiotics and Iconography', in van T. Leeuwen and C. Jewitt (eds), *Handbook of Visual Analysis*. London: Sage. pp. 92–118.

van Leeuwen, T., and Jaworski, A. (2002) 'The discourses of war photography: photojournalistic representations of the Palestinian–Israeli war', *Journal of Language and Politics*, 1(2): 255–76.

van Leeuwen, T., and Jewitt, C. (eds) (2001) *Handbook of Visual Analysis*. London: Sage.

Vattimo, G. (1992) *The Transparent Society*. Baltimore: Johns Hopkins University Press.

Villa, D. (1999) *Politics, Philosophy, Terror: Essays on the Thought of Hannah Arendt*. Princeton, New Jersey: Princeton University Press.

Virilio, P. (1991) *The Aesthetics of Disappearance*. New York: Semiotext(e).

Virilio, P. (1994) *The Vision Machine*. London: BFI.

Virilio, P. (2001) 'From terror to apocalypse?', *Lettre International*, 54, September.

Volkmer, I. (1999) *News in the Global Sphere: A Study of CNN and its Impact on Global Communication*. Luton: University of Luton Press.

Volkmer, I. (2002) 'Journalism and political crises', in S. Allan and B. Zelizer. *Journalism after September 11th*. London: Routledge.

Volosinov, V.N. (1973/1996) *Marxism and the Philosophy of Language*. Cambridge Massachusetts: Harvard University Press.

Warner, C. (1993) 'The man public and the mass subject in Massachusetts', in B. Robins (ed.), *The Phantom Public Sphere*, Minneapolis: University of Minnesota Press.

Wodak, R. (1996) *Disorders of Discourse*. London: Longman.

Yudice, E. (1993) *The Phantom Public*, in B. Robbins (ed.), Minneapolis: University of Minessota Press.

INDEX

CPSIA information can be obtained at www.ICGtesting.com
Printed in the USA
BVOW03s1615160914

367021BV00003B/39/P